DEATH TRAP

As I watched the action at the bunker, I saw the first two men stick their M-16s inside the aperture and empty a magazine into the inside of the bunker. Then Constantino pulled the pin on a grenade, swung around to the front of the bunker and reached for the opening with his right hand. Just as he released the grenade, I saw his body suddenly jerk and fall back on the ground, just lying there. It was obvious that he had been shot from the same bunker into which he had just thrown the grenade.

I contemplated for a moment on what I had seen. A man had been gut-shot from a bunker which had just received at least two ninety-millimeter, high-explosive tank rounds, whole belts of 7.62 millimeter machine guns round, and two magazines of 5.56 millimeter M-16 rounds fired inside the bunker.

What in the hell do they have down there?

PLATOON
BRAVO COMPANY

ROBERT HEMPHILL

St. Martin's Paperbacks

Published by arrangement with Sergeant Kirkland's Museum and Historical Society, Inc.

PLATOON: BRAVO COMPANY

Library of Congress Catalog Card Number: 98-36820

ISBN: 0-312-97657-7

Printed in the United States of America

Sergeant Kirkland's edition published 1998
St. Martin's Paperbacks edition / June 2001

St. Martin's Paperbacks are published by St. Martin's Press, 175 Fifth Avenue, New York, NY 10010.

10 9 8 7 6 5 4 3 2 1

To the men of Bravo Company—
They answered their nation's call
and they did their duty!
—Robert Hemphill

Our experience of war, if given
a chance, is one we would never
surrender or repeat.
—Sen. John McCain

Courage is resistance to fear,
mastery of fear—not absence
of fear.
—Mark Twain

CONTENTS

FOREWORD

JOSEPH L. GALLOWAY

There is no more responsible job than that of an Infantry Company commander in combat. The Army and the Marines take a 24 or 25-year-old captain and put him in direct charge of the lives of 160 grunts. There are no buffers, no cutouts; the captain makes decisions daily, even hourly, that mean life or death to his troops. He can't shirk the responsibility; nor can he hide from his failures. The troops know, and love, a good captain. They instantly recognize, and loathe, a bad one.

Captain Robert Hemphill was a damned fine company commander of Army Infantry in Vietnam from 1 October 1967 to 18 February 1968, in the 25th Infantry Division. He had Bravo Company, 3rd Battalion, 22nd Infantry. He and his men soldiered in the rubber plantations and War Zone C. Hemphill believed in fighting smart and husbanding the lives of his troops. He was a good company commander, and this is his story of those long-ago days. He pulls no punches; he displays the line officer's true love for soldiers and soldiering, true contempt for incompetence in any rank, and general disdain for staff weenies.

It happens that one of the Bravo troops back then was a Spec. 4 by the name of Oliver Stone, who survived to make a movie entitled *Platoon*, which presumably draws on Stone's memories, tempered with a goodly amount of poetic and literary license. This is not that story. This is the story of the real Bravo Company and all its platoons—a damned fine fighting outfit led by a good Captain of Infantry. There were no rapes or murders of NCOs. No spaced out dopers wandering goggle eyed through the triple canopy jungle into the North Vietnamese Army killing zone.

The first time I met Robert Hemphill was at a Vietnam War history symposium at Hampden-Sydney College, in Virginia. He declared in no uncertain terms: "*Platoon* was not about any platoon in MY company. I kept them too busy in the bush to get in that kind of trouble. Oliver Stone was a good soldier. He earned a couple of good medals and a righteous Purple Heart."

I've always thought, and the thought is only reinforced by reading the book Bob has written, that serving honorably and well alongside other good men, under command of a good captain, instills and nurtures a pride of service that no amount of bad press or, worse, public opinion can erode.

If you have to fight a bad war, pray that God and the Army at least grant you a good company commander.

INTRODUCTION

Combat in Vietnam was endless boredom punctuated by moments of intense action. There were exceptions—such as the TET '68 offensive—when those moments seemed to last forever.

This book reflects that maxim. If you are an action freak, you may not like this book. You may be bored by much of the daily routine—the endless "checking out dry holes." You may have trouble comprehending the pressure of weeks in the field with little to show for it, followed by one night back in base camp to relax a little, then back to the field the next day. Yet, there are moments of action and violence in this story that rival any experience of any combat soldier anywhere. This was the lot of the combat infantryman in Vietnam—regardless of his irresponsible portrayal by a revisionist and hostile Hollywood.

The Vietnam combat veteran has faced two enemies because of his service—the enemy in the field in-country and the indifference and occasional hostility of his own countrymen. The combat soldier feels the effects of this second enemy—the failure of his fellow Americans to appreciate his efforts, including his constant willingness to place his very life in mortal danger—to the greatest degree, more so than others who served in Vietnam but who saw no significant, direct combat.

But the development of that enemy was partially his own doing. Trained by the military to maintain a low profile, to not rock the boat, to stay out of the limelight, coupled with some confusion and intimidation brought on by the small, but extremely shrill, anti-Vietnam minority, he was content to return to civilian society and to attempt to resume his former life. He tried to go back to his old job, his old friends, his old hangouts—and he refrained from talking about his Vietnam experiences. When curious people asked him about them, he "Didn't want to talk about it." He did not want to talk about why he went, what positive things were accomplished, and what he learned there.

Largely because of this communication void with those who fought the war, the public, generally, heard only one side. After years of being subjected to a constant barrage of negative information and misinformation, the American public came to believe that the Vietnam War was wrong and that those who participated in it—for whatever reason—were somehow tainted by their service there. This unfortunate course of events, resulting in the premature termination of the support of our Vietnamese allies, might have played out differently had our combat veterans chosen to speak out about their efforts and achievements. They *knew* the truth behind the comment of the North Vietnamese Colonel during the peace negotiations in Saigon that, even though they never beat us on the battlefield, that was totally irrelevant, for they beat us on the streets of America. Our side of the story was never told in time to prevent the tragedy which befell our friends.

This book is my war story. Boring or violent, this is how I remember a portion of my two years there, specifically the five months during which I commanded Bravo Company. This is my story of the combat infantryman and his day-to-day existence under the gun in the field. This is my story of the men of Bravo Company, whom I consider to have been the best soldiers in the history of the United States Army—or any other service, for that matter. They were competent and willing to do their duty, regardless of the danger involved, and they succeeded against all odds. This is my story . . . no, this is *their* story.

The movie, *Platoon*, was written and directed by a former member of Bravo Company, who served during the period I was in command. That was *his* story of his experiences in Vietnam and in Bravo. *Platoon* is not my story, nor is it Bravo Company's story. To my knowledge, many events in the movie did not occur during the time he and I were in Bravo Company. The troops did not have enough free time to get into that much trouble. However, the sense of being there depicted in the movie—the dehydration, the red ant dance, the distractions of fatigue and the elements during an ambush, the frustration in dealing with an elusive enemy—were very real. Although *Platoon* certainly has its merits, the depiction and sequence of some major combat events have been modified in the movie for cinematic purposes.

Field officers and troop commanders historically dislike staff officers, even though most served as staff officers at some point in their careers. Staff officers are often viewed as obstacles in the way of tactical success—and frequently as scapegoats in the face of tactical failure. Troop leaders are sometimes told by staff officers that they cannot do something, usually with good reason. Commanders do not take kindly to such "interference," thus increasing tension between command and staff officers. Commanders frequently address such issues through "command channels," thereby attempting to completely bypass the staff. Sometimes higher commanders will overrule their staffs, and sometimes they will not. Such is life among the officer corps. If I have been unduly harsh to staffers in this book, I would confess that subsequent staff duty since Vietnam has served to somewhat soften my attitude toward those who perform such duty. "Sorry 'bout that."

Although the events in this book unfolded as described, I have taken the liberty of using aliases for some of the individuals involved, except for Division and higher Commanders, and others who have given me permission to use their names. This precaution was taken primarily to safeguard their privacy and, in a few cases, to shield them from embarrassment.

If you like this book, please talk to others about it—about *your* experiences if you were there. Let's keep open the channels of communication and discuss the *positive* aspects of Vietnam, not just regurgitate the negative or dwell on the discomfort. For the infantryman, real war is not comfortable. Like it or not, the Vietnam War occurred—let's make the best of it!

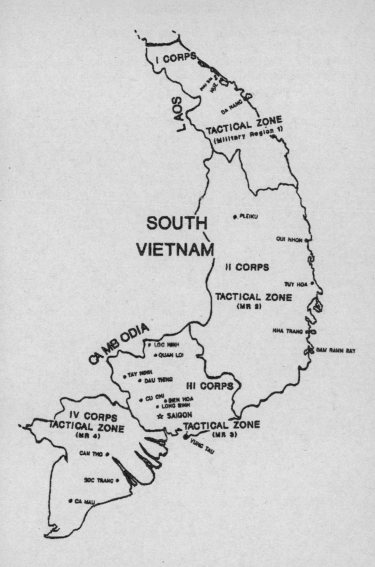

CHAPTER ONE

TAKING COMMAND

Taking command of an infantry company in Vietnam was not exactly like those change-of-command ceremonies you normally see in the Army, where the troops are all in formation, standing tall, wondering why they must suffer in the hot sun or freezing rain, just to make some officer feel important . . . But that's the Army. The outgoing commander takes the guidon from the first sergeant and passes it to the battalion commander who, in turn, passes it to the new commander, who returns it to the first sergeant. Then all three wax eloquent about what a great job the old guy did, and what a great privilege it is for the new guy, and so on. After all the speeches, those troops who haven't passed out in the heat all march off the field, and the officers and "honored guests" go have cake and coffee to appropriately celebrate the occasion. Naturally, no one wants to think about the Article 15s, the numbnuts who won't pull their load, the nights spent freezing their butts off during field exercises while some staff weenies screw things up, and other not-so-glorious things that happen in peacetime combat units.

In Vietnam, it was a little different.

I remember October 1, 1967, just like it was yesterday. My battalion—the 3/22 Infantry, 25th "Tropic Lightning" Infantry Division—the best damn combat division in Vietnam at that time—had walked out of Dau Tieng base camp before daylight to get the jump on the VC base camp watchers.

The Michelin rubber plantation contained numerous small villages, all of which were "suspected" of being VC-controlled. Of course, we couldn't say that out loud, since it may have offended our Michelin "hosts," who had

been gracious enough to leave their plantation buildings
to us while they lounged around in the safety of Saigon,
paying the VC to avoid hitting their valuable houses when
they mortared the Americans. Every grunt in the 25th
knew the villages were VC, whether others liked it or not.
How were they able to figure this out? Probably something about the mines and booby traps that they hit every
time they moved around the villages, or the small arms
fire that they received from the villages, or the mortar
rounds that hit the base camp from the vicinity of the
villages, or. . . . Smart guys, huh?

On October 1st, the battalion's mission was to move
about eight clicks (kilometers) to cordon-and-search one
of these villages. Doing a cordon-and-search meant dropping a ring of troops around a village to prevent anyone
from leaving it, then escorting a few Vietnamese National
Police Field Force guys through to look for suspected VC.
It was important to be in place around the village before
daylight because the VC who stayed in the villages at
night normally left at first light. The idea was to trap them
in the village and let the NPFF police them up. Sometimes
it worked, sometimes it didn't.

At the time, I was the Battalion Adjutant, or S-1, which
meant that I stayed in base camp when the battalion went
on field operations. My job was to make sure the headquarters continued to function and that all the paperwork
was done.

That morning, I was sitting back in Dau Tieng, fat,
dumb and happy, listening to the battalion net through a
speaker box attached to the Prick-25 (Army Radio AN/
PRC-25) we had set up in the office. For some reason, I
was thinking back to the day I arrived in the battalion.

It had been back in mid-September—about two weeks
prior. Although I was a Captain, this was my first time in
Vietnam. I had started life in the Army as a new lieutenant
in Germany and had made Captain about three months
before I arrived in Vietnam. Like all new arrivals in a
combat zone, I viewed my situation with a degree of ea-

gerness and a whole lot of apprehension. The initial greeting of my new Battalion Commander, Lieutenant Colonel Tom Harrold, did not relieve the apprehension one bit.

After looking at the Ranger tab on my shoulder, the jump wings on my chest, and my physical appearance, Falcon 6 ("Falcon" was the battalion's identifier on the radio, and "6" was the standard radio call sign for commanders in the Army) slapped me on the shoulder and exclaimed, "A stud like you needs a company. I'm going to make sure you get one as soon as possible!"

"Thanks, sir. I'll look forward to that," I responded, battling down the sudden upsurge of butterflies in my stomach.

I decided that I should try to influence the decision on which company I would get. I sure as hell didn't want to inherit a bunch of problems and screw-ups for my first company command. I also wanted a unit I could trust in the boonies—it could get dangerous out there!

Checking around the battalion, I found that Alpha and Charlie Companies had the reputation of being the best in the battalion. Delta Company was a brand new company which had just arrived from the states as a "packet" to beef up the battalion. Bravo Company, on the other hand, was not only the worst one in the battalion, but probably the worst in the brigade. As far as I was concerned, Bravo and Delta were out. No way in hell did I want either of those two! Besides, both companies had relatively new commanders. That meant that I was probably safe from being stuck with either of them, even though Bravo 6, Captain Larry Roberts (an alias), was reportedly not doing very well from Colonel Harrold's viewpoint. That left Alpha and Charlie. Alpha 6 was due to come out of command soon, but Charlie 6 had been in command for over six months—an unusually long time. So I concluded that Charlie would open up first, and that was ok with me!

For the next week or so, I started to get to know Charlie company. When they came in from operations, I went down and ate barbecue and drank beer with them. I spent some time in their orderly room, getting to know their routine and problems. I figured that, in a few more weeks, I would be ready to take over Charlie and run with it. I felt a little more at ease as time passed.

Then came October 1st. The battalion had reached its position and established the cordon in plenty of time. The command net was filled with routine traffic as they waited for the NPFF to arrive. Other than making sure that no one left the village, and that their security against outside attack was in place, not much was happening. Falcon 3 Alpha, the battalion Assistant S-3 (Operations Officer), was running the radio net from the base camp.

I was trying to empty my in-box, only half-listening to the radio squawk box.

Suddenly, I was jolted back to reality by a rather frantic radio call. I turned up the volume.

"Falcon 6, Falcon 6, this is Bravo 6-X-ray." X-ray was the call sign for the commander's radio operator.

"Bravo 6-X-ray, this is Falcon 6."

"Bravo 6-X-ray. Bravo 6 is hit!"

"Falcon 6. What happened?"

"Bravo 6-X-ray. The guy in front of him hit a trip wire and set off a grenade. Bravo 6 has shrapnel in his leg. It doesn't look serious, but the medic says he'll need a Dust-off."

"Falcon 6. Roger that. Notify the next in command and call the Dust-off. Break-Break. Falcon 3-Alpha, this is Falcon 6."

"Falcon 3-Alpha."

"Falcon 6. Have Falcon 1 at the helipad in three-zero minutes, prepared to come to the field to stay. Bird will be in-bound for pick-up."

"Falcon 3-Alpha. Roger dat."

"Falcon 6 out."

When I heard that, my heart sank like a load of bricks in the ocean. Those butterflies threatened to take over. No! Not Bravo Company! NOBODY wanted that company! Why were they doing that to ME?!? I should get CHAR-

LIE, not BRAVO! Hell, those guys are shooting each other! They're sleeping on the perimeter! They are the world's worst company! *What'll I DO?*

What I did was grab one of my clerks, SP4 Don Jackson (an alias), who had spent nine months in a line platoon before being sent in to work in the rear. He had field experience here, and I had none. He and I ran upstairs to my room, and I dragged out my field gear.

"Ok, Jackson, tell me which of this crap I'll need to take with me."

"That's easy. Go light. You need your rucksack, rain gear if you want it, four pairs of socks, shaving gear, toothbrush, flashlight, extra mags, webbing, knife, poncho liner, steel pot, weapon, and any personal things you want to take along. I'll load your mags while you pack this stuff up, and I'll lend you my pocket hammock. You can get one for yourself when you come in the next time. Oh, yeah—take a book along. You might get bored waiting for Charlie to come along. After you get out there a little while, you can see what else you want, but this should get you by this time. Don't forget your map case."

"This one?"

"No, not that big one—you ain't mech anymore. Grunts walk slower and cover less ground than tracks. Use the one-sheet size."

"Thanks. Now I gotta move. Bird comes in two-zero."

"Right, sir. Here's the hammock. Pick up the mags when you come downstairs."

Believe it or not, when that helicopter landed, I was standing there, ready to go. It was probably one of the few times I had ever been on time. . . .

As we approached the village, the pilot called for a smoke grenade to mark the landing zone. A few seconds later, purple smoke could be seen wafting its way skyward.

"Roger, Falcon 3. Tally-ho goofy grape."

"Roger purple."

"Coming in."

As the bird sat down, I climbed out, hoisted my rucksack onto my back, picked up my CAR-15 carbine and walked toward Falcon 6, who was standing over by the rubber trees. As I walked up, Harrold had this self-satisfied smirk on his face.

"Morning, Bob."

"Morning, Sir. Helluva day y'all got out here."

"Yeah, it is. Well, there's your company, Bravo 6." He pointed across the perimeter.

"Thanks, sir. Any orders?"

"Go get your guys organized, then come back here and talk to the 3. We move out in about three hours."

"Roger."

And that was my change-of-command ceremony!

But the fun wasn't over yet. I was still the new guy who had to face the company.

I trudged over to the company CP and dropped my ruck by a tree. As I turned around, a lieutenant came up to where I was standing.

"Morning, sir. I'm Lieutenant Phil Mooradian, the company XO."

"Morning, Phil. I'm Captain Hemphill, your new company commander. What're *you* doing out here? Don't you normally operate out of the base camp?"

"Thought I'd come along today for the fun, since it wasn't a long trip."

"Some fun, huh? Get me the platoon leaders, platoon sergeants and field first sergeant here in ten minutes."

"Yessir." He turned to one of the radio operators (RTOs). "Otte, get word to the platoons to have their 6s and 5s here ASAP. Then get Sergeant Johnson. By the way, Captain, these are your RTOs. Otte has the company net, and Webster has the battalion net." (Johnson is an alias.)

I shook hands with each of them. Then they went back to their radios and whatever they had been doing.

Since everyone in the battalion knew this was the worst company, I knew I had to do something to get it going on the right foot. Having had the Company CO mede-vac'd didn't help their spirits any, either. Like everyone else, I had been trying to determine what was wrong with Bravo, and I had come to a conclusion. It had been my observation that Roberts, the previous CO, had tried to be the only chief with everyone else relegated to Indian. In other words, he had tried to do it all himself and had not used his subordinate leaders. I hoped I was right about that, because that was the assumption I was operating under, If I was wrong, I would not get anywhere, either.

A few minutes later, they were all there. I soon discovered that every second lieutenant I had was from OCS: Lieutenant Dick Prairie, First Platoon; Lieutenant Art Gormley, Third Platoon; and Lieutenant Jim Constantino (an alias), Fourth/Weapons Platoon. The Second Platoon had no officer. The Platoon Sergeant, Staff Sergeant (SSG) Joe Hughes, was acting Platoon Leader. Among other things, being OCS Officers meant that they knew what being an enlisted troop was all about. Sometimes it also meant that they got too close to their enlisted soldiers to be good leaders. My platoon sergeants were mostly Staff Sergeant E-6s, one grade below that authorized, and my field first was actually the Weapons Platoon Sergeant. Well, we would see what kind of leaders they were before long.

"Good mornin', gents. I'm your new CO. We're having this little get-together for two reasons—to meet each other, and to let you know what I expect of you. My primary guidance to you is that I expect you guys wearing bars to go act like lieutenants, and you guys wearing stripes to go act like sergeants. In other words, I'll do my job, and I expect you to do yours. I'm not going to do yours for you. Any questions on that score?"

Everyone looked at each other and then, slowly, they all shook their heads.

"All right, then, one more thing—I have been in country for all of a week-and-a-half on my first tour. Some of you guys've been here eight months or longer. I know that you know more than I do about how to fight and survive over here. I expect to put your knowledge to use. When I give you an operations order, and you think you have a better way of doing it, I want you to come to me and tell me. But do it the right way—don't challenge me in front of others. I'll listen to your plan. I believe I'm smart enough to pick the best plan out of a crowd, and I'll decide on the best approach, which may not be mine. In any case, when I decide which plan to use, I expect you to go do it. Questions?"

There were none.

"Okay. Phil, have we been given any heads-up on what we're supposed to do next?"

"Only to expect to move out at about 1500 to a night laager position."

"Good. I'm going over and check in with the 3. It's now 1230. That gives us about two-and-a-half hours before we move. I want the platoon leaders back here in one hour. Do any of you have any questions of me—any kind of question? Now's your chance. No? Okay, see you in an hour. Take off."

After they had left, I turned to the XO. "Not a very talkative lot, are they?"

"They don't know you yet. Give them time—they're okay. I think you just gave them their pride back."

"We'll see. Now, what kind of formation does this company normally use?"

"Usually a 'box' in the jungle—that means two platoons up, two back. Each platoon moves in two files, which gives us a total of four guys cutting trail. With only four guys, it's pretty easy to rotate the machetes to give them a break. No sense beating them to death. Sometimes, when the terrain is a little more open, we move in a column of platoons with plenty of security out. Either one generally works pretty well."

"Okay. Be back soon."

A few minutes later, I found the S-3, Major George Davis (an alias), lounging on his hammock.

"Well, Bravo 6, welcome to the field. How's it going over there?"

"I've decided one thing—I'm certainly not going to follow the guy in front of me very closely!" We both smiled. "I think they know I've arrived. What're we doing next?"

"We should be finished up here in time to move by 1500. We're going right here"—he pointed to the map—"to establish a night laager. Meet me there when you arrive and I will show you your portion of the perimeter. It generally will be from 8 o'clock to 12 o'clock in your direction of march. Order of march will be Alpha, Charlie, Bravo, Delta. Tomorrow, we plan to split off Alpha and Bravo for separate company operations for a few days. We'll get more into that when we get to the night position. Got it?"

"Yeah, no sweat. Looks safe enough for a new company commander."

"Before you go back, want a cup of coffee? I got a jar of instant here that sure beats that stuff you get in C-Rations."

"Sure, thanks." I took out my canteen cup and filled it with water. I dug a small hole in the ground and set it over it. As I was reaching for my heating tablets, Major Davis reached over and handed me a small sliver of white stuff.

"Here, use this. It'll heat it up quicker and hotter. It's C-4."

I learned something new. He was right. In a couple of minutes, we were enjoying one of life's major pleasures—a piping hot cup of coffee. Lesson Number 1—never leave home without C-4 plastic explosive in your pack.

Back at the company with the platoon leaders, I gave them their marching orders. "We form up at 1445 and move out at 1500. We'll move in a 'box' with 1st and 3rd leading and 2nd and 4th following. CP'll follow the lead platoons. 1-6 and 3-6, make sure you maintain contact with Charlie company in front. 2-6 and 4-6 will put out flank security for the company. When we get to the night position, I'll give you your sectors. Any questions? Okay, you're dismissed."

We moved into the night position, fired in our artillery defensive concentrations (DEFCONs) and settled in for the night without further incident.

As I lay back in my hammock, I reflected back on my first day in command. When I had awakened that morning—it seemed so long ago—I had no idea that I would end the day in this hammock in command of an infantry company in the field. Actually, the day had not gone badly at all. The company had moved pretty well, the leaders seemed to have a better attitude than I had first observed, and I looked forward to see how they—and I—performed under fire. Maybe Bravo wasn't so bad after all. As I lay there looking up through the trees, I impulsively smiled to myself. I suddenly had the feeling that Bravo's luck was about to change.

25th Infantry Division
Tropic Lighting
Tropic 6: MG F.K. Mearns

3rd Brigade
Flexible
Flexible 6: COL K. Burrell

(After 11/97) COL L. R. Dunn

3rd Battalion, 22nd Infantry
Falcon
Falcon 6: LTC T. Harrold

(After 6 Feb.) LTC R. Fulton

Company B
Falcon Bravo
Falcon Bravo 6: CPT R. L. Hemphill

(1 Oct 67–18 Feb 68)

1ST PLATOON	2ND PLATOON	3RD PLATOON	4TH PLATOON
"1-6"	"2-6"	"3-6"	"4-6"
2LT Prairie	2LT Wilder	2LT Gormley	2LT
2LT Walker	2LT Lorne		Constantino
2LT Monroe	(SSG Hughes)		

KEY TO CALL SIGNS: 6 " Commander; 5 " Executive Officer or NCO in charge; 4 " 8-4 (Supply Officer); 3 " 8-3 (Operations Officer); 2 " 8-2 (Intelligence Officer); 1 " 8-1 (Admin/Personnel Officer).

CHAPTER TWO

BRAVO BULL

For the next seven days, I learned a lot about being a company commander. First, I learned that it was important to know where the hell I was at all times. (They had tried to tell me that in Ranger School, but I really knew deep down that, when I got to the "Real World," I would have others to tell me where I was. WRONG! I had plenty of people to tell me where to go, but nobody would tell me where I was.) Second, I learned what a "dry hole" was. Since it was rather late in the monsoon season, a "dry hole" had absolutely nothing to do with the weather or terrain. Instead, when we went out into the jungle, looking for Victor Charlie for one or two weeks and found nothing of significance—that was a "dry hole"! Now, "significance" lent itself to various interpretations. In several cases, a lone bag of rice in the middle of the jungle was "significant" enough to get us another week out in our wonderful nature preserve. In other instances, we could win an extension by merely discovering an old base camp, many of which had not seen a live individual since the French Foreign Legion was kicked out of Indochina. However, to those wizards on high, these represented *opportunities to excel*, whatever the hell that meant. To us, it just meant more jungle to hack through, more heat, more rain, more water-filled foxholes, more mosquitoes, more mental pressure, but—most of the time—*no more Charlie!* Someone once said that the war in Vietnam was characterized by long periods of boredom, occasionally punctuated by intense bursts of action. During the next couple of months, we would get our share of the first part.

Monsoon. Just the name conjures up visions of unrelenting torrents of wind-driven rain, constantly beating down on the bowed heads and bent bodies of numerous, hapless souls slogging their miserable way through the knee-deep mud of unprotected rice paddies and sucking jungle floors, slowly hacking away with their machetes at the solid array of bent saplings, bamboo clumps, and wait-a-minute vines that constantly hampered their ability to move . . . *Not quite*! While hacking through the jungle and trying to walk through the mud *was* akin to that description, the rain was far from constant, especially after the first couple of weeks of monsoon. The monsoon, or "wet" season, lasted about six months, generally from early May to mid-November. It would start out with a bang, characterized by wind and frequent rain showers. As it settled in for the long run, we would experience a shower *sometime* each day.

When in the field, it always seemed that our daily rain shower would come just before we stopped moving and settled into our position for the night. That guaranteed that we would spend the night wet—unless we were able to wrap up in a poncho liner. The nylon poncho liner was truly one of the great inventions of the entire Vietnam era. It was light as a feather to carry, but, if a soldier could wrap up in it and stay out of the water overnight, his clothes would be dry by morning. The secret was that the heat from the body would evaporate the moisture through the fibers of the liner. Since I normally slept in a small nylon Vietnamese hammock—which I could carry in my fatigue shirt pocket—covered by a poncho stretched out above me, I normally would go to sleep wet and wake up dry, as long as Charlie did not screw with us overnight. Anything to help us through the Monsoon.

Another aspect of being an American soldier in the field that I grew very fond of was the hot chow and cold beer and sodas that we had routinely every night. *I kid you not!* Although I discovered later that our unit was rather unique, not only did hot food in mermite cans arrive in our field location every night along with our resupply and water jugs, but also the battalion club issued one free beer and one free soda per man each day we were out. These were included in the resupply delivery, iced down in G.I. cans. So, as long as our resupply chopper could get in, we were properly served. Oh, well, as Sherman supposedly said, war is hell.

The day after I took command, I went to the battalion CP to get my mission for the day. As I approached, Colonel Harrold and Major Davis were sitting on a log, having a cup of C-Ration coffee.

Harrold grinned. "Morning, Bravo 6. How's the company?"

"Morning, sir. Well, we made it through the night without getting anybody killed, so I guess we're doing okay."

Major Davis motioned to the ground. "Have a seat. Want a cup of fine coffee from Uncle Sam?"

"Sure, sir. A little coffee never hurt anybody."

After making the coffee, Davis pulled his map into his lap. "Bob, we're going to cut Bravo away for a few days and let you operate on your own. Good way to get used to your company. Here," he pointed to a box drawn on his map, "is your Area of Operations. You are to conduct a search-and-destroy throughout the AO. The Battalion CP will stay in this adjacent AO with Alpha Company. Charlie Company will be north of you here. You will have 105 and 155 millimeter artillery support available from Dau Tieng. Your Forward Observer can call it for you. We can also get you gunships and Tac Air if you need it. Requests for air support will come to me here. That's about it. Any questions?"

I looked at the AO on his map. The one thing that stood out was that the little box was colored deep, dark, rich green—that meant that we would be in rubber trees and heavy jungle. "Umm, nossir. No questions for now." I drew the box on my map and handed Davis' map back to him.

"Okay. That's all I have." Davis replaced his map and picked up his canteen cup again.

Harrold watched me as I stood up. "Good luck, Bob."

"Thanks, sir." I plopped my helmet back on my head and strolled back toward my CP.

"Otte, get the platoon leaders up here. Give them five minutes to get here." I pulled out my map case and plopped down on my hammock near Lieutenant James Ryan (an alias), the artillery Forward Observer. My initial impression of Ryan was that he was an odd one, quiet, somewhat of a loner. He seemed to be very competent in doing his job, but he appeared very distrustful of Infantry officers, especially brand new company commanders. Of course, his most recent experience had been with Captain Roberts.

As soon as the platoon leaders were assembled, I outlined the operation. "This is our company AO for the next three days. We'll do an S-and-D throughout the area. As you can see, there's a lot of jungle out there." I pointed to the map. "We'll follow this trace here, stopping every once in awhile to do a cloverleaf. We'll start out with First Platoon on point out three hundred meters. The rest of the company will follow in a modified box formation with Second on the left, Third on the right, and Fourth in the rear. CP'll follow the lead platoons. I'll call in our night position for resupply when I see how we go today. Questions?"

All shook their heads. "Okay. I want to be moving in three-zero minutes. Go get them ready."

I turned around, untied and rolled my hammock and stuffed it in my pocket. As I stooped down to close up my pack, Ryan spoke up. "Well, Captain, that was a nice simple plan, but you didn't cover fire support. What do you want for artillery?"

I squatted on my back foot and looked up at him. "Available and on call. Call in your DEFCONs when we settle for the night. I'll give you the map coordinates when you need them."

"Captain, I always use my own coordinates. I haven't had much faith with those given me by the other commanders. I sincerely hope you know how to read a map better than they did."

I looked him right in the eye for a few seconds and then turned back to my pack. "Suit yourself, Lieutenant."

Thirty minutes later, the point platoon moved out of the perimeter, and the rest of us soon followed. The nearest boundary of our assigned AO was a north-south road along the edge of the rubber plantation about one thousand meters from the battalion position. Since we were still in the rubber, moving through the first area was relatively easy.

As the point approached the road, Lieutenant Prairie called his position back to me. "Bravo 6, 1-6. Over."

I took the handset from Otte. "Bravo 6."

"This is 1-6. My point element's at the road. Over."

"Bravo 6. Roger. Stay on the same azimuth and cross the road. Be sure you put out security before you cross."

"1-6 roger. We're moving . . . *Get Down!* Over there! Open up!" *Pop . . . Pop . . . Pop! Pop . . . Pop . . . Pop!* AK fire whistled overhead from the direction of the point. "Bravo 6, we're getting incoming from across the road. Looks like three or four of them. We're returning fire now. Don't think they'll last long."

"Bravo 6 roger. Be careful they don't suck you into something bigger." I looked around. As soon as the fire came whizzing over the company, everyone hit the ground. There was nothing for them to shoot at, but they were ready, if needed.

"6, 1-6. They're trying to get away to the south along the road. I think we can get 'em."

I knew Prairie was an experienced platoon leader—and a good one. "Roger, 1-6. Give it a try, but watch your ass. Don't get caught in an ambush. I don't want you going more than a couple hundred meters down the road. Do you roger?"

"Roger, Bravo 6. We're going now."

"Roger. We're moving up to the road if you need help. Out."

As I moved the company up to the road, I heard the sporadic firing and *Crump!* of grenades and M-79 rounds of a running gun battle. I hoped Prairie would watch himself—I did not want to lose a platoon leader or any of his men on my second day in command—or on any other day, for that matter.

About ten minutes later, the radio crackled. "Bravo 6, 1-6."

I took the handset from Otte. "Bravo 6. Go."

"1-6. We got two of 'em. The rest got away into the jungle across the road. We found two blood trails, so we must have gotten a couple of 'em. Over."

"6 roger. Good job. Bring them back here with you and get on back here. Any casualties?"

"6, 1-6. Negative. We're on the way."

"6 out."

I handed the handset back to Otte. He looked at me and grinned. "Well, sir, looks like you earned your Combat Infantryman Badge on your second day in command."

I grinned back. "Yeah, it does. Sure beats earning the Purple Heart, don't it?"

I reached for Webster' handset and called Battalion. "Falcon 3, Bravo 6."

"Falcon 3. Heard some firing out there. Any problems? Over."

"Bravo 6. We ran into a little resistance up here by the road, but it's over for now. No friendly casualties. Got two body count here. Estimate three got away, probably two of 'em hit. What do you want me to do with these two?"

"Falcon 3. Two body count. Not bad for your first day's work. Good job. Any markings on their clothes?"

"Bravo 6. Negative. Just black pajamas and Ho Chi Minh sandals made out of tires."

"Falcon 3. Roger. Search them, take their weapons and leave them. They won't be there long."

"Bravo 6 roger. Out."

When we crossed the road, we left the rubber and entered the jungle. For the next three hours, we cut our way through the jungle, finding nothing. Then . . .

"Bravo 6, 1-6. We've got a base camp in this ravine up here. So far, there's no sign anybody's been here lately."

"Bravo 6 roger. Pass through it and secure the other side. Out. Break-Break. 2-6, Bravo 6. Over."

"Bravo 6, 2-6."

"Bravo 6. 1-6's got an old base camp up ahead. I want you to move up and sweep the camp. 1-6's securing the other side. Move up now. Talk to 1-6 and let him know you are coming. I don't want you two shooting each other up."

"2-6 roger."

"6 out."

For the next thirty minutes, we moved up and swept through the base camp, finding little to make us believe it had been used since the French had left thirteen years earlier. With most of the dozen or so hooches falling down and no sign of recent occupation, it obviously had been abandoned for a long time. We gave it a cursory search and moved on through the jungle.

My destination for the day was a clearing along the edge of the jungle at the base of a long, flat-top hill. Our route was more or less a straight shot to the base of the hill, then to follow the hill for about two clicks (kilometers) to our night position. After we left the old camp, it took us about two hours to reach the hill and to break out of the jungle.

As we reached the hill, I called a rest halt and took out my map to provide our position to Falcon 3. After checking the map, I reached for the battalion push, noticing that Lieutenant Ryan was also talking on his fire support radio.

"Falcon 3, Bravo 6. Got a position for you."

"Falcon 3. Go ahead."

"Bravo 6. Current location's X-ray Tango 505553. We'll be changing azimuth at this time."

"Falcon 3. Roger location."

"Bravo 6 out."

As I handed the handset back to Webster, Lieutenant Ryan spoke up. "Well, Captain, I don't believe it. You gave them the exact same coordinates that I did. Maybe you *can* read a map."

"Yeah, maybe I can." I turned and motioned for the company to move out.

For the next two days, we covered our AO without finding much: a bag of rice here, a bunker or hootch there, an occasional sniper or mortar round, some movement around us at night—the typical dry hole. On the fourth day, we rejoined the battalion and conducted sweeps out of a central defensive position for another three days, with the same results.

On the morning of the eighth day, we returned to Dau Tieng base camp—the first time I had been back since taking command. As we entered the perimeter at the north gate, Lieutenant Mooradian, whom I had sent back in on the second day, met me at the gate with my jeep, designated B-6.

"Welcome home, Sir. Want a lift? I need to show you around the company area while the platoons get settled in."

"Okay, Phil. Otte, tell the platoon leaders to take 'em home. Have them drop their gear and meet me in my office as soon as they get in." I turned to Mooradian. "I do have an office, right?"

He grinned. "Yessir, you sure do, and they know where it is."

On the way to the company area, Mooradian reached into his pocket and handed me a rectangular badge with a wreath around it—the Combat Infantryman's Badge. "Battalion Adjutant said it was all right to give this to you. There's no orders yet, but you're qualified. Congratulations, Captain."

"Thanks, Phil. I've looked forward to this a long time.

Guess I'll probably earn it over and over again in this job." We both laughed.

After dropping my gear in my hootch—which I shared with Mooradian—and getting a tour of the area, I walked into my office in the back corner of the company head-quarters hootch. The platoon leaders, the FO and the First Sergeant were there waiting.

"Okay, I'm going to make this short and sweet. I've been assured there's cold beer and soda waiting at the company club for the troops. Make sure they get one. First priority is to clean all weapons, then get their equipment clean and ready to move out again. After that's done, they can get themselves cleaned up and relax and have fun. But be careful. I don't want anybody falling down drunk tonight. I expect we'll be going out again tomorrow. Questions?"

No questions.

"By the way, I hope to see all officers at the Officers' Club tonight. To celebrate my first week in command, the first round is on me." They grinned as I dismissed them.

I turned to First Sergeant Emelio Suarez (an alias). "Top, I heard something this afternoon as we came in that I didn't like worth a damn. I heard one of the men left back here say how glad he was that the company was in, so he wouldn't have to pull bunker duty for awhile. Well, he's in for a surprise. My combat troops don't pull bunker guard. Their job is to relax a bit and then get ready to go out again. They're available if we get a red alert or some-thing, but the bunkers will continue to be manned by the 'sick, lame and lazy' who stay back here. Understand?"

"Yessir. That's what we'll do if that's what you want."

"That's what I want."

That evening after chow, most of the officers in the battalion gathered at the Battalion Officers Club, which was located in the S-4's building. Since the S-4 was re-sponsible for supply and logistics, this was a very con-venient arrangement, especially at resupply time. The beer and soda which we were issued in the field came from the club.

Our battalion club was organized into six branches: an Officers Club and a Non-Commissioned Officers (NCO) Club for the sergeants, both on the south side of the airstrip near Battalion Headquarters, and separate clubs for the four line companies to the north of the runway. We had one of the most profitable battalion club systems in the Division. The value of club property was estimated at over $25,000.00, which made it more valuable than even the Division Headquarters club back in Cu Chi. (We did not know at the time that we would be fighting six months later to keep our club from being taken over and consolidated at Division level, a fight which we were to win for an extended period of time.)

Anyway, on the evening of October 8th, the officers of the Battalion were in the Officers Club getting raucously blitzed. The other line company commanders were there: Captain Herb Chancey, Alpha Company; Captain Gus Fishburne, Charlie Company; and Captain Bob Culver, Delta Company. Most of us were drinking beer until someone brought out a bottle of Jack Daniels. Feeling that we should at least sample this golden elixir, we proceeded to empty the bottle — and the next as well. At one point, we were even drinking sickly-green Creme-de-menthe like water. I would be no exaggeration to say that we were pretty well anesthetized by 10:00 o'clock when, all of a sudden, *The world caved in!*

Crash! Crash! Crash!

"Incoming! Get down!" somebody yelled — probably one of the more sober ones who could still distinguish incoming mortars from outgoing artillery. We all ducked into a small area under the concrete sairway to the upper floor of the S-4 shop.

I listened as the mortars continued to fall. I was amazed at how quickly I had sobered up when the attack started. I was now cold sober. After a few minutes, I realized that this was no run-of-the-mill, harassing mortar attack. This was getting serious. This could be a prelude to a ground attack — and I and all of my officers were here, cut off from the company by the runway.

I listened. There were no explosions near the club. I left the stairway and moved to the door of the club. It sounded like the mortars were falling on the other side of the base camp in the helicopter parking area. I had no idea how many aircraft were three, but there were usually at least five or ten there overnight.

"Hey, Bob, get your ass back over here before you get hurt!"

"Don't worry, Herb. They're not falling here. I think the helipad is getting most of this for now."

"Captain, come on back. We don't want to lose you." That was Mooradian.

"No, Phil. It's okay out here." I listened one more time. "I'm going back to the company. This could be something more serious, and all the officers are over here. Coming, Phil?"

Mooradian cautiously walked over and stood next to me, listening. "You sure you want to do this, sir?"

"Yep." I then grabbed my steel pot and set out for my jeep. Mooradian hurried up behind me.

"If you're going, I'm going, too."

I started the vehicle, pulled a U-turn, and took off. Since I had not been in Vietnam long enough to learn that VC mortarmen do not use forward observers, I attributed to them our American techniques for indirect fire and drove in blackout so their FOs would not see me. I did not know it yet, but this would prove to be a rather eventful trip.

I drove about a city block, turned right, gunned the engine and raced along the fence surrounding the Brigade Headquarters Motor Pool. I saw the motor pool entrance slip by, then—*WHAM!* I hit something hard with the jeep—and with my head! I glanced over to make sure Mooradian was okay. He just shook his head, looked at me, and grinned. I looked up and saw a spiderweb configuration of cracks on the windshield. Now I realized where our helmets had made contact with a decidedly hostile immovable object. Good old steel pots! I really do not look good with a mushy head.

I stood up in the jeep and saw another jeep crossway in the ditch, its front end buried in the fence. A soldier—presumably the driver—was just standing up and dusting himself off.

"You okay?" I yelled at him over the din of mortar explosions.

"Yeah, I guess so. What happened?"

"Dunno. Go to the aid station and get checked out. See you." With that, I jumped back in and gunned the vehicle down the street, turning right at the end of the motor pool onto the road that led past the Brigade Headquarters and across the runway to the line companies' areas. My jeep drove okay—except for the incessant scraping sound where the left tire rubbed against the smashed-in fender well.

We scooted past Brigade, dodged a jeep coming down the road in the opposite direction in the dark, also in blackout, and started across the runway. It seemed that I was not the only neophyte there, since all the other vehicles that I could see were being driven in blackout. Well, maybe they did not get many mortar attacks there. As I thought about that, I suddenly swerved the wheel to the left as a big two-and-a-half-ton truck came speeding right at us out of the darkness. I ended up in the ditch, entangled in the concertina wire along the runway, as the truck rumbled out of sight.

I backed out of the ditch, returned to the road, cleared the runway, and barreled along toward the company area. Off to my right was the headquarters of the 2nd Battalion, 77th Artillery, our direct support artillery battalion.

Just as I passed the entrance to the headquarters—*WHAM!* "Oh, crap," I thought. Once again, I felt the helmet make contact with the windshield. Once again, I glanced over at Mooradian—but this time, *he wasn't there!*

"Hey, Phil. Where the hell are you?"

"Uhhhh," I heard him moan. "Over here." I heard the voice rise from the roadway.

"You hurt?" I was a little worried, since I did not want to have to look for another XO.

"Noooo, I don't think so. What'd we hit?"

"Another jeep, I guess. Come on, get up and let's see."

I climbed out of the jeep and walked ahead. Sure enough, there was the wreck of another jeep. The driver was just standing there, scratching his head and looking back and forth at both jeeps.

"Boy, looks like you got hit by the same RPG as I did," he gasped as I hurried up.

"Yeah, that must have been it—an RPG. You okay?"

"Yeah, I'm okay, but my jeep isn't. I don't think I can move it."

"Well, just as long as you're not hurt. Where are you from?"

"Second of the Seventy-second arty. This here's the Battalion Commander's jeep."

"Okay. See you."

I went back to my jeep to get it started and get on down to the company. However, that last hit was all she wrote. My jeep had died and given up the ghost. The entire trip from the club to this point had taken no more than five or six minutes—and it looked like I totaled three jeeps doing it. The mortars were still falling back around the landing pad and the threat still existed.

"Come on, Phil," I urged. "Let's get on over to the company. We got work to do."

"Coming, sir."

With that, we set off at a trot toward the company area, reaching it in about five minutes. As I burst into the orderly room, the First Sergeant met me at the door.

"What's the situation, Top?"

"Sir, the bunker line's manned with a few of our stay-behind people, along with some of the field troops from the platoons. The rest of the platoons are in the rear as reserves, down behind the sandbags around the hooches. The whole perimeter is on red alert."

"Yeah, I'd have guessed that. Any other officers around yet?

"Nossir, not yet. The platoon sergeants are standing by."

"Get them in here ASAP. Then get Otte and Webster over here with the radios. Have 'em up on battalion and signed in."

"Yessir," and away he went.

While we waited, I sent Mooradian after our weapons, after telling him to get that jeep in as soon as he had a chance. I did not know whom we had hit, but I had rather keep the ruckus down as long as I could.

A couple of minutes later, the platoon sergeants loped in, along with the First Sergeant.

"Okay, here's what I want you to do. I want each platoon to man your bunkers with all your people, including the 'sick, lame and lazy,' with one squad kept back in reserve. Get them far enough back so you can move them anywhere you need them. Get up on your radios and make a commo check with my guys. I'll be behind the middle platoon. Those damn mortars are dwindling away. If we get a ground attack after them, I don't want them getting through that bunker line. All of you know what to do. Now let's get on out there and do it! Any questions? Okay, get moving."

In ten minutes, everybody was in position and ready for whatever happened. I and my RTOs were in the middle of the open area between the bunker line and the hooches, a sight to behold. There I was, sitting on the ground, leaning back against the radios with a handset in each hand, mumbling for those gook sons of bitches to come on in and take what we could dish out. We were ready for anything they could throw at us, chomping at the bit to get at them—so, of course, nothing came.

An hour after the mortars stopped falling, Brigade reduced the alert to yellow, I called the combat troops back off the line and sent them back to their hooches, sent the radios back to the commo shop, and returned to my office.

Early the next morning, Mooradian towed the Bravo 6 jeep back to the company area. I went out to look at it. Both windshields were smashed, and both front corners were crumpled back so that the front of the vehicle was shaped like an arrowhead. It was obviously totaled, so we would need a new one.

Later that morning, I found out that the other two jeeps that I had hit belonged to the Brigade Commander and the Artillery Battalion Commander. I had totaled three jeeps in about five minutes, and I caught a lot of ribbing from Chancey and Fishburne when they found out about it.

"Why don't you save some of that destructive capability for the enemy?" grinned Fishburne. "That was a lot like a bull getting loose in a china shop—breaking stuff all over the place."

"Yeah," Chancey chimed in. "That's what we're going to call you from now on—'Bravo Bull'."

So, from that obviously minor incident—quite understandable while in the middle of a mortar attack—I acquired a nickname which, though born in jest, came to be well-respected in the months to come, and certain people who knew me well have called me that ever since that day. In fact, it became my unofficial radio call sign. It must have confused the hell out of the VC!

I was not the only one to acquire an enduring nickname around that time. Alpha 6, Herb Chancey, a Florida native, wrote the Governor of Florida and talked him into sending a baby alligator to the officers and men of Alpha Company. They built a small concrete "pond" in front of their orderly room for their new little pet, which he seemed to love. Of course, Chancey became "Alphagator" to us right away.

So, from such humble beginning rose the seemingly

unstoppable dynamic duo of the Bull and the Gator. We—and our companies—would support each other above all other units for the rest of our mutual command periods. That proved to be a very satisfactory combination!

Weapons Available to an Infantry Company

COMPANY ASSETS

M-16 Rifle (5.56 mm) with variations

M-60 Machine Gun (7.62 mm)

M-79 Grenade Launcher (40 mm)

M-72 LAW (Light Anti-Tank Weapon)

81 mm Mortar

60 mm Mortar

90 mm Recoilless Rifle

Hand Grenade

Smoke Grenade, Colors

Tear Gas Grenade

Pistol, Automatic (.45 Cal.)

MECHANIZED INFANTRY

M-113 Armored Personnel Carrier (APC):
.50 Cal. Machine Gun
7.62 mm Machine Gun

BATTALION ASSETS

4.2-inch Mortar

106 mm Recoilless Rifle

DIVISION ASSETS

Artillery:
105 mm Howitzer
155 mm Howitzer
175 mm Howitzer

M-48 Tank:
90 mm Main Gun
7.62 mm Machine Gun

AVIATION ASSETS

Helicopter Gunship:
2.75 mm Rockets
7.62 mm Gatlin Gun

Tactical Fighter (USAF):
Bombs (Various)
Napalm
20 mm Machine Gun

CHAPTER THREE
FALL ACTIVITIES

The rest of October and most of November and December saw a succession of dry holes, occasionally punctuated by harsh reality—that is, AK and RPG fire from a few extremely ill-adjusted and hostile individuals wearing black pajamas and "Mr. Goodyear" rubber-tire sandals. For that period, the good news was that we did not lose very many people. The bad news was that the basic incompetence of some of our leaders became more evident, and we almost went crazy with boredom. The boredom came with humping the jungle, the rice paddies, and the rubber plantations day after day after day, finding very little of importance or interest. Of course, such boredom based on lack of significant contact with the enemy actually *appealed* to some people.

We spent much of October reacting to intelligence agent reports that certain enemy units were sighted in certain locations around the Dau Tieng area, including the Michelin rubber plantation—the local home ground, recreation center and spa for the VC. The basic problem was the validity of the agent reports. They were not compiled by trained intelligence operatives, reporting on their personal observations based on their own field work. No—the intelligence reports to which we responded repeatedly were based on information reported to authorities—American and Vietnamese—by numerous local Vietnamese citizens, for which valuable information they were handsomely and frequently paid. Information gathered from various sources was evaluated and disseminated with reliability ratings stated in a combination of letters and numbers, with "A" and "1" being the most reliable, and "F" and "6" denoting the least reliable. Should we have been surprised that most of the reports for which we spent many weeks in the field checking out were of the "F6" variety, which we dubbed "UR" for "unsubstantiated rumor"?

I cannot say that no one believed these reports. Colonel Kenneth Burton (an alias), our illustrious Brigade Commander of the time, must have believed them. He and his headquarters jumped on every one of those reports, and they felt no embarrassment or guilt about sending us out into the jungle for two weeks to check out that VC battalion just south of the rubber, even though we could not find "hide nor hair" of any such unit ever having been there. Find an extra bag of rice, and we were extended out there for another week, seeking that ever-elusive "body count." Great fun, huh?

We had a few personnel changes in the company during this period. Near the end of October, Sergeant Hughes finally received a map-bearer, a title sometimes conferred on new Second Lieutenants by Platoon Sergeants. Fresh from OCS, Lieutenant Steve Wilder became the Second Platoon Leader. A week later, Lieutenant Prairie was designated as the new Battalion Recon Platoon Leader and left the company. Shortly thereafter, a new First Platoon Leader, Second Lieutenant Richard Walker, reported for duty. Walker, also an OCS grad, seemed to have a good attitude, but his physical appearance left a lot to be desired. Walker must have weighed over two-hundred-and-fifty pounds. Although he stood over six feet tall, he really looked fat. I was very apprehensive about his ability to keep up with the company and function as a platoon leader. Over the next couple of weeks, however, I was forced to reassess my initial impression. Walker was able to fulfill his role very well. Both new officers proved to be very able lieutenants.

On the 2nd of November, a major battle broke out around a Special Forces camp at Loch Ninh in the First Infantry Division's AO, which was adjacent and to the east of the 25th Division's. After another, even more sig-

nificant, battle during an extensive North Vietnamese offensive in 1973, this battle would be referred to as "Loch
Ninh 1." The eastern edge of the Michelin plantation
served as the boundary between the two Division sectors.
The Falcon battalion and the 2/12 Infantry ("Flame") were
tasked to go to Loch Ninh to support the First. Flame
actually went into the battle at the camp, while we drew
the mission of manning the perimeter at Fire Support Base
"Doughboy."

We were to fly by C-130 from Dau Tieng to Quan Loi,
a Brigade base camp in the First's AO, and stage from
there by helo to the firebase. Bravo was broken down into
two parts: one hundred men would fly aboard one aircraft,
and the remainder would travel with the headquarters element. We would be the second line company to depart.

Taking off from Dau Tieng in a four-engine C-130 was
always a hair-raising experience. Although officially rated
as C-130 capable, the runway was unusually short for
such a feat. It required the aircraft to start as close as
possible to the fence behind it, rev up its motors as high
as possible, pop the clutch (or whatever similar apparatus
the aircraft has) and gun it as hard as the pilot could down
the runway toward the fence at the opposite end. The op-
erative word here was "down," since the runway sloped
slightly downward at the other end. With luck and many
a prayer, the plane would grab air just in time to barely
avoid the fence. We did it that day in an aircraft loaded
with one hundred combat-equipped troops.

It was not easy, but we made it over and headed for
Quan Loi. The partial plane load had taken off before the
main element. I and my CP Group were in the second
plane with the majority of my company.

About twenty minutes out, the plane shuddered a bit.
I motioned for the loadmaster to come over.

"What's the problem with the aircraft, Sergeant?"

"Just a minute, sir. I'll check." He spoke into the mi-
crophone attached to his headset, then listened. "Okay,
sir," he said to me. "It seems we lost one engine. That

means we'll have to detour to Ton Son Nhut in Saigon."

"Damn it! We're supposed to be at Quan Loi to link up with a lift company. Will you ask the pilot to contact Falcon 3 and inform him of our situation?"

"Roger, sir." He spoke again into the mike, then back to me. "He's making that call now."

"Thanks."

About forty-five minutes later, we landed at Ton Son Nhut without further incident. We were informed that a replacement aircraft would be dispatched to pick us up and should arrive within the hour. Three hours later, we were still sitting on the runway next to the disabled plane, waiting to be picked up. By that time, we had gone through all our C-rations and much of our water, since the dry season in Vietnam made one very hot and thirsty.

We were finally retrieved around mid-afternoon after a four-hour sunbath, compliments of the U.S. Air Force. Thirty minutes later, we landed at Quan Loi, joined the rest of the company which had been waiting there for us, and caught the lift into the fire base.

Falcon 3 met me as I exited the chopper. "Welcome, Bravo 6. I thought we had lost you."

"Damn Air Farce. Not only did we not make it here on time, but they left us out on the end of the runway for four long hours with no word about a replacement plane. We had no idea what was going on 'til the plane showed up. Sure glad we're protecting their asses out here. So what's going on?"

"We're just doing fire base security. We'll send out ambushes at night and sweeps during the day. Your sector is from that bunker over there to the one over there." He pointed them out.

"Will we be doing ambushes and sweeps every day?"

"Affirmative. All companies will be sending them out to their front."

"Okay. Then I'll leave one platoon off the line. What about the bunkers? We got any digging to do?"

"No, the bunkers are ready for you." He grinned at me.

"Wait 'til you see those bunkers. They will blow your mind."

I looked skeptically at him. "What do you mean?"

"You'll see. They are now called the 'Hay Hole' after the current First Division commander, General Hay. They were originally called the 'DePuy Bunker' after the last commander, who developed them in the first place. But don't bitch about them. They're all we have."

"Okay. Let me get over there and view those works of art. Do we have a meeting tonight?"

"Yeah. We'll call you around 1800 hours. Go get your company settled in."

"Roger." I turned back toward the company. "Otte, get me the platoon leaders ASAP."

I walked over to the company sector to see what the bunkers looked like. It took me awhile to figure them out, but when I did, they were scary. Someone—DePuy, I presume, or more likely, one of his staff officers—obviously tried to make a name for himself by developing a fool-proof bunker complex. The only problem, though, is that *nothing* is fool-proof.

The perimeter consisted of two circles of bunkers. All bunkers on both circles were built alike and were evenly spaced so that each bunker on the inner circle fit exactly between and to the rear of each two bunkers on the outer circle. Each bunker was deep enough for a man to stand upright and shoot through the apertures. The only openings in the bunker were the back entrance and two apertures in front. The apertures faced forty-five degrees to either side. No one in the bunker could see to his front, since the front was a solid sloped embankment designed to reflect RPG rounds. The intent was for the firer to shoot at forty-five degrees to the front of the bunker next to it, rather than having each firer engaging targets to his own front. If all firers in all outer ring bunkers were firing in this manner, they created an interlocking system of cross-fire all around the perimeter. Each inner ring bunker's apertures were sited to allow the firers to shoot to the front of the two bunkers to the right and left front, thereby further interlocking defensive fires from the bunkers. The basic idea was to create a continuous wall of fire through which no human would attempt to venture.

Although I am sure this system had its rabid proponents, I immediately saw several problems with such an arrangement. The sheer effort required to dig such a deep hole each night, particularly by troops who were out on operations all day, would take hours to complete and create very exhausted soldiers. They had little rest as it was, without adding to the problem. If one or two bunkers were knocked out, a hole would be created in the wall of fire through which enemy troops could charge. With the very limited ability to shift fire created by the confining nature of the two apertures in each bunker, troops would have to leave the bunkers to engage the intruders or leave it up to reaction forces to plug the gap in the perimeter. If ammunition ran low, the wall of fire could not be maintained, which would make all bunkers vulnerable. Without the ability to defend themselves in any direction, troops could be slaughtered before they could extract themselves from their holes.

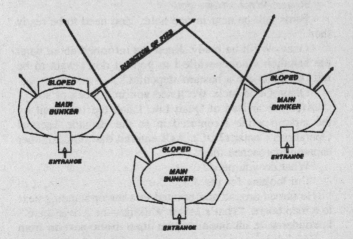

After contemplating the advantages and disadvantages of this bunker system, I decided that I much preferred our method of preparing foxholes with sufficient overhead cover to stop mortar rounds, but with the ability to fire in all directions. I resigned myself to having to put up with these monstrosities while we were there. I was thankful that it was the First Division's commander who had the hots for stardom and not mine.

Our stint in Firebase Doughboy turned out to be very short. The next morning, I was summoned to the CP. As I ambled into the bunker, Major Davis was making a cup of coffee.

"Morning, Major. You called?"

"Yeah. I think I have some good news for you. How would you like to get out of here for a few days?"

"I think I'd like it, depending on where you're going to send me."

"Bravo's next for a standdown assignment. We've been tasked to send a company back to Quan Loi for a week to pull base camp security. Should be easy duty and give your men a bit of a rest. You are to report to the Brigade CP to coordinate your sector and duties."

"Roger. When do we go?"

"Birds will be here in one hour. You need to be ready then."

"Okay. We'll be ready. Keep me informed about what the battalion's doing while I'm gone. I don't want to be left out there like a bastard stepchild."

"Okay. Good luck. We'll see you in a week or so."

After we arrived at Quan Loi, I had the men wait by the airstrip while I reported in to the Brigade Tactical Operations Center (TOC). As I entered the TOC, another captain approached me.

"What do you need?"

"I'm looking for the 3."

He turned around and pointed to a major standing next to a map board. "That's Major Wilkins—he's over there." I wondered if all majors spent their lives next to map boards. Maybe when they died, they went to the Great Map Board in the Sky if they were good little SOBs.

"Thanks." I ambled over to the major.

Major Wilkins (an alias) looked around as I approached. He smiled, stuck out his hand and said, "Hi, I'm John Wilkins. You must be the commander of the company from the Twenty-Fifth that I'm looking for."

I shook his hand and nodded. "Roger that. I'm Captain Bob Hemphill of Bravo Company, Third of the Twenty-second Infantry."

"Want a cup of coffee, Bob?"

"Love one."

He signaled to a soldier at a desk in the corner, who took exactly thirty seconds to produce the coffee. This place must be well-organized, I thought.

"Thanks. What do you want me to do?"

He turned to a small map on one side of the board. "This is the base camp. Your sector is from this point by the road," he pointed as he spoke, "to this point by the walk-through gate. You'll be expected to send out a platoon-size night ambush and daylight sweep each day. The ambush should be out at least two clicks and the sweep should cover at least five clicks. You pick the locations. There's not much out to your front but brush and rubber, no villages or anything. Your men can eat in the First of the Eighteenth mess hall. You can also get in touch with the S-4 and schedule the shower and uniform exchange point if you want to. Otherwise, pick out your CP location and make yourself at home. Any questions?"

I moved over to the map and studied our sector of the perimeter. "That looks like a little over two clicks. That's a lot of sector to cover with three platoons, since one'll be out most of the time. We may have to outpost some of it. We'll be ready to send out an ambush tonight and start the sweeps tomorrow. We'll need maps of this area. I'll send the field first over to get them. Other than that, no comments." I finished the coffee and set the cup on the nearest desk. "Anything else?"

"No, not now. There'll be a staff meeting at 1730 hours which you need to attend. Go ahead and get your guys settled."

"Roger. See you later." I turned and left the TOC.

As I approached the airstrip, I waved the platoon leaders over. As they assembled, the field first sergeant and my RTOs also came up.

"Top, I want you to go over to the brigade CP and see the S-2 about some maps of this area. We'll be needing them ASAP. While you are there, find out where the 1/18th Infantry's mess hall is and arrange for our guys to eat there. First thing, though, is to find me a CP, probably somewhere in that clump of trees over there," I pointed out the prospective location across the airstrip. "Maybe the trees will give us some protection from all this red dust being kicked up by all those aircraft propellers." I had noticed the red clouds which formed rapidly as the pilots reversed engines on the C-130s to stop them. I surely did not want to set up in their backblast area!

Then to the platoon leaders: "Our mission here is to man part of the perimeter and to send out platoon-size patrols to ambush at night and sweep during the day. We'll divide the perimeter into four sectors, with the sector of the platoon that's out being outposted by the other platoons. 1-6, you're first in the saddle tonight. Have your platoon sergeant arrange your chow times with the field first. As soon as I get the CP set up, I'll let you know. Let me know when you get set-up so I can check your area. Now come on and let me show you where your areas are."

After taking the platoon leaders around our portion of the perimeter, I walked toward the clump of trees looking for the CP that the first sergeant and the RTOs were supposed to set up. As I approached the trees, I noticed that it was not really a clump of trees. Instead, it was a *line* of trees and bushes surrounding a double tennis court, adjacent to a large, colonial-style house. I would not have been surprised to see a swimming pool, but, so far, one was not evident.

But where was the CP?

"Otte, where in hell are you guys?" I yelled as I approached the trees.

"Behind the trees, sir. Come on in!"

As I stepped through the treeline, I almost tripped over Otte's radio and pack. I looked around and saw that the CP had been set up in linear fashion between the brushline and the fence around the tennis courts. Once in here, there was plenty of room.

Otte pointed to two trees at the end of the CP area nearest the house. "Sir, your hammock will fit in there if you like it there. Gives you a little area with some privacy where you can meet with your lieutenants."

"Fine." I strung up my hammock and stretched out on it, looking out over the courts, wondering who the hell ever used it. Probably whoever lived in the house. I would have to find out about that.

Later at the staff meeting, I discovered that the house was still occupied by the French family who had run the rubber plantation before the Americans converted the area into a base camp. Members of the family regularly commuted back and forth to Saigon, carrying on the family business, while others seldom left the small French compound set up around the house—and within the protection of the American perimeter. Of course, the compound was off-limits to Americans unless invited. Kind of like having the best of both worlds.

As I left the meeting, Major Wilkins walked with me to the door of the TOC. As I turned to head back to my CP, he laughed and said, "Wait until tomorrow morning. The French may have a surprise for you." I had no idea what he meant—until I awoke the next morning.

Shortly after daylight, I awoke with a start. I set up in the hammock, my instincts sharply tuned, wondering what had awakened me. Then I heard the distinctive *thwock-tlop-thwock-tlop* of a tennis ball being hit back and forth.

I glanced over toward the courts, then did a double-take. Out on the court was a young Caucasian woman—probably in her late teens or early twenties—playing tennis with a withered old Vietnamese man who was obviously her instructor. She had to have been the daughter of the French family living in the compound. In a normal situation back in the States, she would have been considered a reasonably attractive woman who might merit a second look. In that location, she was dynamite!

"Oh, hell," I murmured to no one in particular. "I hope the troops don't hear about this one. I won't be able to get rid of them." I looked around at my CP group. Everyone, to a man, was staring at the girl on the tennis court.

We spent the next week at Quan Loi, repeating the same routine each day and night. It was a quiet time for us, since no one walked into our ambushes, and we found nothing on our sweeps. The French girl came out and played tennis each day at the same time, but she was never seen at any other time. At the end of the week, we rejoined the battalion. The troops had been able to shower and receive new, clean uniforms. The main controversy of the week was that the new uniforms had First Division patches sewn on them. I made sure that the platoon leaders *immediately* lined up the troops and ripped off the offending patches. I had no such problem with my own uniform. I sent back to Dau Tieng for a clean set of fatigues with all my patches already on the shirt and donned them when it was my turn to go through the shower. Gotta keep up the image . . .

On 15 November, we were back in Dau Tieng once more, scheduled to go out again the following day for another stroll through the Michelin plantation. Wandering around among the rubber trees and VC villages was getting a bit old, especially considering the number of mines and booby traps we stumbled over.

I left the mess hall after lunch and wandered into the Battalion TOC. Major Davis was sitting behind his desk, sipping a cup of coffee.

"What are you doing, Major—taking a break?"

He nodded. "Yeah. First one today."

"Anything going on out there anywhere? Anything would be better than another terrain walk in the Michelin."

"As a matter of fact, Bravo 6, we've been given a change in mission. I was about to call a commanders' meeting." He turned to his assistant and told him to get the commanders and staff to the TOC by 1330 hours—thirty minutes later.

"What's going on?"

"The short version is that we're airlifting out at 1600 hours to a village over by Nui Ba Den Mountain. The Special Forces camp there has intelligence indicating a possible ground attack against the camp and village. We'll form a perimeter just outside the village to attempt to draw off any attack."

"1600? That's not much time to get the company back together."

"Announcements at all base camp facilities are being made even as we speak."

"Roger that." I walked over to the phone and called the company. I told First Sergeant Suarez to get everybody back to the platoon areas and to have the platoon leaders standing by at 1345 hours.

By 1730 hours, we had deployed and were setting up our sector of the perimeter outside the village of Phu Khuong. The trip had been short—only a ten-minute flight. The flat terrain was marked only by moderately tall grass and low bushes.

One dangerous situation developed as we landed and spread out to the designated perimeter—*girls*! Shortly after our arrival, I was sitting on my helmet in the area designated as my company CP, going over my map while I waited for the platoon leaders to notify me that they were ready for me to check their positions.

I heard Otte laugh. "Well, Captain, I guess they know we're here for sure."

He pointed toward the village and I looked up. "Oh, hell!" I mumbled. "I guess we'll spend the next couple of hours kickin them out of the foxholes."

Trailing out of the village toward the troops' positions was a procession of five young ladies, all carrying small lacy parasols—the universal symbol of their profession. That's all we needed out there—we may have been on the verge of being attacked, but we had nothing better to do than deal with a bunch of prostitutes.

"Otte, tell the platoon leaders that I'd better not catch anybody with one of those girls. If I do, it's an automatic Article 15. They'd better be more interested in digging in and protecting their own asses than getting some."

I went back to my map study. A few minutes later, I stood up and surveyed the area. No parasols in sight.

"You all stay here. I'm going to check out the area. If anybody calls, come find me." I'd better find out where those VC parasols disappeared to.

As I wandered over toward third platoon, I noticed an open parasol lying over a bush off to the left. I quietly walked over to the bush and peered over it.

On the ground behind the bush was a young soldier fully in the saddle between two tan, outstretched legs, driving hard, oblivious to everything around him—including me. I moved slowly around to his side—still neither one knew I was there—and jumped him big-time.

"What the hell do you think you're doing, soldier?" I yelled at him. He froze in mid-stroke. The girl's eyes flew open in alarm. He stumbled upright, fumbling with his pants, white as a sheet. She jumped up and scurried around, trying to get her clothing together.

"*Stand at attention* when I talk to you!" He snapped to, stood ramrod straight, white as a ghost.

"S-Sorry, sir," he stuttered. His pants fell down around his ankles.

"Get your pants up and get back to your squad! I'll deal with you when we get back to base camp."

"Yessir." He grabbed his pants and took off toward second platoon.

After looking around a little more and finding nothing else, I ended up back at the company CP. I grinned at Sergeant Johnson.

"Well, Top, I think I just made an impression on one of our young soldiers. I caught him in mid-stroke under a bush with one of those young dollies. I probably scared him so bad he won't get another hard-on for a long time."

We remained in position for two days, but the anticipated attack never materialized. Our nightly ambushes and daily platoon sweeps in the area turned up nothing. The Special Forces team received no more reports of impending doom, so we left and returned to Dau Tieng.

Waiting for me at Dau Tieng was a new Artillery Forward Observer, First Lieutenant Frank Bennett (an alias). Lieutenant Ryan was on his way home. LT Bennett was an Infantry officer who had been detailed to the Artillery for six months to serve as an FO. At least he knew where Fort Benning was.

During the previous spring before Colonel Burton became commander, the Third Brigade had fought the Battle of Soui Tre, during which it had achieved the highest single-battle body count of the war, a total of 647 VC bodies buried in mass graves. The burning desire for every brigade commander after that was to record his "Soui Tre," and Burton was no exception. That was likely the reason that *every* report of enemy units sighted—no matter how unlikely—had to be checked out on the ground. There just might be a couple of Main Force regiments lurking out there which we could entice into attacking us so that we could mow them down like weeds and record a high body count. The fact that such units and/or engagements never materialized never dampened his spirit or enthusiasm. Of course, we *did* get a couple of Main Force water buffalo.

There was the day in late November, however, when "Flexible 6"—Colonel Burton's call sign—*thought* he was actually in combat. The Falcon battalion was operating out of a small perimeter in the jungle along the edge of a watershed, which was a clear area of about seventy-five meters on each side of a small stream which meandered through the jungle. The main part of our perimeter was inside the jungle and extended from jungle edge back around to jungle edge. To round out the perimeter, the watershed side was outposted to serve as an early warning in case something came at us from that side. The watershed—particularly during the dry season as it was then—served as a helipad/landing zone for helicopter traffic, both individual choppers for whatever purpose and transport formations for lifting ground units.

Early in the afternoon, we received word that Flex 6 was inbound and would arrive shortly. All company commanders were summoned to the battalion CP to meet with him and Falcon 6. We all wondered what the hell he wanted out there. He was not known to frequent dangerous places such as the jungle where matters could be detrimental to his health.

A few minutes after we had assembled around Major Davis' hammock, discussing how we could arrange a VC mortar attack to greet him, we heard the chopper approaching. The bird set down about fifty meters from the edge of the woodline where we were waiting. Falcon 6 greeted him and escorted him to our location, introducing each of us in turn.

Just as Flex 6 was looking at Falcon 6's map and was about to enlighten us with his extensive combat knowledge—*KA-BOOM! KA-BOOM*! Two explosions resounded from the vicinity of the waiting helicopter. Kneeling down on one knee along with the others around me, I determined that the explosions were from the impact of 82-millimeter mortar rounds, which my mortar platoon—the only one in the field with the battalion on that operation—would return with a vengeance.

Not all of us were down on one knee in the woodline. The last thing we saw of Flex 6 was his ass waving in the grass as he low-crawled—yes, low-crawled on knees and elbows—as fast as he could back to his helicopter. Just as he reached the bird, threw himself through the door, and the pilot pulled pitch to get the hell out of there, a third round landed close enough to blow off one of the doors as the pilot made his turn and gained altitude. As we watched the craft disappear in the distance, we were all smirking at the memory of Burton's unusual departure. This had been a very entertaining afternoon! This experience also must have been very impressive to Colonel Burton—he never bothered us in the field again!

Three days later, we were called home. That means that our operation was terminated and we were to be picked up and taken back to base camp. Bravo Company was designated as last out. Probably the two most dangerous missions a unit could draw during airmobile operations were to be first in during an aerial assault and last out during a unit pick-up. As occurred throughout the Army, those units which did something well usually received that same mission repeatedly. In Falcon's case, Alpha frequently received the mission of first in, and Bravo pulled more last-outs than all the other units combined.

We were notified that we would be working with ten Hueys in the lift company. Since we planned six personnel per ship, that meant that the final contingent would be sixty soldiers. To fulfill that commitment, I would keep back two platoons, along with me and my RTOs. All companies were to leave their Claymore mines in place in their sectors of the perimeter, except those outposting the clearing. Outposts would be brought in and, if anything happened in that direction, the helicopter door gunners and/or the orbiting gunships would handle it. As the extraction progressed and the other companies moved out of their positions, my guys would move in and take over their Claymore generators. By the time we were alone, my men had the entire jungle portion of the perimeter outposted, each of them handling five or six generators. All of them were within sight of their platoon leader, and the platoon leaders were within sight of me. I was located near the treeline where I could see them and watch for the incoming aircraft.

The particularly dangerous thing about this situation was that the VC could very well observe the lift operation and know that most of the units had departed. They did not know exactly how many of us were left, but there certainly should not be very many of us. If they chose to attack while we were thus exposed, it could become detrimental to *our* health. After the next-to-last lift departed, we were, naturally, a bit anxious while we waited during the twenty minutes or so turn-around time that it took the slicks to return. We knew the Bad Guys were out there.

They stayed out there until the helicopters returned. My men had been divided into aircraft loads where they stood and, therefore, knew which bird to run for. As the lead aircraft touched down, I signaled by raising and dropping my arm quickly, which was repeated by the platoon leaders. At that cue, all Claymores in the perimeter were blown in unison—a tactic known as a *Ring of Steel* or a *Ring of Fire*—generators were jerked off the wires, and every man hauled ass for his designated chopper. They had been instructed not to look back or to slow down for *any* reason and to dive into the craft as rapidly as possible.

As I ran across the open area toward one of the birds near the center of the formation—Otte and Webster bounding along close behind me—I heard the *pop-pop-pop* of AK rounds echoing over my head as the VC opened up from the woodline on our little band. As we dove into the choppers, the door gunners opened up on the woodline behind us. As the aircraft lifted off, the two gunships orbiting above us rolled in and conducted several rocket and mini-gun passes along the woodline we had just left. After determining that none of my men had been hit, I chalked up another successful "last-out" and settled back to enjoy the ride home.

During early December, I acquired a new RTO, Specialist 4 Ron Atkinson, a short, red-headed kid who I discovered could hump a radio and overloaded rucksack through the boonies all day without faltering. He had been in one of my platoons for several months, and getting the job as the CO's RTO was a bit of a break for him. He proved to be a very responsive and level-headed soldier. I sent Otte back to the base camp to spend his last couple of months in the Company commo shop. He had certainly done his job well and deserved to get out of the field.

Also during early December, Lieutenant Wilder left the company to take over the Battalion Recon Platoon. Lieutenant Prairie, the previous Recon Platoon Leader, moved up to the S-3 shop to be the Assistant S-3. My Second Platoon was left with no officer, so SSG Joe Hughes once more filled in as acting Platoon Leader.

One bright, dry Saturday morning in mid-December during a 2-day standdown in Dau Tieng, I was given the mission of outposting Highway 14 south from Dau Tieng for about six clicks. The purpose for outposting the road was to provide security for the movement of one artillery battery from a small firebase back to base camp. My plan to accomplish the necessary road coverage was to drop off one squad every five hundred meters on alternating sides of the road. Squads were to sweep continuously through their assigned areas. In that manner, I had hoped to thwart any attempt to attack the convoy.

The main problem turned out to be the locals, *not* the VC. En route to the firebase location, we passed through two villages. As the units moved past them, several young ladies with the ever-present parasols were observed following them out. I hoped people remembered why we were out there.

The mission lasted about five hours and passed without contact. While we had the road secured, a Fullback unit passed by and searched what was left of one of their tracks, which had been blown up by an aircraft bomb which had been converted to an anti-tank booby trap. Those VC were really ingenious.

A week later, the more sinister results of that little five-hour mission came back to haunt us. Captain Ira Mersack, the Battalion Surgeon, informed me that Bravo had five cases of VD from that trip. I certainly hoped those guys enjoyed their little pieces of ass. Had Victor Charlie been around, it could have been the last they ever had.

A week or so before Christmas, Falcon moved out to the watershed area in the jungle south of the Michelin rubber plantation to conduct company operations. The major difference in this operation was that Dufus Delta Company was in the field with us that time, and they had a new commander. I had run into Captain Bill Custis (an alias) in the Third (Mechanized) Infantry Division in Germany the previous year during a Major Training Area exercise. He had been a First Lieutenant company commander, and I was the Brigade S-4 (Logistics Officer), also a First Lieutenant. During an Army Training Test of his company, I had graded the logistical aspect of his company operations. Not only had he and his armored infantry company passed the test, but they had also scored quite high while doing it. Therefore, when he arrived in the battalion, I had informed Colonel Harrold of his past exploits. Harrold could not wait to give him a company. I was not sure how he would do with a straight infantry company without armored personnel carriers (APC), but I thought he would do okay. Boy, was I wrong!

After we had conducted the aerial assault and had set up the perimeter defense for the night, Falcon 3 called a commanders conference. After discovering that I would stay back the next day to guard the perimeter, I relaxed and let my mind wonder a bit.

After the meeting, Custis walked up to me. "Bob, I need a favor tomorrow." It would be his first operation since taking command.

"Sure, Bill. What can I do for you?"

"My FO team is back in base camp doing something in the artillery battalion. Since you are staying in the perimeter tomorrow, could I borrow yours?"

"Okay, I can do that, but be sure to let Lieutenant Bennett run the arty business the way he wants to. Just tell him what you want done and let him do it. He's pretty good at it."

"Sure. Sounds good to me. I'm sure I can use all the help I can get for awhile."

"Okay, Bill. I'll send him over."

"Thanks, Bob. I owe you one."

That afternoon, after Delta returned to the perimeter, Bennett and his team returned to my CP. "Captain, please don't do that to us again."

"Why, Frank? What happened?"

"That dumb son-of-a-bitch put his whole company on line and moved them through the jungle that way. I don't know how the hell they managed to cut trail all strung out like that. He don't have the foggiest idea what he's doing. He's going to get everybody wiped out."

"Okay, I'll talk to him."

That evening after the commanders' meeting, I cornered Custis. "Bill, we have to talk."

"Okay, Bob. What's wrong?"

I told him what Bennett had relayed to me. "Did you do that?"

"Yeah, basically. Why? What's wrong with it?"

"Bill, this ain't a mech outfit. You might be able to take a track and drive through the jungle with it, cutting trail wherever it goes. A man's arm ain't so indestructible. These boys get tired quickly, swinging that machete out there. The secret to moving a leg unit through the bush is to use as small a front as possible, consistent with security, and to rotate them periodically. If you wear them out cutting bush, they won't be fit to fight if you run into Charlie. Do you understand what I'm saying?"

"Yeah, sure. Makes sense. How do you move?"

"We use what we call a box formation." I stooped down, brushed away some leaves and grass to expose clear ground, and drew a sketch with my finger. "That's two platoons up and two back, or one back and one on point. My fourth platoon's always one of the ones in the back. My CP group's here in the middle. With each platoon in a column of twos, that gives me four men in front doing machete duty. That's workable, and the formation's good for whatever comes along. I seldom use anything else."

"Okay, thanks. I'll think about it."

"Good. See you."

Three days later, Bennett's services were requested again by Custis. I let him go again, believing that our little talk had taken care of the movement problem.

Once again, Bennett reported back to me that Custis was still moving through the jungle in a formation similar to a line, although he had modified it a bit. He still had too many wielding a machete.

I saw him again that evening at battalion. "Bill, I thought you understood what I was telling you the other day. Bennett told me that you're still using a line in the jungle. I just want to tell you that until you figure out how to move through the jungle without endangering your men so much, my FO team's no longer available. It's easy enough to get killed out here without helping Charlie do it. I won't expose them to more danger than necessary."

"Okay, if that's how you feel." He turned and walked back toward his CP.

Two days later, the whole battalion was on the move. Alpha, Bravo and Delta were working our separate AOs. Charlie was playing Palace Guards with the Battalion CP. Alpha and Bravo were several kilometers in the jungle, and, to our west, Delta was working its way north along the edge of a watershed, clearing about one hundred meters into the woodline.

Late in the morning, about three clicks to our east, Alpha ran into a base camp and had a bit of trouble with VC going down through tunnels and coming up behind them. Chancey finally worked out of that one with only a few casualties. As they later moved out of the camp toward the west, they had been hit with a short 8-inch artillery round, which created more casualties, including two dead, than the VC had done. It was certainly *not* their lucky day.

I had heard nothing significant from Charlie Company. Delta had made some progress along the watershed about two clicks to our west when it ran into trouble. Custis reported to Battalion that he had found an occupied bunker complex, but he did not know how many VC were in it. He was calling an artillery fire mission to the rear of the area and would take steps to reduce the obstacle. That was all he reported for awhile.

We had checked out a couple of old base camps but had found little to worry about. It had been a rather uneventful day for us, especially in view of all that had happened to Alpha. We continued to move through the jungle toward the watershed.

All of a sudden, the battalion radio crackled. Delta was giving a sitrep. The essence of what he said was that he was getting shot up from the bunkers and had already lost three or four and had twelve or fifteen wounded. He needed a reaction force.

"Bravo 6, Falcon 3."

"Bravo 6."

"Falcon 3. Did you monitor Delta's situation?"

"Roger. Want us to go and take care of Delta?"

"Roger, Bravo 6. Their location is X-ray Tango 546334. Good luck."

"Roger. Out. Break—Break. Delta 6, Bravo 6. Fear not, son. We're on the way."

"Delta 6. Roger. We'll be waiting."

"Bravo 6. Okay, we'll try to flank them and come up behind them. I'll let you know when I want you to cease firing."

"Delta 6 roger."

"Bravo 6 out."

I plotted a direct route to Delta's location and we took off, moving as fast as we could within the constraints of security and cutting trail. The route would take us through the moderately thick jungle lying between Alpha and Delta. Although the jungle in that area required some machete work, it was not impenetrable. We were able to move through it with fairly quickly. I just hoped that we had not run into a continuous line of fortifications through that area. If we had, we would be moving headlong into it.

As we approached Delta's position, we passed around what we thought was the bunker complex area. We ran into only one sniper in the area where I had anticipated some problems, but that sniper wounded one good soldier. I left the fourth platoon to medevac him and pushed on. As we approached the rear of the complex, I called Delta to cease fire and I sent my point platoon—Gormley's third platoon—to try either to reduce the problem or to gain sufficient information to allow us to make our attack.

Fifteen minutes later, I heard from Gormley. "Bravo 6, this is 3-6."

"Bravo 6."

"3-6. We made it all the way through the bunker complex. The complex had only three old bunkers in it, only one of which was occupied. We killed the two gooks with AKs which were in it. Everything's quiet now."

"Bravo 6. Do you mean to tell me that only two VC with AKs shot up a whole company?"

"3-6. Roger. That's all there was here."

"Okay. Secure your area. We're coming up."

I changed mikes. "Delta 6, Bravo 6."

"Delta 6."

"Bravo 6. My element's cleared your bunkers. You can hold your fire so you won't hit my people. We've got two dead VC. I'm coming up now. Request you meet me at the nearest bunker."

"Roger."

"Bravo 6 out. Falcon 3, did you roger?"

"Falcon 3 roger. Good job. Out."

We moved up to the bunkers, and I joined Gormley. "Good job, Art. Anybody hurt?"

"Nosir. Not in my platoon. But you ought to look out front."

I walked around the bunker and was astonished at what I saw. Directly in front of the bunker was a large bomb crater, with the area around it cleared out to the woodline. American soldiers of Delta Company were lying all around the edge of the crater. Apparently, they had tried to take the bunker by frontal assault, a tactic of last resort when absolutely nothing else works. What a damn waste! I thought to myself. I was livid!

I looked up and saw Custis walking up. He looked a little frightened. "How many did you lose?" I snapped out.

"Five killed and eighteen wounded," he stammered. I could tell he was shaken by this.

"Why in hell did you try to attack this bunker across this open area right into the mouth of the firing? That was fuckin' *stupid!* You got good American soldiers killed and hurt here today by you damn stupidity. Why did you do it?" I was really heating up now.

"I don't know. I thought we could take it."

A cold calm came over me and my voice took on a hard, steely edge as I looked him straight in the eye. "Custis, I'm only going to say this once, so you'd better hear it clear. If I *ever* see or hear of you doing something else this stupid again, I promise you that I will *personally* blow your stupid idiotic brains out myself. Do you understand?"

He just nodded.

"Now get your men taken care of and get out of my sight. We'll secure the area. I want to know when you are all medevac'd and ready to move." I turned and walked to the other side of the bunkers, assigned security missions, reported to Falcon 3 and plopped down on top of a bunker to wait for Delta to finish screwing around.

Two weeks later—after only a month in command— Custis was relieved of command of his line company and

made Headquarters Commandant back in base camp for
awhile. Later, he was sent to Cu Chi, where he spent the
rest of his Vietnam tour running the Division's replacement training center. He was not trusted with the lives of
troops again on that tour of duty.

The biggest thing of interest during late December was
the Christmas truce, the first of three which the Allies had
negotiated with the enemy. The other two would be New
Year's Day and the Vietnamese holiday period called Tet.
Although Christmas was to be observed by a truce, we
would still have to remain in the field as part of the command's overall defensive posture.

Two days before Christmas, still in the watershed area,
we set up a perimeter where we would remain through
Christmas. We continued our offensive operations from
that location until the truce began. Each night, Battalion
placed Lieutenant Steve Wilder's Battalion Recon Platoon
across the watershed as an ambush.

On Christmas Eve, Colonel Harrold's resupply pack
contained a little surprise: two bottles of Jack Daniels
Christmas Cheer. That evening after chow and our nightly
meeting—knowing that there would be no fighting that
night because of the truce—we opened the bottles and,
within an hour or so, we emptied them. I can tell you that
I was feeling no pain anywhere.

As we sat there and continued drinking the whiskey,
someone suggested that we sing Christmas carols. We
sang a couple in subdued voices. Then, in the spirit of
good will to all, we decided to serenade the VC. So there
we were, singing carols at the top of our voices so all
could hear.

After an hour of that, we stopped and listened as all
hell broke loose across the clearing where Wilder was set
up. A minute later, a 61-millimeter mortar round landed
harmlessly in the middle of the clearing.

Falcon 3 went to his radio and came back a few
minutes later. "Seems that a VC unit came through Recon's ambush and started setting up mortars right in front

of his position. We were obviously their target. Wilder sprang the ambush and got most of them. The rest ran away. Wilder has secured the dead VC and their equipment and is moving his ambush down the watershed a ways."

Falcon 6 looked at him—a bit bleary-eyed—and said, "Tell young Steven he did a fine job. Tell Flex 6 that I don't appreciate getting hit during the Christmas truce."

"Yessir, but I don't think Flexible has control over VC truce violators."

"Oh." He sat back down.

The next day, as I was nursing a terrible headache, I thought about what we had done the previous night. Getting drunk in the field and singing at the top of our lungs was really stupid and dangerous—although it had readily worked to our advantage due to the ambush. However, the most significant event of the evening was that they had hit us in violation of the negotiated truce. What would they do during New Year's and Tet? Maybe nothing. Only time would tell . . .

CHAPTER FOUR

HAPPY NEW YEAR!

I will never forget the little New Year's party we had to welcome in 1968. Of course that is a misnomer—it was not little, and it was no party! Our principal guests for the evening were the officers and men of the 271st and 272nd Viet Cong Main Force Regiments of the 9th VC Division. There were a lot of fireworks, and the little bastards spent the night.

Three days earlier, the Falcon battalion—minus Delta Company which was cooling its heels in the rear as usual—had made a helicopter assault into a rather large clearing astride a well-used dirt road in War Zone C leading from near the Cambodian border toward Saigon. The clearing was about three kilometers from the border and the large Viet Cong/North Vietnamese Army sanctuary area beyond, and about two kilometers south of a "T" intersection with another road running parallel to the border.

The mission for this little excursion was to set up a 2-battalion fire support base in an area noted as a major infiltration route for NVA units coming into the Third Corps Tactical Zone. This was to have been the biggest of three FSBs in the area, all of which would be able to provide fire support to each other. Our landing was supported by the FSB already established near the Special Forces border camp at Katum to our northwest. Our base was named FSB Burt.

Our sister battalion, 2/22 Mechanized Infantry ("Fullback"), was scheduled to arrive by road later the same day and to occupy the western half of the perimeter. We had the eastern half and would join Fullback at the road in the north and in the south. Once the perimeter was

established, heavy-lift helicopters would begin bringing
the artillery, which would consist of one battery of
155mm howitzers and three batteries of 105's, including
our old buddies, Charlie Battery, 2/77 Field Artillery.
Once all this stuff was in place, the two battalions would
begin company operations out of the base. At least, that
was the game plan.

Alpha company was first in, as usual, and except for
scattered sniper fire, had met little resistance. Captain
Herb Chancey, the "Alphagator," moved his people to
their positions in the center of the battalion sector of the
perimeter without major incident. He also pushed a squad
out to the western side of the perimeter in the area assigned to Fullback to provide security of the landing zone
until the mech arrived. Next in was Chargin' Charlie, and
Captain Gus Fishburne moved his unit to their sector, tying into Alpha's right flank and extending to the road in
the south where he would tie in with the mech later. Fishburne also was tasked to provide an ambush platoon to
the south along the road each night.

Then we came in. I had assigned Lieutenant Gormley's
third platoon to the perimeter to plug the gap between
Alpha's left flank and the tie-in point with the mech along
the road on the northern end of the perimeter. After he
closed into his position, he sent out a listening post (LP)
for security. I designated Lieutenant Walker's first platoon
to conduct a nightly ambush about one click to the north
along the road. Each night, he was to move his platoon
out to the site and return each morning. SSG Hughes'
second platoon and Lieutenant Constantino's fourth
(weapons) platoon drew the assignment of battalion reaction force—or reserve—and, therefore, set up their position inside the perimeter. Fourth platoon also would
provide 81mm mortar support to the battalion sector. I
established my company CP to the rear of Gator's CP near
the center of the battalion sector. My command group set
to work filling sandbags to build the CP bunker, which
we might need if we were hit. I picked a place to string

my hammock near the bunker, dumped my rucksack, and went to check Gormley's perimeter positions and crew-served weapons emplacements. When I returned, I checked out the bunker—it looked a little small for the seven of us. Oh, well, maybe we won't need it, I thought.

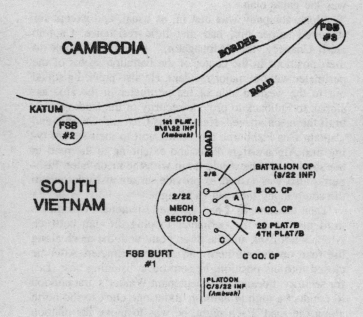

Later that afternoon, we heard the familiar rumble of the M113s and the *boom-boom-boom* of the .50 caliber machine guns as the track commanders reconned by fire as they moved along the road. *Fullback was coming!* Not that we had been very sneaky coming in—the artillery preparation of the LZ, the helicopter gunships firing rockets, the smoke ship laying down a smoke screen, the dozens of helicopter loads coming in—but those guys really made a lot of noise when they traveled! Of course, just being around those tracks made us very uneasy, since they couldn't be hidden. Those things attracted RPGs like a magnet! I had been in mech in Germany, but after three months of sneaking through the jungle, I really didn't want to be near those things now. They definitely could shorten one's life span!

Mech units did not like to set up their perimeter inside the jungle if they could set up in the open looking into the jungle. That gave their fifties full effectiveness at anything coming out of the jungle, plus their armor protection gave them more flexibility concerning their vulnerability to incoming fire. With everything in plain sight, the tracks could cross-cover each other. On the other hand, we liked trees above us to disrupt incoming fire and to provide cover and concealment. The battalions linked up at the road to the north and south which bisected the clearing where we were set up. Fullback had all 3 of their line companies—there were no "D" companies in mech units. Fullback had only one ambush out since mech units generally refrain from such "leg" silliness—they might get hit by fifties during the dawn mad minutes and other recons by fire. They did push out several LPs, though.

We used the road running through the middle of the perimeter as our landing zone, supply point and such. We came prepared to stay for awhile.

One thing—strategically speaking—that we didn't know at the time, but which became obvious to us around the end of January during the TET holiday period, was that this particular road was one of the main enemy infiltration routes toward Saigon. We noticed that it looked quite well-used for such a remote area. When we were there—one month before TET—they had already started infiltrating supplies, units, etc., south. That meant we were sitting astride their main supply and reinforcement route in that area, and they didn't like it a whole hell of a lot.

We went out there expecting to interdict some of their normal dry-season operations in an area which they used as a sanctuary, along with War Zone D to the southeast

and Cambodia three kilometers to our north. Over the next
several days, we would come to realize how seriously they
wanted that road kept open. We were interfering with an
important segment of their country-wide plans.

For the next three days after setting up the fire base,
we conducted company reconnaissance-in-force (RIF) operations. This had been known as a search-and-destroy
mission until some idiot in Saigon decided that it was not
pleasing to American sensitivities to go around searching
and destroying things, even though that's what most ar-
mies actually do to varying degrees in a war. This is especially in a limited or guerrilla war where it is important
to deny logistical support and personal comfort to the insurgents. So we were doing the same thing but using a
different name for it. The problem was that we were doing
a lot of RIF'ing but finding very little to destroy. Whatever you called it, we were going almost all day in that
oppressive dry-season heat and staying awake half the
night to be alert in case we had some unwelcome visitors.

As the New Year approached, we were looking forward to the truce—yes, I said *truce*! The allied and enemy
high commands had worked out a cease-fire for Christmas, New Year's and the Lunar New Year (TET). The
Christmas truce was for 12 hours, New Year's for 24
hours, and TET for 3 days. During Christmas, we had
been hit only once, so we had high hopes for the New
Year's break. We will discuss what happened during TET
later.

The good part about the truce was that we could only
conduct defensive missions, such as security ambushes—
but no RIF's! Maybe the guys would get a chance for
some rest. So, at 1800 hours on New Year's Eve, the truce
began.

New Year's Eve passed rather quietly. On three oc-
casions during the night, Walker had reported that his security guys on the northern flank of his ambush position—
nearest the Cambodian border—had reported the sound of

movement. However, nothing came of it. Walker thought that it could be wild pigs or some other animal wandering around through the jungle. We had been known in the past to blow an ambush on VC pigs, dogs, and water buffalo who had had the misfortune to wander around through the wrong part of the jungle. At least no member of the human species approached the ambush site, as far as he knew. There were no Tokarov pistol souvenirs on that night!

One little thing bothered us, though. During the night before the truce began, one of Alpha's LPs had reported movement near his position and had blown his two claymore mines. The movement had then stopped. The next morning, they found four dead bodies. All four had worn black pajamas, and two carried Tokarov pistols—the sure sign of an officer. They certainly resembled a recon party, and we wondered just what it was they were reconning.

One hour after daylight, Walker's platoon passed back by Gormley's LP and entered the perimeter. As the platoon sergeant went over to the LZ to draw the platoon's C-rations for the day, Lieutenant Walker ambled over to the company CP.

"I tell you, Captain, I'm glad to see these truces. Nothing happened out there last night. Think our luck'll continue?" He plopped down on his helmet—I will never understand how that helmet managed to hold up so much weight without cracking—good stuff those Americans make, yes?

"Don't know, Rich. Depends on how many more movement reports you send in. What was that all about last night?"

"Well, Sergeant Watts' security team up near the 'T' heard something moving around behind them in the jungle, but it wasn't close enough to identify."

"Did the movement sound like something trying to move quietly through the undergrowth or was it thrashing around?"

"No, there wasn't any thrashing. More like rustling limbs and cracking underfoot."

"That pretty much rules out pigs and water buffalo. Judging by Alpha's results a couple nights ago, I'd say you had visitors from Cambodia last night. If it happens again tonight, pay more attention and try to find out what you've got out there."

"We're going out again tonight?"

"Yeah. I'm putting you out one more night, then I'll swap you with second platoon for a couple of nights. Now, go get some chow and some rest. We'll plan a get-together around 1600."

"Yes sir. Food and rest. It's something to live for." Walker hauled his bulk up off his helmet and headed back to his platoon area.

I picked up my CAR-15 and, motioning for Spec 4 Jerry MacKenzie (an alias), my new battalion RTO, to stay, I walked over to the Battalion CP. The CO and the S3 were finishing their C-rations as I walked up.

"Quiet night, Bravo 6?" asked the S3, Major Davis.

"Pretty much. Walker reported some movement north of his ambush site, but he didn't know what it was. Based on his description and what happened with Alpha's LP, my gut feeling is that we had another recon party checking us out last night. Sounds like they moved around toward Fullback's side. Seems they learned from Alpha not to get too close to us."

"Where do you think they came from?"

"Can't say for sure, but it seems likely that they came over the border from their hiding place in Cambodia, especially since we're only three clicks away."

Falcon 6 had been listening to this exchange. Now he leaned forward, brows deeply furrowed, and said, "Those recon patrols are starting to worry me. I don't know what they have across the border, but they are not going to recon forever. We need to keep our guard up!"

Another brilliant observation, I thought. "Well, at least this truce crap's over at 1800 tonight. No more games."

"Wrong, Bravo 6," Davis chimed in. "We just got word that the truce has been extended until 0600 tomorrow— at Victor Charlie's request."

"Great friggin' deal. I wonder what he's got in mind for that additional twelve hours."

Sergeant Major Norman Butte (an alias) walked over and handed the colonel a cup of fresh, hot, genuine C-ration instant coffee that he had made for him, along with some genuine C-ration crackers smeared with generous helpings of genuine C-ration peanut butter that he had prepared for him. I found it gratifying that the Battalion Sergeant Major finally had found something useful to do way out here in the bush—to wait hand and foot on the colonel. Ass-kissing was the best one could expect from such a useless egg-sucking SOB. . . . Of course, the real problem was that Falcon 6 let him do it.

Harrold took the coffee and crackers, leaned back, and, with that overly serious look still on his face, said, "I don't know what they'll do, but we need to talk about it. Get the other commanders over here."

Davis jumped up, said "Yessir," and gave instructions to the radio operator.

Chancey hurried over from his CP to see what was going on. A few minutes later, Fishburne ambled over, puffing on his big cigar. They both pulled off their helmets and sat on them.

I looked at Gus—"Tell me, where the hell do you get those brown round things sticking out of your mouth way out here? I thought we were in a combat zone and had supply shortages."

"Don't know. Just lucky, I guess. Keep finding them laying around in the jungle." He grinned and puffed away.

Harrold looked at his three company commanders. "Bravo 6 and I have been discussing our situation here. His ambush reported some movement last night which he thinks may have been another recon party heading toward Fullback's sector. Fullback hasn't reported anything, but that's not surprising. The mech aren't very big on LPs or anything other than an occasional 'mad minute' to clear out whatever is in front of them. Any other reports of activity in your areas? How about you, Gus? Your ambush report anything to the south?"

The other commanders shook their heads.

"In case you haven't heard, MACV has extended the truce until 0600 tomorrow, at the request of Victor Charlie. That means nothing offensive until then. That also means that the countryside is open for them to move without interference. They are not going to recon forever. We don't know what they have across the border, but they probably have significant forces over there. The body count that Alpha got a couple of nights ago were from our old friends, the 272nd Regiment, according to the G2. We know from experience how good those guys are. I'm worried about them taking advantage of this truce extension to hit us tonight. We have absolutely no intelligence about what's over there in Cambodia. But these recon patrols indicate to me that they are planning something soon, and we think tonight's as good an opportunity as they'll get. There will be no artillery interdiction fires, no air interdiction, no B-52 'Arclights,' nothing to stop them. They can move right in until your ambushes and LPs detect them. The damn problem is, there's nothing we can do about it until your guys hear them. Of course, we don't know if they are coming tonight, but if Bravo 6 is right, they just might pay us a visit. I want all ambush patrols and LPs to be especially alert. I want them to have extra claymores out there. I want the perimeter on fifty per cent alert, and I want double ammo ration passed out. S3, get the fire support coordinator in here, and coordinate with Fullback's S3. I want DEFCONs all around this perimeter re-checked and re-fired. Have all batteries on standby tonight, ready to fire all protective fires, including beehives if necessary. Fellows, that's about as close to an ops order that you will get today. Any questions?"

No questions.

"Okay, go get your soldiers ready and get some rest. This may be a long night."

New Year's Day passed rather uneventfully. There were no offensive actions and no artillery fires. We had taken defensive measures for our own protection, including reinforcing our LPs and pushing them out about 600 meters during the day for early warning. Everybody just had a peaceful day. We did not let our guard down, but did nothing provocative—that was the idea of the truce.

Walker got his platoon ready to go back out on the ambush—I put them back out on the road to the north toward Cambodia, this time about one-and-a-half clicks from the perimeter. Third platoon was still in well-prepared positions on the perimeter on the north side, plugging the gap between Alpha and Fullback, and second and fourth platoons were in prepared and sandbagged positions inside the perimeter as the battalion reaction force. All Bravo Company positions on and within the perimeter had good overhead cover over their foxholes. Fourth platoon had its mortars set up to cover the Falcon sector to provide any fire support that might be needed.

As evening approached, Lieutenant Walker and his platoon saddled up and went back to their position to the north. I had talked to Walker several times to make sure he left no sign that he had been there, and I told him to enter after dark and exit before daylight as quietly as he could since I wanted to continue to use the same area and not reveal his position. In retrospect, I am not sure that we could have moved anywhere around there without someone knowing where we were, especially in platoon size or larger. It was very difficult to try to sneak in and out to cover up everything we did. I am sure that there was some indication to the enemy that we had patrol positions around the area, even if they did not know exactly where our positions were. Around the company CP, I settled into my hammock, which was strung right next to the bunker. Lieutenant Bennett, the artillery FO, slept on an air mattress and ground cover nearby. Since this was the dry season, he could do that. The RTOs generally slept inside the bunker, keeping the radios just outside the opening.

The evening passed until around 2330 hours, when I got a radio call from Walker. Walker said his security guys reported some movement. I told him to make sure all his people were awake, down low and quiet—prepared and alert. A few minutes later, I got a call from Walker saying he had movement to his rear, which would have been opposite Fullback's northern portion of the perimeter. After another ten minutes, he reported that the movement had quieted down, like whoever or whatever it was moved a bit and then stopped. He reported nothing else for a while, and nothing came through his ambush position. This was reported to Falcon 3.

About 0030 hours, we heard the distant sound of mortar shells going down the tubes and 82mm and 61mm shells started landing in the perimeter. Most were landing in the clearing—in fact, they appeared to be specifically aimed at the clearing—which meant into Fullback's area and along the road where our supply point and LZ was set up. We had a few rounds over in the trees, but they were basically ineffective. The fact that most rounds were falling in the clearing meant that either they were more afraid of the tracks or they did not know where our positions were. A rather large number of mortar shells came in, probably 100–200 rounds. I also received word that Katum and the third fire base were also being hit with mortar fire. At that point in the festivities, it looked like it was just another mortar attack. However, just like any other incoming fire, the perimeter was alert and ready, just in case something else happened. This initial mortar attack lasted about a half-hour and then stopped abruptly.

Gormley called to let me know that his platoon CP had received occasional 61mm shrapnel, but it was mostly spent fragments. Nothing was very close. Perhaps this mortar attack should have told us something.

As the mortars started to fall again in Fullback's rear,

Walker's coarse whisper seeped out of the squawk box. "Bravo 6, 1-6"

"Bravo 6." I also spoke in a low voice to keep the handset noise down at his end.

"1-6. We can hear mass movement all around us. All sides, including between here and the perimeter. I can also hear them on the other side of the road. Over."

"Roger. Stand by." I thought about his situation for a minute or so. I decided that it was probably best if they tried to stay down and defend themselves in that position, rather than trying to move through what was out there, plus taking the chance on receiving fire from our perimeter. We obviously did not want to shoot our own people.

"1-6, I'm not going to bring you in now. There's too much around you out there. I want you to stay in that position. Stay low, get everyone into a small perimeter there for a perimeter defense, and be prepared to defend yourself. Try not to be discovered. Lie low, don't make any noise, and try not to let them know you're there. If I don't hear from you, I'll get back to you from time to time. If we have to, we'll communicate by breaking squelch. Do you roger?"

He roger'd in the affirmative by breaking squelch twice, which told me that the enemy was very close. In Bravo company, we routinely communicated with LPs and ambush patrols who were afraid of being detected by nearby enemy soldiers by breaking radio squelch once for "no" and twice for "yes."

"6 out."

As I reached for the battalion radio in MacKenzie's hand, I heard Fullback in the north open up with their .50 cals, punctuated by automatic return fire, including the easily-recognizable sound of AKs. It sounded as if the mech company that joined us on the north was having some sort of probing attack on their perimeter.

I switched handsets again. "3-6, Bravo 6. Give me a sitrep. What's that fifty fire I hear? Do you have targets?"

"3-6. Negative. The LP heard movement, but we

haven't seen anything on the perimeter yet. Sounds like the tracks are doing a little recon-by-fire. Maybe they'll scare them away with the fifties. Our only problem right now is these mortars are getting closer. Over."

"Okay. Keep your eyes open and your head down. Bring in your LP before he gets shot up."

"3-6. Roger."

"6 out. Break—Break. 1-6, this is Bravo 6. If you monitor, break squelch."

Two clicks.

"Okay. Be sure you have cover between you and the perimeter. I don't want you catching Fullback's fifties. Do you roger?"

Two clicks.

"Have you been discovered at all?"

One click.

Okay. Keep your head down. Bravo 6 out. Break—Break. 4-6, Bravo 6. Any fire requests?"

"6, this is 4-6. Affirmative. Alpha 6's FO has us plotting a mission to his left front now. Should be going down the tubes in zero-one."

"6 roger. Make it good. Be advised that if we're committed, it's all of us. You go out of action and become eleven-bushes."

"4-6. Roger eleven-bravos. We'll be ready."

"Keep your heads down. 6 out."

I reached back to MacKenzie for the other handset. "Falcon 3, Bravo 6."

"Falcon 3."

"Bravo 6. 1-6's got movement all around him. Sounds like a major troop movement. He's not been discovered, and I think he would be if he moves. In the dark, he would be better off staying where he is and defending himself. I've told him to sit tight and keep his head down. 3-6's LP also reported a lot of movement to his front. He's coming back to the perimeter. What's going' on across the' perimeter?"

"Falcon 3. It looks like some sort of small probing

attack against Fullback, but Fullback's pretty well beaten them back. No one's getting past the line of tracks."

"Roger. I bet no one's asleep on *this* perimeter! Bravo 6 out."

The firing in Fullback's area lasted fifteen to twenty minutes and then petered out. Then we started receiving sporadic mortar fire again. This time, some of the mortar fire shifted over to our side a bit, though most of it was still in the clearing.

Third platoon on the perimeter continued to be watchful. Gormley's LP came in. He had been out in the same general direction as Walker's platoon but on the other side of the road. That cleared third platoon's field of fire to their front.

"Bravo 6, 3-6. LP's in."

"6 roger. You're clear to engage anything that moves to your front. Be sure no one's shooting at ghosts. Everybody's jumpy, and I don't want 'em getting excited over nothing."

"3-6. Roger."

After a lull that seemed like an eternity, all hell broke loose in front of Alpha company in the center of our portion of the FSB perimeter. I also heard the mech sporadically firing its fifties down the road to the north, along with occasional bursts from our M-60s from our side of the road.

I grabbed the battalion push. "Falcon 3, Bravo 6. Request sitrep on Alpha."

"Falcon 3. Alpha 6 has two elements in direct contact to his front. Appears to be holding his own at this time. Be aware that Charlie battery is loading beehives. Initially, they will be fired into Alpha's area over your head. They'll warn you before they fire. Over."

"Bravo 6 roger."

"Falcon 3. Also be aware that the big boys are preparing to fire 'Killer Junior'. Alpha's FO has them on standby. Over."

"Roger. We'll be listening. My 1-6 continues to lay

low and remain undetected. My Foxtrot Oscar's monitoring the Redleg push for fire in that direction. The FDC knows their location. 3-6 has no fire on the perimeter, although a few mortar rounds are keeping him awake."

"Roger. Hang tight. 3 out."

As the firing got serious in front of Alpha, I noticed that the firing had spread around to Charlie's sector. The volume of fire became intense in both locations. Since the rest of the perimeter was relatively quiet, it seemed that Falcon—inside the woodline—was getting the main attack. The main enemy effort at the moment was in Alpha's sector, and much of the incoming fire was sweeping throughout the perimeter, along with the incoming mortar fire, particularly into my CP and reaction force positions behind Alpha. My guys were laying low in their bunkers and behind their sandbags to keep from being hit. Bennett and I were down behind the CP bunker, working the radios, trying to keep in touch with the situation.

As I monitored the radio, I heard the Gator: "Falcon 6, Alpha 6. Got a sitrep for you. Over."

"Alpha 6, Falcon 3. Falcon 6 is monitoring. Go ahead."

"Alpha 6. Got all three line elements on the perimeter engaged. Center element is most heavily engaged. I don't know what we've got out there, but this is big. They're hitting us hard with machine guns, AKs and RPGs. I've got my Foxtrot Oscar calling in beehives to my front. I hope these things work. I've never used them before. We're not getting any mortars now. It sounds like they shifted them down to Charlie 6's location or back to Bravo's. I have my 4-6 element preparing to react to 2-6's sector. Is Bravo 6 available if I need him? Over."

"Roger, Alpha 6. Be advised we have tac air and gunships coming in. FAC is due on station in one-five mikes. When the fast movers come in, we'll have to check-fire the arty if we bring them in close. Gunships can shoot stand-off. What's your recommendation?"

"Alpha 6. If these beehives work, I want to keep 'em coming. Maybe you can bring in the air to the rear. It looks like these dinks are gonna keep on coming. Maybe we can stop some of the follow-on echelons. Over."

"Roger, Alpha 6. We'll work on it. Anything else?"

"Not now. Alpha 6 out."

"Charlie 6, Falcon 3. Sitrep. Over."

"3, Charlie 6. I've got machine gun fire on my left flank toward Alpha's position. I'm getting some mortars around my right flank element along the road. One mortar round ricocheted off one of Fullback's tracks across the road. So far, I have only sporadic fire except on the left. My ambush element is hunkered down in a defensive posture and has not been discovered. Charlie battery is right behind me, and they've been getting some mortars. One of their folks told my RTO that their landlines have been knocked out. Their FDC is using runners to give fire directions to the guns. Their officers are down on the individual guns. We're holding for now. Over."

"Roger, Charlie 6. Did you monitor Alpha 6's situation?"

"Roger, 3. Also monitored your comments about air support. Send 'em on!"

"Roger, Charlie. Falcon 3 out."

Bravo continued to get sporadic mortar and automatic weapons fire in the treeline from the perimeter fighting. It was funny watching my guys shoot their mortars: all you could see above the sandbags were arms slithering up the sides of the tubes, dropping in their rounds and slipping back down behind the sandbags. No heads or bodies could be seen. We were returning mortar fire to targets outside the perimeter, along with the artillery. I noticed that there was little arty fire on the mech side of the perimeter. After the initial probe ran into the mech's fifties, they must not have liked it and backed off. The fifties chewed them up and threw whole arms, legs and heads everywhere. After that carnage, it appeared that they came to our side where all they had to contend with was M-60s, M-16s, grenade launchers, etc. In fact, we found a sketch map later which indicated that the probe on the mech side may have been a diversion, and that the main 2-prong attack was planned for our side in Alpha's and Charlie's sectors. Of course, we were not privy to that great piece of intelligence at the time.

By 0130 hours, the pressure on Alpha company was increasing dangerously all along his perimeter, and action was picking up momentum in front of Charlie. Bravo 3-6 also had been engaged on the perimeter, but he was not under undue pressure.

"3-6, Bravo 6. Sitrep."

"3-6. We've had several squad-sized probes, particularly along the road. Almost like they're just trying to get us to keep our heads down. We've been able to drive them all off. The biggest problem here is the RPGs. They're mostly firing them at Fullback's tracks. I can see two tracks burning on our left. The VC are infiltrating their RPG gunners to shoot at the tracks. No other attacks over there. We're knocking off the gunners as they shoot, but we can't see them before then. They're still coming, but we're okay for now. I don't think. . . ." The radio went dead.

"3-6, Bravo 6. Over." No answer.

"3-6, this is Bravo 6. Respond! Over." No answer.

"3-6, Bravo 6. Do you hear me?" What the hell happened to Gormley?

"Bravo 6, this is 3-6. Sorry I lost you. My CP just took a direct hit from a 61-millimeter mortar. Over."

"You okay? Give me a casualty report."

"3-6. Everybody caught a little shrapnel, but nobody's serious. Got a little ringing in our ears. Doc's checking everybody out now. Scared us more than it hurt us. Over."

"Okay, 3-6. Get back to me as soon as Doc checks everybody. I want to know if anybody's going to the aid station. Are you functioning okay?"

"Roger, 6. No problem. I'll get right back to you. Over."

"Roger. Out."

I turned to Bennett. "What's going on with the beehives? Alpha 6 seems to think they are coming his way. Since they have to travel by here, I'd like to know their status."

"Roger, sir. I'm checking that out now."

Beehive rounds were artillery rounds filled with small steel flechettes, or darts, which shoot out of the tube at reasonably close range into oncoming personnel and can reduce human beings to hamburger. We had never been exposed to them before, but we had been informed that we should have some kind of cover between us and the howitzer to keep us from getting poked full of little holes. No one had ever been known to survive getting hit by those little bastards. Supposedly, they were so devastating that there never had been more than fifty rounds used in one defensive fight before, and that had been at Soui Tre. The same players from Soui Tre were here again—Bravo Company and Charlie Battery. As far as we knew, the flechettes came out of the end of the tube like shotgun pellets and cut a swath in front of it. So much for bad information.

Because of the automatic fire sweeping across the perimeter from time to time and the random mortar rounds, Lieutenant Bennett and I were down behind the CP bunker, and the rest of my CP group—all five of them—were inside our 5-man bunker.

Bennett took his handset from his ear. "Captain, they have already fired several beehives toward Alpha's right flank. Must have gotten by us okay since nobody complained."

"Damn! I told them to let me know!"

"The thing now is that they are about to shoot two more. This time the target is Alpha's center. They are going right over this CP. We are to protect ourselves."

"When?"

"In two minutes."

I turned to the RTOs in the bunker. "Atkinson, let 2-6 and 4-6 know that two beehives are coming right over us, and they have to take cover." PFC Ron Atkinson had taken the radio from Otte earlier.

I turned to Bennett. "We'll put this bunker between us and the guns. Let's go!" Bullets were still flying around, so the lieutenant and I crawled around in front of the bunker and took cover between it and a spindly sapling. We made sure we kept our asses down out there.

We lay there for what seemed like an eternity, waiting for them to fire the two rounds. Suddenly, two explosions went off right next to us, throwing dirt and debris all over us.

"MacKenzie, tell those bastards to hurry and fire those rounds. These mortars are getting too damn close out here!"

After a moment, a voice came back from deep inside the bunker, "Sir, those *were* th' beehives!"

"Holy crap! Let's get out of here!" I scurried back around the bunker with Bennett hot on my heels, and we both piled into the bunker on top of the others. So much for shotgun blasts.

I picked up the battalion mike and called Falcon 3. "What the hell happened with the beehives? They exploded out here, not at the tube. My Foxtrot Oscar and I were almost perforated."

"Bravo 6, Falcon 3. I checked with the Redlegs. It seems those rounds can be set for muzzle blast or shot out with a delay fuse to go off away from the tube. The last two were fired with a delay."

"Great time to find that out. Better late than never, I guess. Bravo 6 out."

"Bravo 6, 3-6. Over."

"Bravo 6."

"3-6. Doc checked everybody out. All present for duty. Some of us have a few more holes in our bodies and a ringing in our ears, but nothing serious. Over."

"Good to hear. Any change in your situation?"

"Negative, Bravo 6. Nobody's trying to overrun us yet."

"Okay. Keep in touch. Looks like we may have to bug out of this location soon. I'll let you know. 6 out."

I switched mikes. "Falcon 3, Bravo 6. Got a sitrep."

"Falcon 3. Go."

"Bravo 6. 3-6 on the perimeter has sporadic contact, mostly with RPG teams shooting at Fullback's tracks across the road. Looks like they got two tracks so far. My guys take out the teams when they shoot, but they can't see them before then. 3-6's CP took a direct mortar hit. Shook 'em up a little but nothing serious. They're still functional. 4-6's supporting Alpha's sector through Alpha's FO. Over."

"Roger. Keep me informed. Out."

Three more beehives went off nearby. I stuck my head out to listen to the battle. The enemy mortars had been shifted back toward the center of the perimeter. The re-supply point must have been taking a helluva beating! The automatic weapons fire and grenade explosions remained intense in Alpha's sector, but the fire in Charlie's sector was still sporadic. I crawled out of the bunker, took a breath of acrid air, and settled back against the bunker wall. I wondered if we were going to get to play in this little game. I did not have long to wait.

The battalion radio sputtered to life. "Alpha 6, Charlie 6, this is Falcon 3. Sitrep. Over."

"3, Alpha 6. I have penetrations in 2-6's and 3-6's areas. I've just committed 4-6 to the perimeter. They're sweeping back toward 2-6's area to try to restore the bunker line, but the fighting in some places is hand-to-hand. Request you have Bravo 6 standing by. I have negative contact with 2-6 at this time."

"Roger, Alpha 6. Stand by. Charlie 6, go ahead."

"Charlie 6. I have major contact against 1-6 on the left and 2-6 along the road. Fullback has lost one track across the road to RPGs. My ambush is still undetected. If this keeps up, I'll probably have to commit 4-6 soon. Will keep you advised. Over."

"Roger, Charlie. Falcon 3 out."

I called to Bennett, who was still inside the bunker: "Have Alpha and Charlie fired their DEFCONs yet?"

"Yes, Captain. They have been firing an' adjusting them for the last hour. They both have the 155s firing 'Killer Junior' their way as well."

"I thought those big explosions sounded awful close. I'm surprised we didn't get any shrapnel here. Trees probably protected us."

"Killer Junior" was a direct fire technique developed by the 155mm artillery battalion, whose radio call sign was "Killer." They fired high explosive rounds into the trees over friendly heads. The intent was that the tree limbs would explode the rounds and the hot shrapnel would project forward and rain down on enemy heads. In previous engagements, it reportedly worked very well. Tonight, we would see first-hand exactly how well it worked.

"Bravo 6, Falcon 3."

"Bravo 6."

"Falcon 3. Alpha's situation is critical. His perimeter is breaking down. He has committed his reserve. How soon can you be ready to move with all available?"

"Bravo 6. Zero-five mikes."

"Roger. Let me know when you are ready. Out."

"Atkinson, get 2-6 and 4-6 over here ASAP. Tell them they've got 30 seconds to get here or I'll have their asses! RTOs and FO team, get ready to move now. Weapons and webbing only. Now move!"

I shrugged into my webbing and picked up my CAR-15. As I turned, Sergeant Hughes and Lieutenant Constantino came rushing up, darting from cover to cover.

"Okay, listen up. We're moving to counterattack in Alpha's sector. There are at least two penetrations, and it sounds to me like all hell's broken loose over there. We're going in on line, 2-6 on the left and 4-6 on the right. I want you to stay tied in together all the way to the perimeter positions. Understand? I want no gaps. Keep one squad in reserve in case you need to plug a hole in your line. I'll be right behind you. I want you to sweep through right up to the bunker line. Focus on any enemy in the area and kill them. Watch out for Alpha's men. We don't want to shoot them. At the perimeter, take over Alpha's holes. In your sector, you are in charge, no matter who's there from Alpha. Use any Alpha survivors in your platoon. Alpha 6 will provide guides to show you their limits. Questions? Good. Get your men ready to move in zero-two. Weapons and webbing only. Put 'em on line, tie in with the other platoon and move when I give the word. Now get out of here!"

Two minutes later: "Bravo 6, 2-6. Ready."

"Bravo 6, 4-6. Ready."

"Roger. 6 out."

"Falcon 3, Bravo 6. We're ready."

"Falcon 3. Okay, Bravo 6. That was quick. Your mission is to restore Alpha 6's perimeter. Let me know when you are in position. Good luck. 3 out."

That was my kind of Op Order—short and sweet. "Gator, Bull. Over."

"Gator. You coming my way, Bull?"

"Roger that. We're on our way to save your ass. Need two guides at your CP to point out your flank limits. We'll be sweeping your area and assuming your perimeter. Assuming we're successful, we'll be taking charge of your sector. Agreed?"

"Roger, Bull. We need you, buddy."

"My Foxtrot Oscar'll join yours and work the artillery when we get there. Have yours on the Redleg push to talk to mine while we're moving. Copy?"

"Roger. He's calling yours now."

"Okay. Tell your folks to keep their heads down. We're on the move. Bull out."

I turned to the CP Group. "Okay, let's go. Stay low and keep up with me."

I took off at a crouch over to where second and fourth platoons had deployed. They were already out of their holes and down on the ground in movement formation.

Since they had previously reconned the routes to Alpha and Charlie, they knew the direction to go.

"Okay, stay low, move quickly, and shoot anything that you can't identify as friendly. Stay on line and keep dressed right and left as best you can. We've got surprise. Let's use it. Now move out!"

In one motion, both platoons rose up off the ground like a line of ghosts in the night and surged forward, moving at a slow trot with weapons ready. We ran into several shadowy figures just behind Alpha 6's CP bunker and blew them away without slackening our pace. As we approached the bunker, I signaled the platoons to hold up. They stopped and quickly dropped down into prone firing positions.

I went up to the CP. "Hey, Gator, it's Bull! Where're our guides?"

Chancey stuck his head out. "Man, I'm glad to see you! I thought I was a goner. The guides are coming out now."

"What's your situation?"

"I have radio contact with only 1-6 on the left. He's holding his own for now, but his right flank is exposed. 4-6's radio got shot away on the counterattack. Best I can tell, some of 2-6's and 3-6's holes got overrun, but they're still holding a few holes. Some of the men are behind the holes firing at VC inside the holes they just left. That's all I know."

"Okay. I'll join you in a few minutes." I turned to Bennett. "Get in there and keep the arty coming. I want it within one hundred meters of the perimeter. I want 'Killer Junior' fired forward of the bunkers and beehives locked and loaded. Find out where that Tac air is. I don't care about the gunships. I want big bombs five hundred meters out. The bigger, the better. And I want nape standing by on station. Move!"

I signaled for 2-6 and 4-6 to join me. As they reached the bunker, I gave each one guide. "Make sure you stay tied in with each other. 2-6, be sure you link up with Alpha 1-6 on the left when you reach the perimeter. 4-6, try to establish contact with Charlie company. These guys'll show you where they're supposed to be tied in. Pick up Alpha's people as you go. Okay? Now get back to your platoons and go when I give you the signal. You're looking good so far, but the best is yet to come. Go!"

They scampered back to their platoons. As soon as they were ready, I gave the signal. Once again, they rose as one and surged ahead, this time at a fast walk. As they moved forward, they fired from the hip as ghostly moving objects appeared and fingers of automatic weapons fire reached out to them. They managed to keep their formation and swept everything before them, firing across the front, changing magazines, firing again. M-60s were fired from the hip, with ammo bearers and gunners scrambling to re-load as smoking guns ate 100-round belts almost as fast as they could be loaded. Artillery shells and butterfly bombs were falling beyond the perimeter. Spent shrapnel was falling all around as the men moved forward. The din was deafening, but they advanced virtually unimpeded. As they closed in on the perimeter positions, they absorbed Alpha's survivors as they passed by. They granddad and machine-gunned everything dressed in black along the way and inside the holes. As they jumped into the holes, they lifted out the dead and wounded and gave them to Alpha's men to take to the rear. Taking over the positions, mostly open holes, they established their fields of fire, with squad leaders and platoon leaders ensuring they knew their sectors. Just to be sure, they fired all their final protective fires to the front. Then on command, they held their fire—and there was silence to the front. They waited . . .

Returning to Alpha's CP, I called to Bennett: "Check-fire the arty, but have 'em standing by. The air can keep on coming. I want to break up the *next* attack if I can."

Both platoon leaders sent out fire teams to link up with their flank units. 2-6 had no trouble tying in with Alpha

1-6, but 4-6's team took small arms fire trying to contact Charlie.

They took up positions where that contact point should have been and reported back.

"Bravo 6, 2-6. All secure. Two whiskeys being treated. Linked up with Alpha 1-6. We have one problem. Few of these holes have overhead cover. Over."

That was amazing—only two wounded in all that melee they just had come through.

"Roger, 2-6. Make do with what you have. Try to get some cover up in case they start again. 6 out."

"Bravo 6, 4-6. Samo-samo. One serious whiskey being evac'd with Alpha's people. Four light wounds, no evac required. Can't find Charlie's element. I have a team sitting at the coordination point. We also have some overhead cover problems here. Over."

"6 Roger. Okay, 2-6 and 4-6. Stay alert. Do the best you can in those positions. It'll be daylight in a couple of hours. They're not likely to continue much beyond that. Tell your men they did a great job so far, but this party's not over yet. Sounds like Charlie's catching hell. We'll probably catch the next echelon any time now. Stay in touch. Out."

"Falcon 3, Bravo 6."

"Falcon 3."

"Bravo 6. Alpha's sector's secure. We have assumed control of the perimeter. Had only one serious whiskey. Only problem is that our right flank is open. Can't find Charlie 6's left flank."

"Bravo 6, this is Falcon 6. That was the quickest action I have seen. Are you sure the whole sector was secured? Over."

"Affirmative."

"Falcon 6. Great job! We're trying to find out Charlie's situation now. Will let you know. Anything further? Over."

"Negative."

"Okay, Falcon 6 out."

My RTOs and I walked over and crawled into Chancey's bunker, which was larger than mine had been. We had room to relax and think in there.

I looked at Herb. "Man, you look beat. You okay?"

He heaved a big sigh. "Yeah, Bull. You really saved us tonight. I've never seen anything like it. I thought we would all be overrun. They came at us and kept coming. Over and over again. When I lost contact with my platoons, I thought they would be in here next. Where are my platoon leaders?"

"Two are back at the aid station, one serious but he'll live. The other two are assisting my lieutenants. You want them back here?"

"Yeah. I'll put them to work doing something else."

"Okay. Atkinson, tell 2-6 and 4-6 to send Alpha's LTs back here to the CP. Gator, what's going on with Charlie 6? I've been a little out of touch."

"Yeah, a little. Charlie 6 reported major attacks on his two perimeter platoons. Said he was holding out so far. At least two tracks belonging to Fullback's platoon to his right have been blown up. They've moved reinforcements in to replace them."

"Sounds familiar. Gormley says two of those to his left have been hit. RPGs seem to work pretty good against those 113s. It looks like they found a way to get them while avoiding the fifities. They hit them in the side from in front of us. Of course, Gormley's getting the teams as they fire on the tracks. Always did like to keep down the life expectancy of RPG teams. Better check my other guys. Atkinson, hand me the mike." He moved the radio over to where I could reach it.

"1-6, Bravo 6. If you monitor, break squelch."

Two clicks.

"Is there any change in your situation?"

One click.

"Is the enemy too close to allow you to talk?"

"This is 1-6." His whisper was barely audible. "They moved around us toward the perimeter. Some came back this way after Fullback opened up on them. Then they went around toward 3-6's location. There appeared to be three waves coming through. All wore black, as far as we could tell. We're laying real low in a perimeter next to our ambush position. We haven't seen anything in the last half hour."

"Okay, good report. Don't talk so much. Let me know if anything changes. Bravo 6 out."

"3-6, Bravo 6. Sitrep."

"3-6. Situation hasn't changed. They're still after Fullback's tracks. It looks like three or four are burning now. I heard vehicles running, so I think they reinforced that platoon. Whatever's left of it. Over."

"Roger. Let me know if anything changes. We're in Alpha's area now, in case you need us. Bravo 6 out."

I turned back to Chancey. "Who've they got now as reaction force?"

"Recon platoon. That's all that's left."

"Yeah. If they commit them, guess they'll have to ask the mech for help. They don't seem to be doin' much anyway, except for those platoons on our flanks."

The battalion radio jumped to life. "Falcon 6, Charlie 6."

"Falcon 3. Go ahead, Charlie 6."

"My ambush just took a direct hit from one of our aircraft bombs. Reports are confused, but they appear to be in pretty bad shape. They'll have to stay there, because the situation here's going from bad to worse. I know they have kilos and whiskies. Over." That *was* bad—they had both killed and wounded.

"Charlie 6, Falcon 6. I'm very sorry to hear that. We're having the FAC shift those aircraft to the east. Let me know how bad off they are as soon as you know. Over."

"Roger. Whoever's controlling those air strikes really screwed up. Those guys never knew what hit 'em. Looks like we have at least three kilos, including the platoon leader, and at least ten whiskies, some serious. But that's only sketchy so far."

"This is Falcon 6. Roger. What is *your* situation?"

"Charlie 6. Both line platoons have some hand-to-hand combat. I'm in the process of committing my reserve platoon to the center. I'll let you know what happens. Over."

"Roger. Falcon 6 out."

Fifteen minutes later, Fishburne called again. "Falcon 6, Charlie 6. I need help. Over."

"Falcon 6. Give me your situation."

"Charlie 6. My two platoons are losing it. My reserve platoon is decisively engaged on the right flank. The enemy has an RPD set up and firing inside my perimeter. And I've got some damn gook on top of my bunker trying to throw a grenade inside. Every time he leans over, we empty a magazine at him and his grenade explodes outside. He may get lucky one of these times. Over."

"Okay, Charlie 6. I'll send Romeo to help you. Try to hold on 'til they get there. Over."

"Hot damn! The artillery just blew away that dink on my bunker with a beehive. They took that RPD out, too! I owe those guys a big one!"

"Good news! Now hold on. Romeo's on the way."

"Roger. Out."

I looked at Chancey. "Looks like Gus is in worse shape than you were. At least you didn't have someone trying to toss a grenade in your lap."

"Yeah. Glad they got the bastard."

Bennett's fire support radio crackled into action. I asked him what was going on. He waved his hand and listened intently for a couple of minutes, a wide grin spreading across his face. "This is great! Listen to this! Charlie Battery's XO was down on the gun nearest your Charlie 6's bunker. Since they had no land lines, he was helping with the gun. Right after they loaded a beehive, he noticed the gook on top of Charlie 6's bunker trying to grenade him. He also noticed an RPD machine gun firing beyond the bunker. He had them swing the gun around by the trails. Then he sighted down the tube and jerked the lanyard. That beehive turned that dink into

ground buzzard bait and also knocked out the machine
gun. All's now quiet around that bunker. Love it!"

I looked at Chancey and grinned, motioning toward
Bennett. "Sure is easy to please an artilleryman, even an
infantryman playing at artillery."

Suddenly my radio came alive. "Bravo 6, 2-6. We've
got a lot of movement to the front. Sounds like the next
attack's coming."

"Bravo 6. Okay, 2-6 and 4-6, give it to 'em. I'll try to
get some nape in there. Let me know how it does."

"2-6. Roger. Over."

"4-6. Roger. Over."

"6 out." I looked over at Bennett. "Nape on station?"

"Yessir. FAC's standin' by."

"Okay. I want that nape on the ground one hundred
meters in front of the perimeter on the first pass. I want
it danger-close. I'll adjust for the second pass. And I want
it down ASAP!"

Bennett turned to his radio. After a couple of minutes,
he turned back to me. "Nape's coming in hot right now."

"2-6, 4-6, this is Bravo 6. Nape's coming in hot.
Should be about one hundred meters to your front. Adjust.
Over."

"2-6. Roger."

"4-6. Roger. Here it comes!"

The jet screamed by, and I heard the familiar popping
of exploding canisters. The second jet repeated the performance.

"2-6, Bravo 6. How's that nape?"

"2-6. In a good spot. I heard some screaming out there.
Keep it coming! Over."

"Roger. Out. 4-6, give me a report on the napalm."

"4-6. Agree with 2-6. It's about seventy-five to one
hundred meters out. Keep it coming."

"Bravo 6, 2-6. Here they come!"

"Roger. Give 'em hell. Out."

I turned to Bennett. "Give the FAC an adjustment. I

want it fifty meters closer. I want two passes and I want it now!"

A crescendo of weapons fire erupted to the front. The *pop-pop-pop* of AK fire echoed around outside the bunker. Mortar shells were falling to our rear, but very few landed in our immediate area. The jets screamed by and the napalm canisters popped, then lit up the countryside as the chemicals blazed up. The steady staccato of M-60 fire and *rat-atat-tat* of M-16 automatic fire, punctuated by the *Crump! Crump!* of grenades and grenade launchers, completed the symphony of death. The good news was that I heard more of ours than theirs.

"2-6, Bravo 6. Sitrep."

"2-6. That last nape was almost on top of us! Really caught the gooks off guard. They're still coming at us head-on, but we're stopping them forward of the holes, with the help of the nape. Nothing hand-to-hand or anything like that. Those M-60s are really smoking! Over."

"Okay, 2-6. We should have at least one more pass with the nape. Keep your final protective fires going as long as you need to. How's your ammo holding out? Any casualties?"

"2-6. Ammo's okay. Alpha left us some in the holes. We're not running low yet. No casualties reported. Over."

"When you get a break, send someone back here to resupply. Alpha's got plenty here. Out.

"Break-Break. 4-6, Bravo 6. Sitrep."

"4-6. My left flank squad is getting most of the action in my area. 2-6 seems to be getting the main attack. We are firing more across 2-6's front into the flank of the assault than to our own front. No casualties so far. Ammo status is good. Over."

"Roger. Watch for them to change direction. Let me know if you run into Charlie's flank. Out."

I sat back and listened to the firing. The crescendo was subsiding. The M-60s were still firing, supplemented by an occasional burst of M-16 fire. Three more sorties of nape came in, and butterfly and high explosive bombs could be heard in the distance.

"Bravo 6, 2-6."

"Bravo 6."

"2-6. They appear to have broken contact. I think the nape broke them. We have negative incoming at this time. Over."

"Roger. Give me a casualty and ammo status."

"We're redistributing ammo. I'm sending a runner for resupply. I have four whiskies being evac'd back to the aid station. None serious, but Doc wants them to be looked at. They should be back."

"Roger. I'll be at your position in zero-five. Out."

I looked at my watch. 0430. Time flies when you're having fun. I was glad my genuine $19.00 black-face Seiko glowed in the dark. I turned to Chancey: "Well, Gator, it'll be getting daylight in another half-hour or so. Maybe they've had it for one night. Heard some gook firing his AK along the road in the middle of the perimeter a while ago. What happened?"

"After Recon was committed to Charlie's area, Falcon 3 arranged for Fullback to send over a couple of tracks to reconstitute our reserve. I think they went after the AK shooter and got him. In fact, there may have been a couple of them chased down back there."

"What's Charlie's situation?"

"Best I can tell from listenin' to th' radio, Recon successfully swept his area and restored his perimeter, with the help of a lot of beehives from Charlie Battery and some 'Killer Juniors' fired over that way. Fighting is pretty much wound down over there, except they are getting some sniper fire from time to time. Funny thing happened. They had one sniper in a tree that wouldn't come down, so they called in a 'Killer Junior.' No more sniping from there."

"Bravo 6, Bravo 6, this is 1-6." Walker's hoarse whisper was taut, on the verge of panic.

I grabbed the mike. "Bravo 6."

"Bravo 6, we just caught a grenade in the middle of our perimeter! We have guys hurt bad!" He was shaky but under control.

"Calm down, 1-6. Are you under attack?"

"I don't think so. They're going on past us."

"Keep your voice down. Tell me what happened."

"This is 1-6. The VC were all around us, pulling back from the perimeter. It was pretty noisy, with all the artillery and stuff. We were lying low. Nobody seemed to know we were here. Then a couple of dinks found our claymores along the road and started following the wires back into here. We shot 'em, but somebody on the other side of us must have heard us and tossed a grenade at the sound of gunfire. Nobody tried to attack us, so he must have thrown the grenade and moved on. We can still hear movement behind us and across the road. Over."

"Roger, 1-6. Tell me about your casualties."

"1-6. The grenade landed right by our medic. I think he's dead. At least three are hit pretty bad. Six or seven more are hit but I don't think they are serious. Over."

"1-6, are you hit?"

"Negative, Bravo 6."

"Okay, 1-6. As soon as it gets daylight and we know you're clear out there, we'll get you back here. I can't do it any quicker and take the risk of getting the rest of you shot up. As best you can without risking detection, do what you can with first aid. Start making poncho litters to get those who can't walk back here. Do you understand? Over."

"Roger, Bravo 6. We're trying to do that now. It's hard without a medic. Over."

"Roger that. Let me know as soon as the movement stops. Take it easy, son, and do the best you can. Watch your security. I'll get you out of there as soon as I can."

"Roger, Bravo 6. I understand."

"6 out."

I turned to Atkinson and MacKenzie. "Come on, you

two. Let's get out of this bunker and see what's going on."

I climbed out. We were still getting some sniper fire, but all the other fire had ceased. As soon as the RTOs were out and saddled up, we moved out toward second platoon's location. As we approached his platoon CP, Hughes climbed out and met us.

"How's it going, Sergeant?"

"It's pretty quiet out there now, sir. Haven't had anything since they tried that last attack."

"Let's walk the line. Show me your left flank position."

Hughes picked up his rifle and headed out through the few trees that remained. As I followed him, I noticed that streaks of breaking dawn were beginning to appear in the eastern sky. In the early morning twilight, I began to make out the destruction that had occurred there overnight. The dead VC lying all around attested to the ferocity of the fighting. The remaining trees had been reduced to splintered trunks by all the "Killer Junior" and other high-explosive fire thrown in there. Most of the jungle undergrowth had been shot away by a variety of weapons, including a number of beehive rounds fired into the area. The thought crossed my mind that it was good that it was the dry season, because the area would be all swamp during the monsoons.

Hughes and I stopped at each hole, letting the men know how well they had done and how proud of them I was. There was little need for much encouragement, for the adrenaline was still running high from the night's activities. They had done well and they knew it, and they were satisfied that their leaders also knew it. Not many members of Bravo company had been hurt, and their morale was soaring. As expressed by one soldier: "Well, Captain, I guess Bravo put the max on those little bastards, didn't we?" They sure did!

As we left his last position, I turned to Hughes. "Put them on 50% stand-down on a one-hour rotation and let 'em get a little rest. Push an LP out two hundred meters.

Make sure all Alpha's casualties have been evacuated, including the KIAs. There are a lot of dead gooks around here, so watch out for sleepers. Make sure all are dead. If any are still alive, get them to the rear under guard for treatment and interrogation. As soon as everything quiets down, sweep out in front of your position for four hundred meters to make sure nothing is hiding out there. Send a detail out to start dragging bodies and equipment back inside the perimeter. Pile the VC back near Alpha's CP. If you should find any Americans, take them back to the aid station. Questions? Okay, see you later."

I went through the same routine with 4-6, who had finally linked up with Recon in Charlie's sector. Then I walked back to Alpha's CP.

"3-6, Bravo 6."

"This is 3-6."

"Bravo 6. Get ready to send a squad out to assist 1-6's move back to this location. Send your medic with them. I'll give you the word after I see if we can get more medical support."

"3-6 roger."

"Bravo 6 out, Break-Break, 1-6 Bravo 6."

" '1-6"

"Bravo 6. How's it going out there?"

"1-6. We've done the best we can with what we've got. Our medic is the only kilo, but some of our guys are hurt bad. When can we come in?"

"Soon. Everything seems to have quieted down. I'm sending you a squad from 3-6 with medical support. They'll help you get back in. Sit tight. We're still getting sniper fire."

"Roger."

"6 out."

I turned to my company medic. "Wilcox, go back to the battalion aid station and get some help for 1-6. I want you to go, too. 3-6 will send a squad with you for security. A litter jeep would help if they can send one out. They've got at least one dead and three seriously wounded.

They've got other wounded as well. Meet 3-6 on the road to the north at the perimeter. Any questions? Get there as quick as you can with whatever you can. I want 1-6 back here ASAP! Now go!" (Wilcox is an alias.)

"3-6, Bravo 6."

"3-6."

"Bravo 6. My Doc's trying to rustle up some litter help from higher. He'll meet your squad on the road at your perimeter. Get them up to 1-6's location ASAP. He needs help badly. Over."

"3-6. Roger that. My guys are standing by at the road. Over."

"Roger. Let me know when they start out. Touch base with Fullback's guys on your left. Out."

"Falcon 3, Bravo 6."

"Falcon 3."

"Bravo 6. Request you inform Fullback that we'll be sending out assistance to bring 1-6 back in. Medical assistance and security will be moving out as soon as they can get their act together."

"This is Falcon 3. This may be premature. I'll have to clear it with Falcon 6 and Flexible. Over."

I felt my anger rising and my face muscles tighten. When I spoke, my voice was deliberate, level and cold. "Falcon 3, this is Bravo 6. Be advised that my last transmission was not a request. I'm advising you of my actions. I don't give a rat's ass who you want to clear it with. Either advise Fullback that some of my people will be to his right front, or I'll do it myself. You do your staff job and I'll do my job. I have dead and wounded out there and they will be brought back as soon as I can get them back. Do you roger? Over."

"Roger, Bravo 6. I'll call Fullback. Be advised Falcon 6 monitored your last transmission. Over."

"Bravo 6. Roger. Out."

I really hate staff officers! If they had a brain, they'd either sit on it or take it out and play with it. I cannot stand all this bureaucratic crap when something important has to be done. Damn them!

"Bravo 6, 3-6."

"Bravo 6. Go."

"3-6. Your Doc's here. He has three other medics and four litters. He even has a litter jeep, but the driver won't go forward of the bunker line. Over."

"Roger that. The casualties will have to be brought back to the jeep. Get them going now. Tell Doc good job."

"Roger, Bravo 6. They're moving now. I passed the word to Fullback's right flank platoon leader. He'll pass the word back up his line. You know they lost most of their tracks in that platoon? Doesn't look like anybody else over there even got hit. Over."

"Roger, 3-6. Good job. Out."

"1-6, Bravo 6. Over."

"Bravo 6, this is 1-6. Over."

"Bravo 6. One of 3-6's elements is headed your way with medical support. Lookout for them and don't shoot 'em up. As soon as they take care of your guys, get back in here as soon as you can. Let me know when you start back."

"1-6. Roger that. I'll send someone out to the road to look for them. Over."

"Roger. Out."

I turned to my RTOs. "Come on. Let's go to third platoon."

We walked over to Gormley, standing beside his CP bunker. I could see the hole in the sandbags where the mortar round landed. He turned as we approached.

"Morning, Captain. Have a good night?"

"Great! Another night like that and I'll feel like I earned my CIB."

"More than most people who get them."

"Yeah, I know. You okay?"

"Yessir. Total casualty count is one serious and two light WIA's. The serious one is a shoulder wound. He's back at the aid station. The rest have been treated and are back in their positions."

"Good. We'll wait here 'til your guys get back with the first platoon. Let's go walk your perimeter. Have you sent out an LP?"

"Yessir. I pushed one out when things got quiet."

"Okay. I want you to sweep forward of your perimeter to make sure we're clear out there. Have a detail start bringing bodies back here in the perimeter. Stack the VC somewhere to your rear. If you find any Americans, get them to the aid station."

Gormley nodded. We made the rounds and talked to the men remaining on the perimeter. They were doing fine, but understandably were not as pumped-up as the second platoon, since their night was somewhat less active. Then we went back to 3-6's CP to await first platoon.

About thirty minutes later, my company push crackled. "Bravo 6, 1-6. Over."

"Bravo 6."

"1-6. We're heading back to the perimeter. We have the kilo and three whiskeys on stretchers. The rest can walk, but we'll be moving slowly. Your Doc tells me that we are not likely to lose any others."

"Roger, 1-6. Come on in. We've got a jeep at the perimeter to take your litters. I'll meet you there. Out."

It took about forty-five minutes for first platoon's point to reach the perimeter. Specialist Larry Robinson was the first man to pass through.

"Damn, Captain, I'm really glad to see you! That was hairy out there last night!"

"You, too, Robinson. Glad you guys made it back."

Walker was not far behind Robinson.

"Good morning, Rich. Welcome back. Have your litters loaded on that aid jeep. Doc Wilcox will get your others to the aid station. How many do you have?"

"Our medic is dead. Three guys are pretty serious. Seven others are hit less seriously."

"All from one grenade? You sure it wasn't a satchel charge?"

"Yessir. We were in a pretty tight perimeter, trying to hide and make as small a target as possible. The grenade landed right in the middle."

"How did it miss you?"

"Doc was in the way. I owe him my life. I wish I could thank him."

"Don't let it get to you. It's the luck of the draw. Are you okay?"

"Yessir. I'm okay."

"Good. Get your people in, get them fed and resupplied, and let them relax and rest awhile. They've earned it."

"Yessir." He walked over to the jeep.

I went over to the perimeter and spoke to each one as he came back through the perimeter. After getting a report that everyone was accounted for and the casualties were taken care of, I turned back toward Alpha's position.

As we passed near the battalion CP, I heard someone approaching me. I glanced up and saw two silver stars coming my way. The Division Commander, Major General F. K. Mearns ("Tropic 6") was bearing down on me with that long, purposeful stride. I knew that we had a lot of choppers coming in, but I assumed they were mostly medevacs. I did not know that the gladhanders and other vultures had already started arriving.

I glanced at the RTOs. "Stand at attention as best you can." I saluted the general. "Good morning, sir."

"Good morning, Captain. Which company do you have?"

"Bravo, sir."

"Okay, Bravo 6. I want to tell you that was a mighty fine counterattack you led last night. Mighty fine!" Seems he had already been thoroughly briefed by someone— probably that ass-kisser Davis. Or— he could have been overhead watching the whole thing for the last six hours, right up there with the tac fighters, gunships and artillery shells flying from three directions—not very likely!

"Thank you, sir. The men deserve the credit. They did the work."

"Please pass to them my congratulations."

"Yessir. Your people will be getting some award recommendations for these guys. I'd appreciate it if you could expedite the approvals. In fact, if you brought Purple Hearts with you, we have plenty of guys at the aid station who deserve them."

"You can count on my help there, Bravo 6. Good job, son." We saluted, and he moved on to find someone else to pigeon-hole. Well that's what generals are paid to do, I guess.

As we approached Alpha's CP, MacKenzie interrupted my thoughts. "Sir, Falcon 3's calling a meeting of the commanders in one-zero."

"Thanks, MacKenzie. You two get on back to our own CP. If anything happens, you know where to find me." As they walked away, I shook my head slowly, thinking about Davis: "Screwed-up idiot!"

Ten minutes later, Gator and I ambled into the battalion CP. Falcon 6 had gone to find Tropic 6, but Davis was there, looking like he had been through a war or something. I guess we all did. Charlie 6 had already arrived and was quietly sipping on a cup of coffee.

"Gus, you okay? Sounded like you had a little fun out there last night." I plopped down on a pile of sandbags and looked closely at him. He looked totally drained of any recognizable feeling or spirit.

"Bob, I thought we were goners for sure. That damn gook on top of my bunker tried his best to get a grenade inside. The only thing that saved us was that beehive from Charlie Battery."

"Glad you made it, Gus. Lot of close calls last night."

Chancey heaved a sigh of relief. "Yeah, tell me about it."

Davis picked up his papers. "Let me run down a couple of things with you. First, as you may know, Tropic 6 and

Flex 6 are in the area. Falcon 6 is out with Flex 6 and Fullback 6 right now. Next, let me give you some preliminary casualty figures. Counting killed and wounded requiring medical attention, Alpha 6 lost about fifty per cent of his company and Charlie 6 lost two-thirds. Bravo's losses were one HHC medic dead and eighteen wounded. Many of the wounded were treated and returned to duty. Those who weren't and the dead are being medevac'd back to Cu Chi. We're still trying to get all of Charlie's ambush platoon back here. We sent a platoon of tracks from Fullback to help haul them back. Bravo's ambush has completely closed back into the perimeter. As for enemy dead, we won't know until we recover them all and count them."

"We're starting to drag bodies back into the perimeter now," I interjected.

Davis nodded and droned on. "We're getting a couple of days stand-down. Katum has some limited base facilities at the Special Forces camp. The 4/9 Manchus are coming in to take over our portion of the perimeter for a few days. It's now 0810 hours. Their first lift is due at 0900. After they all close, the same birds will be used to ferry us to Katum. Until then, Bravo will withdraw back to your original positions and prepare to move. You will go into Katum first and set up the perimeter for the others. Alpha and Charlie, man your sector as best you can with the men you have available. We don't expect any further action at this time. Charlie will follow Bravo with Recon and the CP Group, and Alpha will bring up the rear. We will man the perimeter there, but we'll do no patrolling. The Civilian Irregular Defense Group, or CIDG, will provide area security for us. As you arrive, I'll be there to point out your sectors. We'll talk more once we close in there. I'll give you the word when it's your turn to move to the road for pick-up. Fullback and Manchu will be patrolling around the fire base and dragging the VC bodies back to the center to be buried in a mass grave like the one at Soui Tre."

"Yeah, we have to maintain the similarities here. Tying this to Soui Tre means a lot of publicity and glory for higher headquarters. I'm sure the press vultures will have all the gory details for the evening dinner news." God, I hated reporters. They got in the way more than they helped.

Davis rustled his papers. "By the way, the MACV and USARV Surgeons are coming out to examine and interview Sergeant Jerome from Alpha. If you haven't heard, he was stuck out on LP when the attack started. As he made his way back to the perimeter, a beehive went off nearby. Seems one of those little darts went all the way through his body and he never knew it until later when it started itching. They can't understand how that could happen. Okay, any questions? That's all I have for now." (Jerome is an alias.)

I went back to the CP and briefed the platoon leaders about what we were going to do. As they left, Atkinson walked up.

"Captain, got a minute? I want to show you and the lieutenant something."

I nodded. Bennett and I followed him around to the front of the bunker where we had taken cover from the beehives the previous last night. There, he pointed out a line of flechettes stuck in the top edge of the bunker and another dozen or so stuck in the spindly tree. We were that close to being thoroughly perforated.

I looked at Bennett. "Well, chalk up another one for Divine Intervention." He nodded dumbly, staring at those little darts.

I wandered back to the edge of the road. From that location, I could survey most of the perimeter. I could see the artillerymen burning their ammo boxes and extra powder charges, with flames soaring high above the clutter and debris of the fire base. Across the perimeter, the mech were jockeying their tracks around, repositioning them to plug holes in the perimeter, while pulling back the burned-out hulks of blown-up personnel carriers in which men died hideous deaths last night, caught up in fiery furnaces of burning aluminum and exploding ammunition. They had lost all four tracks in each of the two platoons that had joined Falcon. In the middle of the road through the perimeter, numerous dustoff choppers were busy ferrying out the wounded as the aid station finished with them, as they had done continuously since about 0300 hours. Those pilots were the real heroes of Vietnam, continuously amazing the infantryman—attempting to come in under almost any condition, no matter how hostile, to transport the wounded and injured back to hospitals in rear base camps. An infantryman would undergo any hardship to respond to a downed dustoff. We appreciated what they did for us. Throughout the area in and around the fire base, men were beginning to pull in the VC bodies, throwing them in piles. Bulldozers from the artillery were beginning the task of digging large pits to serve as mass graves for a lot of little men dressed in black. When the pits were finished, the piles of bodies would be tossed in, covered with lime and the dirt plowed back in on top of them. They had done the same thing at Suoi Tre. One could still fly over the Suoi Tre site and view the scars which still remained on the ground in the jungle clearing from the mass graves, which the jungle still refused to take back.

A major battle had been fought there. Finally, another 3rd Brigade commander ("Flex 6")—this time Colonel Leonard R. Dunn, Jr. (an alias)—had been allotted his "Suoi Tre", which had been the providence—and general's star—of one former commander and the ultimate goal of all "Flexible 6s."

We did not know it at the time, but that little 12-hour New Year truce extension had cost two crack regiments of the 9th VC Main Force Division over five hundred dead—that we found and buried—and probably at least two hundred more that they carried out of there, which was their normal procedure. They also lost hundreds more wounded, as well as a failed objective. Our casualties

paled by comparison. The artillery had fired almost two
hundred beehive rounds, the most of any single battle to
date.

After the swarm of reporters, news cameramen, and
photographers had accompanied and followed the colonels
and generals who came to revel in the carnage, this battle
made the next-day news back home. However, by the time
the reporters descended on Burt, the Falcon battalion—
the ones who had fought the major part of the battle and
who had paid the requisite price—had closed in at Katum.
That left Fullback's commanders, most of whom had seen
little of the battle, to expound to the press on the horrors
of combat. It was Fullback's guys who were photographed
tossing black-clad bodies into mass graves. The guys who
deserved most of the credit were either busy rebuilding
howitzer emplacements, or were in Katum, trying to get
a little rest and to reconstitute their lost combat power and
to replace their casualties. We left it to the bystanders—
the colonels, the generals, the staff officers—to tell the
story of Fire Support Base Burt, but the guys in the open
foxholes, the squads, the platoons, and the companies—
the guys struggling across the fire-swept clearing, the guys
trying to survive in cut-off and exposed ambush sites, the
guys on LP cut off from their perimeter, the guys sighting
down isolated howitzer tubes at the oncoming hordes before jerking their lanyards—these guys knew the *real*
story of Burt. These guys knew in their hearts and minds
that they had made a difference that night. They had won
a big one for the home folks. No one else may have given
a damn for what they did, but *they* gave a damn. They
knew what they had done. They had max'ed the final
exam.

That had been one helluva long, long night.

CHAPTER FIVE

BUZZSAW

January 15, 1968, started out like most other days that month, but it turned out to be one that was burned into my memory with the intensity of a blowtorch. I wish that I could forget that day, but I never will. I was at the height of pride in my unit and in my ability to command, and had the feeling—common in Bravo Company, particularly after the battle at FSB Burt—that we were almost invincible, that we could handle any situation, as we had done for at least the previous three-and-one-half months. However, that day became a reality check. That was the day when fate brought us tumbling back to earth, back to the realization that *nobody* is invincible, that *nobody* gets by without paying his dues. The jungle was the great equalizer, and on that day, *the jungle ate our lunch!*

Five days after the Burt battle, Falcon had returned to the fire base and resumed its old sector. Manchu had gone on to other things elsewhere, but Fullback and the artillery were still there. The main difference was that Colonel Dunn's brigade CP had moved in. I guess he wanted to see what action felt like at ground level as opposed to 1,500 feet overhead. Whatever the reason, he and his renowned "shoot-from-the-hip" philosophy were there.

While we were at Katum, all companies had been resupplied and had received sufficient replacements and returned wounded to look like companies again. We had been able to get clean uniforms, rest a bit, drink a few beers, read the papers, write a few letters home to let the folks know that we were all right—all the things that help mend body and soul. By the time we went back to Burt, Alpha and Charlie were totally functional again.

Bravo company had also received a few replacements,

but we had managed to stay relatively intact. A little rest was helpful, but our morale was sky-high. Once again, we had been called on to save another company. Once again, our luck had held, and we had been able to render service to our fellow man. During the three-and-one-half months I had been in command, we had reacted to every other company in the battalion—some, including Alpha, more than once—and had been successful each time. A few of those successes had been blind luck borne on the wave of aggressive action, but successes they were. During that time, Bravo had never requested assistance in return, never called for a reaction force, never needed one.

On the day we returned to Burt, the first thing I noticed after the choppers flew away was a definite stench. At first, I thought I had detected the brigade CP, but as we took over their position, Manchu Bravo 6 told me that they had received orders from brigade to leave several VC bodies lying around outside the perimeter to rot. The idea was to impress upon the VC that, if they attacked again, they might have a hard time joining their ancestors. You see, they believed that the present life was only a brief respite in their journey to reside with their ancestors forever in the afterlife. However, they could only continue that journey after a proper burial. Ergo, if they were not buried, but were allowed to stay out in the tropical sun and rot, they would not likely join their family and friends in the Great Beyond. So thought these higher headquarters geniuses. I don't know, maybe they were right. Until the fire base was dismantled in mid-February, there were no other ground attacks—mortars and rockets, but no ground attacks. We were lucky, though. Alpha company in the south received the brunt of the stench, especially when the wind was right.

Contributing to the overall aroma of the area around Burt was the fact that not all bodies had been covered up in the mass grave. Some had been piled in the ditches along the road and covered with rocks. Since a pile of rocks is not air-tight like a mound of dirt, they were also very noticeable. I am not sure whose brilliant idea that was, but we cursed them whenever we had to walk down that road.

I also had another, more pleasant, surprise waiting for me at Burt—a new Platoon Leader for Second Platoon, Second Lieutenant Randy Lorne (an alias), again fresh from OCS. Once again the thought crossed my mind that all those new ROTC and West Point officers must really be too good to get down and dirty in the combat zone. I guess too much money had been invested in their education to get them killed before they could make Captain and be allowed to get other people killed. Or they all must know someone important . . .

The day after we returned to Burt, we were assigned a RIF AO for the day, to the east of the firebase. As I was picking up my webbing to get ready to go out, the radio interrupted the relative silence.

"Bravo 6, 3-6"

"Bravo 6."

"3-6. I have a man who needs to talk to you. Request you see him before we move out."

"Roger. Send him over. 6 out."

Five minutes later, Spec 4 Roger Ayers (an alias) arrived at the CP, saluted and stood at attention.

"At ease, Ayers. What's your problem?"

"Well, Captain, I-uh-I've got a drip and it hurts pretty bad."

"Where did you git it?"

"Back in Dau Tieng before we moved out here."

"You ought to know better than dipping your wick in something strange without a rubber. It's pretty damn stupid to expose yourself unnecessarily. You understand?"

"Yessir."

"It ain't the first time, either, is it?"

"Nossir."

"Well, it had better the *last* time!"

"Yessir. Can I go back to base camp and get this taken care of?"

"Sorry. I've got no way to get you back today. You can check back tomorrow."

He winced. I could see the pain in his eyes. "Yessir." He saluted and returned to his platoon.

I noticed Sergeant Johnson watching me with a smirk on his face. I grinned.

"I can assure you, Top, that he'll be in serious pain before I let him get on a chopper out of here."

I strung out Specialist Ayers for four more days before I let him go back for treatment. It proved to be an effective measure. Although he had had VD several times in the past, he never contracted it again—at least not as long as I was in command.

For the next week or so, the rifle companies took turns conducting RIFs in the general area around Burt. On January 13th, during our second stroll through the woods, an incident occurred which aptly illustrated my rather unflattering description of Flexible 6 (Colonel Dunn) and his staff.

We had been out to the extent of our area of operation (AO) without incident and had returned to within five clicks of the fire base, walking the artillery around us as we moved, when I heard fire from my point platoon. I grabbed the handset.

"2-6, Bravo 6. What's that fire I hear?"

"2-6. We received AK and RPG fire from our right flank. Appears to be two or three AKs and one RPG-2. Probably an enemy ambush patrol scared out of hiding by the arty. No one was hit. We're returning fire and preparing to execute fire-and-maneuver to get them. Over."

"Roger, go ahead, but be careful. Let me know what happens as you go. There might be more there than you can handle. I'll keep the arty going beyond you. I'll bring it closer if you need it. Over."

"2-6. Roger, 6."

"6 out."

I turned to Bennett. "Did you hear what I told 2-6?"

"Roger, sir. We'll keep it going. Let me know when you want to adjust it."

"Okay." I reached for the Falcon push. "Falcon 3, this is Bravo 6." My voice was measured with no hint of excitement or panic.

Falcon 3. I hear shooting. Over."

"Roger that. 2-6 on point has some incoming. I'm waiting to see if he can handle it before I commit more force. Seems to be three AKs and one RPG flushed out by the arty. We're continuing to work the arty. Maybe we can ruin their whole day. Just in case this is something bigger, I want a FAC and gunships standing by. I'll call if I need them. Then they can come up on my net. Over."

"Roger, Bravo 6. We'll get on that now. Be advised that Falcon 6 is in the air on aerial recon. I expect that he will be coming your way."

"Roger. Out."

Back to the company push. "2-6, 6. Sitrep."

"2-6. No change. We're moving on them to their flank now."

"Roger. Standing by."

With the Falcon radio, MacKenzie stepped up to my side. "Sir, Falcon 6 wants a sitrep to pass to Flex 6."

"Tell him what I just told the 3. Tell him I'll get him a sitrep just as soon as I get a chance here."

After a moment: "2-6, 6. How's it going?"

"2-6. My maneuver element is now receiving fire from the same location. I don't believe we have anything more than we thought, but my fire support element hasn't got 'em yet."

"Roger. I don't want your maneuver element shot up. Pull them back to your location and use your whole platoon as a base of fire. I'll use 3-6 as a hammer. Let me know when you're ready. Over."

"Roger, out."

MacKenzie tapped me on the shoulder. "Flex 6 is on Falcon push and wants a sitrep. Seems pretty upset."

"Flex 6 is always upset or drunk. Tell him the same

thing you told Falcon 6. He'll have to wait 'til I get a break here."

Back to the business at hand. "3-6, 6. Did you monitor my last with 2-6?"

"Roger, Bravo 6. We know where the firing is and we're ready."

"Roger. Stand by. Out. Break. 2-6, 6."

"Falcon Bravo 6, this is Flexible 6. Sitrep. Over." How did that bastard get on my company push? I am trying to fight a contact here.

I looked up and saw a small observation helicopter— that would be Falcon 6—and a big Huey up above him. I shot a bird in that general direction and went on about my business.

"Flex 6, I'm trying to fight a contact here. I'll get you a sitrep as soon as I have a chance. Out. Break. 2-6, Bravo 6. Over."

"Bravo 6, this is Flex 6. I want a sitrep *now*! Over."

Then I heard a great, booming voice from beyond. "Flexible 6, this is Tropic 6. *Get off* Bravo 6's net and let him fight his battle. Out." God bless you, General F. K. Mearns, wherever up there you are! I glanced up again and saw a third dot—the Division Commander's Huey— way, way up there. I swear, this had to be the first war in which combat was a spectator sport.

"2-6, Bravo 6. Are you in position?"

"Roger, Bravo 6. We are about two hundred meters forward of 3-6."

"Roger. Out. Break. 3-6, 6. Move out now. Flank the target to the right. Over."

"3-6. Roger, moving now. Expect to close in zero-five."

"Bravo 6 out." I dropped the handset. "Bennett, shift that arty three hundred meters to the rear *now*!"

"Yessir."

MacKenzie interrupted my train of thought. "Sir, Falcon 6 came back on the push and asked for a sitrep when you have a chance." I nodded.

"2-6, 6. You still receiving fire from the same position?"

"Roger, 6."

"Okay. 3-6 is coming around to your right. He'll tell you when to cease fire. I want you to pour all you've got in there, starting now. Do you roger?"

"Roger. Here it goes!"

The firing increased from 2-6. "3-6, Bravo 6. Sitrep."

"3-6. We're about half way there. I can still hear the AKs."

"Okay. When you approach the enemy position, give 2-6 word to stop firing."

"3-6. Roger."

"6 out."

The other horn: "Falcon 3, Bravo 6. Where are the FAC and gunships?"

"Falcon 3. FAC just came up and should be trying to reach you now. Gunships are en route but not yet in sector. Over."

"Roger. Out."

Back onto my company push: "Falcon Bravo 6, this is FAC. Over."

"FAC, Bravo 6. Roger, glad to see you. You have nape?"

"Affirmative. Can deliver in zero-five."

"Roger, FAC. Need you to stand back until I see what we've got here. Over."

"Roger, standing by. Out."

About that time, I heard 2-6 abruptly cease fire. The AK sound continued. Then to the right, I heard 3-6 open fire. After about three minutes, the firing stuttered to silence.

"Bravo 6, 3-6. Report five enemy KIA, four AK-47s and one RPG-2 captured. We're spreading out into a perimeter, but there doesn't seem to be anything else here. We had no casualties. Over."

"Roger, 3-6. Watch your ass and make sure that's it. Make sure they've got no tunnels or spider holes to jump you from. I'll have 2-6 join you there. We'll move up to your location. Good job. Out. Break. 2-6, 6. You monitor?"

"2-6. Roger, we're moving now. We also had no casualties. Over."

"Okay, good job. Talk to 3-6 as you close. The rest of us are moving now."

I turned to Lieutenants Walker and Constantino, who were standing where I could see them. "Okay, move out. First platoon, push out a point to make contact with 2-6 and 3-6."

I picked up the Falcon push. "Falcon 6, Bravo 6."

"Falcon 6."

"Bravo 6. I have a sitrep for you and Flexible 6. Action successful. Used 2-6 as base of fire and 3-6 as maneuver. Results are five VC KIA, four AKs and one RPG captured. No friendly casualties. No other bad guys located. You can send air support home with my thanks. Request disposition instructions for enemy kilos. Over."

"Roger, Bravo 6. Do you have an LZ?"

"Roger, 6. One ship can get in here."

"Roger. Okay, we'll send a bird after them. Should be there in one-five mikes. Over."

"Roger that. We'll be standing by. Over."

"Falcon 6 out."

Back to the company push: "FAC, Bravo 6."

"Bravo 6, FAC."

"Roger, FAC. Looks like our little action is over. Appreciate your response. Have a cold one for me."

"Roger, Bravo 6. Glad to be of service. Out."

We closed up with the second and third platoons, established a defensive position, and waited for the aircraft. After the VC were picked up, we returned to the fire base with no further activity.

On January 15th, it was once again Bravo company's turn in the saddle. Our RIF AO was in deep jungle out to about eight clicks southeast of Burt, and our specific mission was to check out a suspected VC base area. Those highly-intelligent folks at brigade thought that there might be some remnants from the Burt fight still hanging around the area. Intelligence got that idea from the helicopter pilots and others who had reported seeing people carrying stretchers back toward and into Cambodia. They also figured that maybe some of the wounded from that fight still might be residing in underground hospitals or aid stations and were being transported during darkness the three clicks back to Cambodia.

We lined up and headed out from the fire base perimeter. The jungle was pretty thick, so we moved with a four-man front and with third platoon on point about three hundred meters to the front. We had been out in the AO about two hours when I heard firing from the point platoon.

"3-6, Bravo 6. Sitrep."

"3-6. We're taking a lot of incoming fire from our front and left flank. Sounds like an M-60 machine gun and a couple of AKs. Also there are at least two RPG gunners out there. The automatic fire is coming from one location, I think from only one bunker to the left front. The RPGs are moving around on our left flank. My point squad took the brunt of the fire and is still separated from us by about fifty meters. We are pinned down now but we're returning fire as best we can. Over."

"6. Roger. Give me your location. In the clear."

"3-6. Grid is 442775 on an azimuth of 210. Over."

"Roger. Hold tight. Put your people in a small perimeter for protection and start trying to get your point squad back. I'm going to throw some arty to your front. When it splashes, give me your adjustment. You may be able to use it to cover you getting to your point. Do you roger?"

"Roger, 6."

"Okay, 3-6. Let me know what's happening. Out."

I turned to Bennett, who already had the guns on standby and was planning the mission. "Get 105 fire out ASAP. Put a round in front of 3-6's point squad and let him adjust it. Once he puts it where he wants it, I want a battery five, then wait for further orders."

"Roger, sir. First round will be out in zero-one."

"3-6, 6. What's going on?"

"3-6. Okay, we're still getting automatic fire. We've got some of the point back in here. Everybody in the squad was hit. Squad leader is a kilo. We're still working to get the others. Evidently, there are several bunkers, but the auto fire seems to be coming from only one bunker about thirty meters to our left front. We're still mostly pinned down here. We've seen two VC with RPGs but we got both of them. At this time, we're getting no more RPG fire. Over."

"Can you pinpoint the bunker location?"

"Roger. I see the bunker's outline from here. Looks like an ant hill. Between bursts, we can even hear them chattering."

Bennett broke in. "Splash out."

"Roger." Back to 3-6: "3-6, splash out."

"3-6 roger. *Hey! That was pretty close to the point!*"

"Did they take shrapnel?"

"Negative. It's about one hundred meters in front of them. Undergrowth and elephant grass is pretty thick there. Splash location looks okay to me."

"Okay, I'm going to bring in a lot more. Keep your heads down. Should give you a chance to get the rest of your guys back."

"Roger."

To Bennett: "Okay, battery five on those coordinates." A "battery five" required the firing of five rounds per each of the five howitzers in the battery, or twenty-five rounds. That should give those dinks in the bunker a good reason to hug the bottom of the hole, even if we do not hit them.

About two minutes later: "Splash out!"

"3-6, splash out. Battery five coming. Count 'em."

"3-6. Roger."

The artillery crashed into the jungle ahead of 3-6. This barrage should have kept the bunker from being reinforced before we could get our people out. Since I still did not know what we had walked into, I wanted to isolate the area around Third Platoon until we could control the situation. The fact that brigade suspected a base area did not necessarily mean a large area. Sometimes as few as two bunkers were described as a base area.

"Okay, Bennett, put them on standby, laid in on those coordinates." He nodded.

I heard the automatic fire resume up ahead. "3-6, 6. What's your status?"

"3-6. We got all my point back here. There is at least one kilo. We are in a small perimeter here, but the auto fire started again from the same bunker. We are still pinned down."

"Roger. I'm sending 1-6 up to take care of that bunker. If you get fire from any other location, let me know ASAP."

"Roger."

"6 out."

I picked up the Falcon push. "Falcon 3, Bravo 6."

"Falcon 3."

"Bravo 6. Sitrep. My point element is taking automatic fire from at least one bunker. His point took the initial burst and has at least one kilo. He's gotten all his point back to his position, but he's pinned down there. We used arty to cover his consolidation and to try to prevent enemy reinforcement. I'm sending another element to take out the bunker. Request you start backing up air support. I'm not sure yet what we've got there, but I may need more than artillery. We'll also need a dustoff standing by, but I don't yet know where we'll bring him in. He may need a jungle extractor. Over."

"Falcon 3. Roger. I'll let you know when they come up. Anything else? Over."

"Negative. Bravo 6 out."

Back to the company push: "1-6, Bravo 6."

"This is 1-6. Over."

"Can you pinpoint the firing ahead of you? You should

be able to distinguish firing from two distinct locations. 3-6 is returning fire received from a bunker about thirty meters to his left front. Over."

"1-6. I hear firing, but it's hard to distinguish two locations from here."

"Okay, 1-6. I want you to move up to the left front until you are even with 3-6's location. You should be able to distinguish the two locations by then. When you get there, turn toward and flank the bunker and take it out. Move as quietly as you can without machetes. Watch your security. There may be other bunkers in the area, although this is the only one firing on 3-6. After you take out the bunker, provide security for 3-6 to extract to this location. I don't want you to turn until you can distinguish the bunker's location. I want you to talk directly to 3-6 on this push so he can guide you in and make sure you don't shoot each other up. Over."

"1-6. Roger, Bravo 6. We're moving now. Over."

"Roger. Let me know before you make your turn. I want to make sure you know where you're going."

"1-6. Roger."

"6 out. Break. 3-6, 6."

"This is 3-6."

"1-6 is coming up on your left flank to take out that bunker. Continue firing at it to draw their fire and keep their attention on you. Talk to 1-6 to guide him into the bunker. Make sure you don't get shot up or shoot him up. Cease fire when he approaches the bunker. Do you roger?"

"3-6. Roger."

For the next few minutes, I listened to the firing up ahead and to 1-6 and 3-6 occasionally exchanging location and checkpoints. We had been pretty successful in the past with this tactic. All the rifle platoon leaders had performed it at least once in the past. The idea was to provide a base of fire to engage the target and to draw their fire and attention, while a maneuver element flanked the bunker and took it out. The tricky part was to have

the maneuvering platoon accurately close on the bunker
without either platoon shooting at each other by mistake.
Due to the location and number of weapons, this encounter could have the potential to be a bit more complicated
than some of our previous experiences.

"Bravo 6, 1-6. Over."

"6—Go!"

"1-6. Moving in this jungle and elephant grass is not
easy, but from the sound of the firing, I should be pretty
much to their flank and ready to make my turn. From here,
I can hear firing in two different places. I can hear M-60s
and M-16s from the right. From the left position, I hear
a few AK rounds, but mostly it sounds like M-60 fire. Is
it correct that the VC in the bunker have a 60? Over."

"Roger, 1-6. We think they are firing a captured M-60.
Okay, your objective is the left location. 3-6 says those
bunkers look like anthills, so watch out for them. When
you get close, let 3-6 know so he can cease firing. Go get
them!"

"Roger, Bravo 6. We're turning now."

"6 out."

Again I sat and waited, listening to 1-6 and 3-6 coordinating their movements. Abruptly, all sound of firing
from that direction stopped. 3-6 had ceased firing, but so
had the VC. As the meaning of that dawned on me, the
hairs on the back of my neck bristled. "Oh, hell!" As I
grabbed for the handset, the radio crackled again.

"3-6, 1-6. Where the hell is that bunker? The firing
stopped and I can't see them in this mess."

"1-6, 3-6. You're too far to the right. *Move left! Move
left! The bunker is on your left!*"

Suddenly it sounded like the world opened up. The
sounds of M-60 and AK fire were punctuated with the
stacatto of M-16s and the "*Crump!*" of grenades.

"1-6, Bravo 6. What's going on up there?" No answer.

"3-6, Bravo 6. Sitrep. Over."

"3-6. 1-6 is taking fire from his left flank. They walked
right in front of the bunker and the dinks opened up on

his flank. Sounds like they hit 'em pretty hard. I can't see much from here. Over."

"Roger, out." I turned to Bennett: "Get a battery two one hundred meters to the left of those last coordinates, and I want continuous fire walking back and forth out there in front of 1-6 and 3-6."

I turned back to the mike. "3-6, Bravo 6. I'm putting another 105 barrage one hundred meters to the left of the last coordinates to put it in front of 1-6. Adjust it as best you can. They'll keep shooting for awhile. Keep your heads down."

"3-6 roger."

"1-6, 6. Sitrep. Over." Still no answer.

"1-6, 6. Respond! Over."

"Bravo 6, Bravo 6, this is 1-6 X-ray. Over." That was Walker's RTO, and he was obviously panicking.

"Bravo 6. What's your situation? Over."

"Bravo 6, Bravo 6. This is 1-6 X-ray. 1-6 and 1-5 are dead! Everybody's down all over the place! The artillery is killing us! Please stop the artillery! Can you help us? Over."

To Bennett: "Add one hundred meters now!"

On the company push: "1-6 X-ray, this is Bravo 6. Calm down, son. We're shifting the artillery now. Who's left in charge? Over."

"Bravo 6, this is 1-6 X-ray. I guess I'm in charge. All the sergeants are down. Over." Great! A Spec-4 in charge.

"This is Bravo 6. Okay, son. What is going on now? Are you still getting fire? Over." The firing seemed to have stopped except for an occasional burst.

"Bravo 6, this is 1-6 X-ray. Everybody's on the ground. Several are shooting back. Nobody's shooting at us right now. I can hear the gooks chattering in the bunker. They sound real excited, too. Over."

"This is Bravo 6. Okay, 1-6 X-ray. Do you know where 3-6's location is? Over."

"Bravo 6, this is 1-6 X-ray. No, Bravo 6. I know they are ahead of us, but I don't know where. Over."

"This is Bravo 6. Stay low and try to get everybody you can under cover from that bunker. I'm sending 2-6 up to help you extract your people. Don't let anybody get up and try to run. They'll probably get shot if they try it. Pass the word about 2-6, and also tell them to try to crawl away from the bunker back toward you. Do you understand? Over."

"Roger, Bravo 6. Over."

"6 out. Break. 2-6, 6. Did you monitor?"

"2-6 roger."

"Bravo 6. Okay, move your element up to assist 1-6 and 3-6 to extract their people and equipment. 4-6 will move up with the Charlie Papa and establish a defensive perimeter. I want you to get *all* of 1-6 and 3-6 back to that perimeter. That's personnel and equipment. If you have a problem doing that, let me know ASAP. Do you roger?"

"2-6 roger. We're moving now."

"6 out. Break. 3-6, 6. Sitrep."

"3-6. We have all personnel back at my location. I have two kilos and six whiskies, three serious. We're down low and receiving sporadic fire at this time. We shot two more RPG guys trying to come around our flank. Over."

"Bravo 6 roger. 2-6 is on the way to your location to help extract you back here. Make sure he knows where 1-6 is located. Over."

"3-6 roger."

"6 out. Break. Bravo 1-6 X-ray, this is Bravo 6. Over."

"Bravo 6, Bravo 6, this is 1-6 X-ray. Over."

"This is Bravo 6. Tell me what's going on up there. Over."

"Bravo 6, this is Bravo 1-6 X-ray. Everybody's under cover, I think. Most are back away from the bunker at least fifty meters. We dragged the dead and wounded back, too. We have three who I think are dead and eight wounded. Doc says five are really bad and need dustoff ASAP. Over."

"1-6 X-ray, this is Bravo 6. Okay, I understand. Bravo

2-6 is on the way to get you out of there and back to this location. Your people will need to help them get all your casualties and equipment out of there. We don't want the VC to get any more of it. What is the enemy situation? Over."

"Bravo 6, this is 1-6 X-ray. They are shooting at us when they see us, but they are still in the bunker. We can hear them chattering once in a while. When they shoot, we shoot back to let them know we're ready for them and to make them keep their heads down and stay inside. We used most of our ammo, though. Over."

"This is Bravo 6. Okay, here's what I want you to do. Take the ammo from the dead and those too seriously wounded to fight and distribute it to the others. That should give them enough to defend against an attack if the gooks try it. Do you understand what I want? Over."

"Bravo 6, this is 1-6 X-ray. Yes, Bravo 6. We can do that. Over."

"This is Bravo 6. Fine. Okay, 2-6 is on the way. When you hear him coming up to your rear, fire two shots in the air to let him know where you are. Tell the others, but do it quietly. Let me know if anything changes. Do you understand that? Over."

"Bravo 6, this is 1-6 X-ray. Roger, Bravo 6. I understand that. I want you to know that Doc says the platoon leader and the platoon sergeant and the first squad leader are dead. The other squad leaders are all wounded. Over."

"This is Bravo 6. Okay, I understand. I'm sorry to hear that, but I know you'll do a good job in getting everybody back. You've given me a good report, son. You watch out for 2-6, okay? Over."

"This is 1-6 X-ray. Roger, Bravo 6. Over."

"6 Out. Break. 2-6, 6. Did you monitor my conversation with 1-6 X-ray?"

"2-6. My X-ray monitored it all and gave me the info. We'll get them back. Understand two rifle shots?"

"6. Roger. Let me know when you find them. Out."

I swapped hand sets. "Falcon 6, Bravo 6. Sitrep."

"Falcon 3. Go."

"Bravo 6. 3-6 has all his people together. 1-6 X-ray has his people back away from the bunker. He's getting sporadic fire, and his people are returning it as best they can. 1-6, 1-5 and one Sierra Lima are kilos. The other Sierra Limas are whiskeys. Right now, it looks like five kilos and fourteen whiskeys in those two elements. I'm now moving the rest forward to conduct an extraction. 4-6 is setting up a defensive perimeter, while 2-6 is forward to assist the extraction back to this perimeter. Incoming fire is sporadic in both areas. 3-6 has killed two more RPG gunners. All fire appears to be coming from one or two bunkers. I'm now using Redleg to isolate the area from reinforcement, so I believe we are facing the same people and positions we started with. Roger so far?"

"3. Roger, Bravo 6."

"Okay, I'm going to continue to need priority of arty fire. I'm not going to use gunships right now unless we start catching more fire. I want them standing by to protect Dustoff. If you've got a FAC in the area with nape, I can use that. Meanwhile, I need Dustoff on standby until we can make some sort of Papa Zulu in here somewhere. It looks like they need to bring jungle extractors with them. Finally, I need a reaction force. I don't know what I've got in here, but I don't believe we can fight our way out if we have to, and still bring out our casualties and equipment and cut a PZ. End of report. Over."

"Falcon 3. Roger, Bravo 6. We have FAC and gunships en route. Dustoff is also en route with extractor. I'll get right back on a reaction force."

"Roger, 3. Bravo 6 out."

As I handed the mike back to Atkinson, I heard the battalion radio crackle again. "Falcon 3, Alpha 6."

"Falcon 3."

"Alpha 6. Alpha is ready to respond if you want us to. We're saddled up and standing by. If Bravo needs help, we want this one bad."

"3. Roger, Alpha 6. I'll get back to you if we need you. Out."

The Alphagator is ready. That made me feel a little better. We had reacted to Alpha and the other companies several times, but this was the first time we had needed a reaction force. Good old Gator!

The fourth platoon and CP group had closed to about 75-100 meters behind 3-6's location. 4-6 spread his men out into a defensive perimeter and waited. I started out of the perimeter toward 3-6's location when MacKenzie stopped ahead of me and handed me the battalion push. "It's Falcon 3."

"Falcon 3, Bravo 6."

"Falcon 3. Be advised that Fullback Bravo is en route to your location. Over."

"Bravo 6. Fullback Bravo? Where are they coming from? The firebase?"

"Falcon 3. Negative. They were moving south on the road from the perimeter. They are now due east of your location. They'll make the turn from there and break trail to your location. Fullback Bravo 6 is monitoring this push, and he has your push if you want him to switch. We figured the mech can help you haul your casualties and knock down a PZ. They can also help get your element back into here."

"Roger. We'll expect them. Out. Break. Fullback Bravo 6, Falcon Bravo 6. Do you monitor?"

"This is Fullback Bravo 6. Roger, Bravo 6. We just made the turn. My point is about one-and-a-half clicks into the jungle. Request you shackle me your location. I want to be sure we're going to the right place. Over."

"Roger, Fullback. Since we're in contact, they know where we are. No sense compromising our CAC-Codes. My coordinates in the clear are 452778. Copy?"

"Roger, Bravo 6. Good copy. Echo Tango Alpha for my lead element to your location is one-five mikes. We're pushing it as hard as we can through this heavy stuff."

"Roger, Fullback. Request you come up on my push.

My 4-6 element on the perimeter will guide you in when
they hear you. If you'll arrive near the head of your column, I'll meet you at the perimeter and brief you. Over."

"Roger."

"Bravo 6 out."

As I switched to the company push, I heard a rather
long exchange of gunfire to the front.

"2-6, 6. What's that firing up there?"

"2-6. The firing came from 1-6's area where one of
my elements just went to help them. I'm trying to get a
report now. Over."

"6 roger. I'll stand by until you find out what's happening. Out."

After five agonizing minutes: "Bravo 6, 2-6."

"6. Go."

"2-6. My element found 1-6's location after one of
their men fired two signal shots. Then part of my element
went charging ahead to try to knock out the bunker to
take the pressure off 1-6's extraction. Either the bunker
opened up on them or they hit a trip wire or something.
Anyway, three are whiskeys. They are all now back at 1-
6's location. They never did get the bunker. The remainder of the element is now assisting 1-6 in extracting all
their casualties *and* mine, too. Over."

"6 roger. Control those people! I don't want any more
casualties up there if we can help it. How's the extraction
coming"

"2-6. We're consolidating all casualties behind 3-6's
location, but we're going to need help to get them and
their equipment back. Plus we're getting sporadic fire
from the front. I think they shoot when they see something. We're trying to give them as little a target as we
can in this grass and undergrowth. Over."

"Roger. Fullback Bravo is coming to assist. We should
be able to use his tracks to haul some out. Let me know
when you've consolidated everything behind 3-6. Try to
get all casualties, weapons and equipment back to that
location without creating any more casualties."

"2-6. Roger. 3-6 has all his unit back here now. We've expanded the perimeter to accommodate them. We're still working on 1-6."

"Roger. 6 out."

As I handed the mike back to Atkinson, I heard the rumble and crashing of approaching tracks breaking trail through the jungle. For our sake, I was glad they were not reconning by fire with their 50s.

"Bravo 6, 4-6."

"Bravo 6. Go."

"4-6. Fullback's lead element just contacted the perimeter. Fullback Bravo 6 is with them."

"Roger. On th' way."

I turned to the RTOs: "Come on. Atkinson, tell 2-6 that I'll be sending Fullback's elements up to him. Use one element to his front and one to start hauling casualties back here."

I walked over to the perimeter as one M113 pulled up and stopped in front of me. I saw four more stopped forward of the perimeter.

"Where's Bravo 6?" I asked the driver.

"Inside, sir."

I waved my thanks as a bare head, covered by a radio headset, stuck up through the open cargo hatch in the rear. He looked around to get his bearings, saw me, grinned, and motioned for me to come inside the track.

As I climbed through the rear hatch door, I thought the mech commander looked familiar. We shook hands. "I'm Bob Hemphill."

"Bill Morrow. Where do I know you from?" (Morrow is an alias.)

"I was thinking the same thing. You weren't in Germany, were you?"

"No."

"Then it must have been Benning." I noticed the Ranger tab on his sleeve. "What Ranger class were you in?"

"Ranger 8, 1965."

"So was I. That's the connection. Hey, I really appreciate you coming in here to help us. You got here pretty quick."

"Glad to oblige. What is your situation?"

"My point platoon stumbled into an unknown-sized bunker complex. Looked like anthills to them in the undergrowth and elephant grass up there. His point squad took a burst of machine gun fire which got most of them. The rest of his platoon then took automatic and RPG fire. I sent first platoon up there to help get them out, and he apparently walked in front of one of those bunkers and they opened up on them broadside. Didn't help that the gooks seem to be using an M-60, or something that sounds like one. Second platoon is now helping first and third to pull their men and equipment back away from those bunkers and to consolidate them back behind the point platoon's initial position. What I need you to do is to send three of your platoons up there to help 2-6. I'd like you to deploy one in front of 1-6's location and one in front of 2-6's consolidated position to provide security for the extraction. Your other platoon could start hauling casualties back here. I need your fourth platoon to start carving out a PZ for Dustoff."

"You sound like you had mech experience. Okay, we can do that." He listened a minute and spoke into the headset. Then he looked up at me. "The others are closing now. My point platoon is moving forward."

"Okay, thanks." I stood up in the hatch and motioned for Atkinson to hand me the company push. "2-6, Bravo 6."

"2-6."

"6. One of Fullback's elements is coming up now. Show him where 1-6's location is and have him provide security forward of that area. Have somebody from 1-6 go with him to show him where those bunkers are. Be on the watch for RPG teams. We don't want them blindsidin' th' tracks. Roger so far?"

"Roger."

"When the second element comes up, do the same in front of your consolidated location. Use his third element to start hauling casualties back here. Tell your doc to make sure the most serious are transported back first. Fullback's medics can help ours. We should have a PZ cut by that time. Roger?"

"Roger, Bravo 6. I see them coming now."

I watched as the follow-on mech platoons passed through, deploying forward to secure our extraction. I glanced back to the rear as four other tracks started knocking down trees to make a clearing. I heard a burst of 50 fire from up ahead. Must be the tracks moving in front of 1-6 and taking the bunkers under fire. I heard little return fire.

I reached for the battalion push. "Falcon 3, Bravo 6."

"Falcon 3."

"Bravo 6. Fullback Bravo has arrived. He's deployed two elements forward to secure my extraction and one element to assist that extraction. His other element is clearing a Papa Zulu. What is the status of Dustoff? I estimate five kilos and eighteen whiskeys, most needing medevac."

"Roger, Bravo 6. Dustoff is standing by. We have two birds on station with a third on the way. They will rotate in and out until all are taken out. You'll need to bring your kilos back here with you. We'll get them out from here."

"Okay, as soon as we have a useable PZ and the first load of whiskeys arrives, I'll bring in the first one. Have them come up on my push. Over."

"Falcon 3. Roger, Bravo 6. They should contact you momentarily."

"Roger. Bravo 6 out."

"Falcon Bravo 6, this is Dustoff 13. Do you have a PZ? Over."

"Dustoff 13, Bravo 6. PZ's about ready. Coordinates are 460782. Approach from the east. PZ's cold but bad guys are in the area. We'll try to keep them down. I'll call you down when the first load of whiskeys arrive. Over."

"Roger, Bravo 6. Standing by."

The mech up front were still firing their 50's sporadically. I stooped down and said to Morrow: "I'm going over to the PZ to control the medevac."

"Okay. My second and third platoons are in position and have suppressed three bunkers with their 50s. They have negative incoming. When we get all your guys out, I'll pull my tracks back to this location and provide you perimeter security. They'll be firing as they pull back. When all this is over, we'll give your company a ride back to Burt before we rejoin our battalion."

"Sounds good. We'll need to haul my kilos back, too. The birds won't pick them up out here."

"Okay, no problem."

"Catch you later."

I climbed out the rear hatch door and walked over to the PZ. Fullback's platoon leader, Lieutenant Andrews (an alias), came over to me.

"Sir, I think we have a pretty good PZ here that we can use anytime."

"Yeah, it looks good. We can get one ship at a time in here. When you finish, will you secure it?"

"Roger, sir. We'll deploy around it to try to keep the bad boys from knocking down our birds."

"Okay, fine." I heard the rumble of tracks behind me. "Here comes the first load."

I reached for the handset as I tossed a smoke grenade into the clearing. "Dustoff 13, Bravo 6. Smoke out. Come on in."

"Bravo 6, Dustoff 13. Tally-ho goofy grape."

"Roger purple."

"Coming in."

As I heard the chopper roll in, the first track appeared at the PZ. I walked over to the track. "Hurry and get those guys out there. Bird's inbound now."

For the next half-hour, one track after another brought

in wounded, and people scurried back and forth, carrying them to the PZ in ponchos flapping in the wind from the helicopter rotor blades. One Dustoff bird after another swooped down, loaded up and peeled off back toward the south, heading toward the nearest field hospital with their critical cargo. It was a wonder to watch, knowing that this feverish activity would save the lives of all or most of those they flew out.

After the last WIA was lifted out, I took the handset from Atkinson.

"1-6 X-ray, 2-6, 3-6, this is Bravo 6."

They answered in turn.

"Bravo 6. I want you to marry up with your Fullback counterpart and load all the extra equipment and your kilos on the tracks. Coordinate the move-out with your counterpart. When they get the word to pull back, I want you riding with them. They will give us a lift back to base. The move-out'll be directed by Fullback Bravo 6. 2-6, I want you to assist 1-6 X-ray in getting his people organized and on the tracks. Do you roger?"

All roger'ed in turn.

"Bravo 6. Let me know when you're loaded and ready to move out. Out. Break. 4-6, Bravo 6. Come to my location."

"4-6 roger."

The sun was getting low in the western sky as I walked back to Morrow's track in the middle of the perimeter. I glanced at my watch. 1835. It's going to be dark before we get back to Burt if we don't hurry, I thought.

As I approached the track, Lieutenant Constantino walked up.

"Jim, I want you to go over there to Fullback Bravo 4-6's track and coordinate your platoon's ride back to Burt. You'll load all your people and equipment on the tracks. It's up to Fullback when we leave, but you'll need to do this ASAP. When you get everything loaded, let me know."

"Okay, sir, on th' way." Off he went.

I stuck my head in the hatch door. "Bill, how long before you plan to move?"

"As soon as your guys are loaded up. I'll let you know when they are ready."

"Okay. I'd sure hate to be out here after dark."

"I don't intend to. We'll go back along the same trail we made coming in. If we don't run into trouble, we should have you back in Burt within thirty minutes after we depart. Then we'll have to road march back down to our battalion in the dark."

"Not worried about ambushes?"

"I'm always worried about that, but we'll be using our 50s to discourage that sort of thing. Besides, sometimes moving fast is the best ambush preventative."

Within ten minutes, we were moving back through the jungle. The mech had thoroughly hosed down the entire visible bunker area with their 50s, but there was no more hostile fire at us. Either the good guys had gotten all the bad guys—which I seriously doubted—or they had decided to stay back and leave us alone. They probably still smarted from the January 1st Burt fight. We still did not know the extent of the bunker complex. Somebody would have to come back through there another day to see what was present. When they did, I would have bet that they would send in something bigger than one company!

True to his word, Morrow had us back at Burt within thirty minutes after we began moving. My men and equipment were unloaded and my kilos were taken to the aid station for pick-up. As I left his track at the perimeter to join Colonel Harrold and Major Davis, who had come to the perimeter to meet us, I shook his hand. "Bill, thanks for your help. If you ever need us, just call."

"You're welcome, Bob. Always willing to provide our services to a Ranger classmate. Tough luck about your casualties. Looks to me like you handled it as well as you could. You look pretty down. Shake it off. Things like this happen sometimes, no matter how good or how careful you are."

"Well, I'm not used to losing my people. First time I ever lost an officer or senior NCO. It's not easy to swallow this. Take care, Bill. You've got a cold beer waiting back in Dau Tieng anytime you want to collect it. See you."

He waved as I closed the hatch and turned to Atkinson. "Tell the platoon leaders to get their people back to their positions, and to tag all their extra gear and take it to the company CP for pick-up. Tell 2-5 to take care of first platoon as well. Have him send 1-6 X-ray to the aid station. I'll see him there. After you do that, you two go back to the CP and tell Top to collect the gear at the supply point to send back to the rear on the first supply ship. When you get that done, try to raise Bravo 5 in the rear and tell him to expect this stuff and to secure it until the unit returns. Then tell him to send out all available replacements, including NCOs, on the next supply ship. Also tell him that, as soon as all this is done, I want him out here, too. Questions? Okay, go. I'll be with Falcon 6 for awhile if anybody needs me."

They left as Harrold and Davis came over to where I was standing, watching the mech lumber past the perimeter positions, heading south down the road. As they cleared the perimeter outposts, I heard the 50s start reconning-by-fire to their front and flanks. I bade them a quiet "Bon Voyage" and wished them well.

"Welcome back, Bravo 6. I'm glad you made it back here." That was Harrold. I wanted to say, yeah, I made it back, but some of my best soldiers didn't. I wanted to say that I didn't want any of that glad-handing crap right now. I wanted to say, "Leave me alone with my grief." But I bit my lip and said none of those things.

"Right, Colonel. Some of us made it back, but too many didn't. I want to tell you that you made the right decision in sending in the mech. Another leg unit would not have been able to clear a PZ for Dustoff or haul out our casualties and equipment."

"Yeah, I thought they'd be helpful to you. The 50s probably didn't hurt, either."

I shook my head. "No, they didn't. They were pretty useful."

"Look, Bob. We need to go back to the CP and talk about today. Flex 6 wants to see you and me when you get your unit settled in. A sort of after-action report."

"Yes, Colonel," I sighed. "I can imagine what Flex 6 wants after what Tropic 6 did to him day before yesterday. Okay, if you'll give me thirty minutes, I'll meet you at the CP."

"Okay, Bob. See you there."

"Bravo 6, I'd like to tell you something that happened today." Davis' voice had lost much of its arrogance as he related to me what had happened in Alpha company. While our action was going on, and it appeared that we were in a pretty deep mess, Alpha 6-X-ray was monitoring the radio. When I reported 1-6's predicament, he passed the word to the men that Bravo was in trouble. Alpha 6 was not aware of what was going on. When he emerged from his bunker a while later, he was surprised to see his whole company lined up at the perimeter, locked and loaded, ready to go out. When he asked what was going on, several troops told him that they heard Bravo was in trouble, and they wanted to go help Bravo. They were ready to go. He told them that he had already volunteered Alpha as a reaction force, but that Falcon 6 was trying to get a mech company from Fullback. If that failed, Alpha would go. Meanwhile, he sent them back to their positions and told them to stand by.

I choked up a little when I heard Davis' story. The *men* of Alpha company had gotten together *on their own* to go help Bravo. That was certainly a silver lining in an otherwise very dark cloud. It told me that they appreciated our coming to their assistance in the past.

I nodded at Davis. "Thanks for telling me that." I turned and walked off toward the aid station. I would deal with Harrold and Davis later. I had something more important to do now.

I walked over to the road near the aid station. On the ground next to the road lay my five dead soldiers, covered only by a poncho someone had thrown over them. As I stood there looking at them, a chopper came in to take them back to graves registration. The wind from the chopper blades blew up one corner of the poncho, and by the glow of the moon, I saw them one last time: Lieutenant Richard Walker, Master Sergeant Ernest Martin, Sergeant Thomas Watts, Sergeant Kenneth Howell, and Specialist Charles Irby. All were fine leaders, cut down in the prime of life. I would miss them greatly. Bravo company would never be exactly the same without them.

They were loaded on the bird, and it lifted off, turned, and gained altitude quickly. This was not a safe place to be flying around at night.

First Platoon's RTO walked up.

"Specialist Peyton reporting, sir." He saluted, which seemed a bit out of place here.

I returned the salute. "I just wanted to tell you that you did a helluva job up there today. That wasn't easy, but you handled it well."

"Thank you, sir. It was hard seeing the Lieutenant and the Sergeant killed, especially by our own artillery fire."

"Tell me about it."

"The Sergeant and the Lieutenant were hit by the initial burst, but they weren't dead. Because of his size, the Lieutenant made a big target as he lay there in the grass, and the gooks in the bunker kept shooting into him. I think they finally killed him. Sergeant Martin was lying next to me. He was wounded, but he was alive. Then the artillery started coming in. It was too close, at first. One round landed right next to Sergeant Martin. That's what finally killed him. I caught a couple pieces of shrapnel from that same round, but it ain't serious." I noticed the bandage on his arm. "The arty then shifted beyond us and landed just beyond the bunkers. The squad leader also got hit by the first machine gun blast. I think he died right away. It was really hard seeing the Lieutenant and Sergeant Martin die."

I placed my hand on his shoulder. He had done a lot for a young soldier. "I know it was. Now you can return to your platoon. Sergeant Hughes will help you get them organized. Then get some rest. Make sure you have an LP out so we won't get hit again. Good night."

"Good night, sir." Good troop, I thought as he hurried away.

I looked up at the running lights of the helicopter as it disappeared into the night. I shook my head slowly. What could I have done to prevent this? How could I have better reacted to head off this buzzsaw we had run into today?

These questions really bothered me a lot. I have repeatedly relived that day and searched my conscience in reviewing my actions that day to see if there was anything I could have done differently which would have prevented the loss of my fine soldiers. In spite of the thinly-veiled accusations of the Brigade Commander that night—which Colonel Harrold strongly disputed with him—I believe that there was nothing else that I could have foreseen to do. We did everything we did the normal way we do it, which I believe was the right way, and which has been consistently successful in the past. We just happened to have the misfortune to run into a buzzsaw that day. We had a point squad out, which did its job. We had a point platoon out, which did its job. We had no intelligence about what might be there, other than the suspicion that some casualties or other enemy unit personnel might still be hanging around from the fight of January 1, based on reported helicopter sightings. We went in there to check them out and to find out. We found out. Unfortunately, as we moved through the jungle, they saw us before we saw them. When we made contact, we used maneuver and fire support to attempt to eliminate the enemy positions, to isolate the battlefield and, eventually, to break contact.

The other company commanders would tell me years

later that they could see that this action had affected me quite a bit. I would remember standing there that night in the firebase with the bodies of the five guys, and how really bad I had felt. That was the only lieutenant I ever lost, and the only senior NCO I ever lost. We had lost a few soldiers from time to time, but never this many at one time, and certainly not such a deep cut at our leadership. It bothered me every time any of my people were killed or seriously hurt. But this had been the worst— even worse than we would experience during the upcoming Tet Offensive which would break on the scene a couple of weeks later.

We never walked into another buzzsaw during the remainder of my five months in command. We never again lost so many fine soldiers at one time.

Concerning the enemy bunker complex we had found, two other companies went through the area a couple of days later, and found that it had been vacated, but, judging by the overall size, the number of bunkers, the facilities, etc., it looked like we had stumbled on a two-division-sized base camp. It had been occupied by something the day we ran into it. We never knew for sure, but the speculation was that at least one regiment could have been there. We had hit the security bunkers out around the base camp. It became apparent that the whole company could have gotten wiped out that day, had it not been for the actions of one sergeant—Sergeant Howell, the point squad leader of the point platoon. He died doing it, but he probably saved the company. As he traveled behind the point man and the machete man, he thought he saw something ahead. He held up the squad as he went up to check it out. That turned out to be an ant hill. The squad moved on. A few minutes later, he saw something that also looked like an ant hill. As he went up to check that one out, it turned out to be a bunker, and he got hit in the chest by a burst of automatic fire from it. That action set off the firing. Had he not done that, the whole platoon—and perhaps the whole company—could have walked right into the middle of that base camp and been fired on from all sides, wiping out the entire unit. But the point platoon and the point squad were doing their job in providing early warning to the rest of the unit. Unfortunately, we lost some people while they were doing it, but they saved a lot of people.

That was a day I would never forget or, in some respects, never get over.

CHAPTER SIX

TET STARTS

January 31, 1968, the day the TET Offensive started, was the beginning of two weeks of the hardest combat that US forces faced in the whole Vietnam War. The first day of TET for my command, Bravo Company, 3/22 Infantry, was one of tremendously conflicting emotions for me, and my men.

We were based outside the village of Dau Tieng in III Corps, north of Saigon and Cu Chi, the home of the 25th Infantry Division, near Tay Ninh. Dau Tieng was just south of War Zone C on the edge of the Michelin rubber plantation, which was definitely Viet Cong country. In fact, it was generally believed among the Americans that the Michelin buildings inside the base camp were never hit because Michelin paid protection to the VC.

On January 26th, which happened to be my birthday, the battalion convoyed by jeep and truck from Dau Tieng through the smaller Ben Cui plantation, through beautiful downtown Cu Chi to a new perimeter position along the Saigon River about eight clicks east of the town. In retrospect, I imagine there were plenty of hostile eyes watching and chronicling our progress, but they let us pass without incident.

Our mission was to work along the Saigon River and its tributaries to root out any enemy bunkers or other facilities that were expected to be there. The daily battalion drill was to send two companies a day out on sweeps along the river, while the other two stayed back to guard the perimeter—and the battalion CP, of course. Because of our encounter with two regiments from the 9th VC Division at Firebase Burt on 1–2 January, we were real careful to leave sufficient force to secure our operating base. As part of our normal night defenses, each company also sent out platoon-sized ambush patrols to interdict any likely probe or reconnaissance of our perimeter. This was a proven method of advance warning and security. At Burt, those guys had given us enough warning of the impending onslaught to make sure everyone was alert and ready, even though they had spent the night completely surrounded.

We closed into our new perimeter late on the afternoon of the 26th. Part of the perimeter line wound around and through a patch of woods, while the rest of the positions were in the open fields outside a small village about a click away. By the time we set up the perimeter, sent out the listening posts, sighted in the crew-served weapons, prepared the individual positions, and had chow, it was pitch dark.

When the platoon leaders were ready, I checked out the company's positions and weapons. Each position we used was not much more than a two-man foxhole with sufficient overhead cover to stop an 82-millimeter mortar round. Since we had pulled 82mm tail fins out of the second layer of sandbags, we felt reasonably secure with two layers of sandbags with something sturdy to hold them up. Foxholes were sufficiently deep to allow the occupants to get below ground level when they needed to and still fire to their front and flanks. This gave them the ability to fight from each position independently if necessary. Through the experience of quite a few firefights and serious battles, we were quite satisfied that this type of position was best for us.

We had seen, first-hand, what some other divisions had done, and some of those things scared us. As previously stated, the Big Red One ("If you're gonna be one, be a Big Red One") had a policy that every Infantry unit would dig a sophisticated series of interlocking bunkers *every night* in the field—they called it an NDP (Night Defensive Position).

In an NDP, each bunker was deep enough to stand up

in, had complete front cover with small apertures on each
corner designed to cover the front of the next bunker on
each side, and small entrances in the rear. The idea was
to produce a "wall of lead" by the continuous interlocking
fires of automatic weapons. The scary thing was that you
couldn't see to the front at all! There was little provision
made to react to the very serious possibility that a bunker
may get knocked out. That was the obvious—obvious to
us, anyway—key to penetrating the defenses. Get up close
enough to one bunker to lob in a satchel charge, knock it
out and then move inside the automatic protective fires
laterally to the next bunker. Take out two in this manner,
and a big unprotected hole was opened up in this "impenetrable" fortress. With no ability to see to the front,
and limited ability to see to the rear or side, each remaining bunker was a sitting duck—with no good fields of fire
for its own defense.

There was one other vulnerability with an NDP—
"walls of lead" are great but—what if you ran out of
ammunition? "Walls of lead" tend to lose their effectiveness when the lead is gone. Of course, that can happen in
any type of position, however, when your defense is based
on continuous automatic fire instead of on selective aimed
fire, it can happen a lot quicker!

One of the more important problems with the NDP
system was that it took a long time to prepare. Troops
who had been moving all day—or fighting their butts off
if they were lucky enough to find somebody to shoot at—
would then have to spend most of the night digging.
Throw in night ambush patrols and the need to move out
again the next day and the troops didn't get much rest.
No wonder those guys were always tired! The marginal
benefits which the NDP system may have offered were
more than offset by troop fatigue, unless a semi-fixed position, such as a firebase, was being prepared. On the other
hand, *our* units normally closed into our night positions
by 1700 hours, received our resupply birds, and prepared
our positions before dark. That gave our guys a chance to

get some rest—presuming that they were not on ambush or that we did not get hit that night. That made them much sharper when we moved out the next day, or when we got into our next firefight.

We started patrolling the riverbanks on the 27th. Companies staying back for perimeter security provided the night ambush patrols. With two companies out and two back each day, that meant two platoons were out each night. Although ambush positions were changed each night, one was generally placed on the other side of the village, and one was normally sent east to watch the approaches to and from the river.

For the first four days, the riverbank sweeps produced little more than long-abandoned bunkers, a few small rice caches and an occasional indication of someone passing through. There was no sign at all of enemy personnel or of recent bunker construction. Considering the high level of activity we had had since the first of January, this operation had degenerated into nothing more than spending the day beating the bush and wading across chest-deep canals, making sure that we were wet and tired when we settled in for the night. This was downright boring!

Most of our time in combat units in Vietnam was spent chasing down ghost battalions and regiments, and checking out numerous other intelligence reports sent down by Brigade and Division HQ. The problem with these reports was that they were generally "agent reports" which were rated F-10 ("unsubstantiated rumor"). The "agents" in these cases were almost always Vietnamese peasants who said they saw something. The real reason why these fine citizens were so willing to help us find all those VC and NVA units was that they were *paid* for their information. No matter what they told us, they were paid. We normally presumed that they were routinely collecting from both sides. Seldom did these F-10 reports yield anything except the opportunity to go hiking and camping in the Great War Zone C Nature Preserve. Ah, Nature!

For the last half of January, we had been spared the

opportunity to check all those F-10 "dry holes." For some reason, those agent reports had not been coming down from Division. We were happy to be spared that. Our presumption was that all our activity that month had made us generally unavailable for such shenanigans, especially after the big fights on 1–2 and 15 January. In any case, the intel system was generally quiet during the month, and we became a little complacent.

As slow as the days were, the night ambushes along the river approaches were producing a little more activity. Although no enemy soldiers came through the ambush sites, the patrols were able to observe through starlight scopes some fairly large unit movement—as large as companies sometimes—toward the south. We were certain that they knew where we were, since we were so obvious with choppers coming and going and our guys moving around in the open. Plus, all the villagers knew we were there—kids were even trying to sell us Cokes. So our presence was no secret. The units moving through were obviously trying to avoid contact with us. Maybe they had all heard of the way we had kicked their compatriots' asses all over War Zone C! "Regulars, by God!"

We thought a lot about some of these events, except for the lack of intelligence reports. We wondered what the night movements meant. Why were enemy units moving around without trying to engage us? With no sign of enemy hide-outs along the river, that meant that the units were probably not based in this area. They were just passing through. What was their purpose? We had no idea what was going on.

The morning of 31 January dawned bright and clear, which meant that it was going to be a hot one. Hot and dry. We would need a lot of water today. Bravo and Delta Companies were in the saddle—meaning that we were to conduct the riverbank sweeps that day. We left the perimeter at about 0800 that morning, with Delta leading. The plan was for us to move to the river in column, then to split up, with Delta going left to the north and Bravo right to the south. We passed the village, moved along one small tributary toward the river and, about three clicks out, approached the canal we had become intimately familiar with. We halted, spread out and took cover while Delta negotiated the canal.

Then it was our turn to get wet. The canal proved to be almost neck-high that day. As a passing thought, I wondered how much buffalo crap was mixed in this brown, murky water-or whatever other kind of dung. Didn't matter, though. After all the weeks and months of rainy season, swamps, jungle, canals, bomb craters and other uncharted bodies of scum, a little buffalo crap never hurt anyone. Normally, I didn't think about it, but I guess I was feeling a little morbid that day.

We had just made it through the canal and the third platoon—on point—had just turned south along the river, when the battalion squawk box blared out.

"Bravo 6, Falcon 3-X-ray. Over."

MacKenzie picked up the handset. "Bravo 6-X-ray."

"Message to Bravo 6 from Falcon 6. Return to this location ASAP. You'll lead back, Delta will follow. Copy?"

"Roger, copy. What's going on?"

"Lots going on. Can't tell you over this push. Looks like all those Saigon warriors are finally going to get the chance to *earn* those CIB's. 3-X-ray out."

Now what the hell did he mean by that? Shrugging, I took the company handset from Atkinson.

"Falcon Bravo, Bravo 6."

All platoons answered in turn.

"Okay, we've been called home. Seems like something's going on somewhere, don't know what. We'll lead back, Delta'll follow. We'll move in reverse order. 3–6, you take point. I'll move up behind 1–6. Now let's make time, but keep your eyes open. Move out."

All platoon leaders "roger'd," and we started back across the canal. Delta had also turned around and was waiting until we made it across before they started back.

We were making pretty good time, moving well, when I heard a commotion up around the point platoon. I listened a moment and heard no firing, so I took the RTOs and headed toward their location to see what was happening. When I arrived, I could not believe my eyes.

The whole platoon was in a circle in the middle of a dried-out rice paddy, around a rampaging water buffalo, which was jabbing its head right and left, trying to gore somebody. Every weapon in the platoon was trained on it—rifles, M-60s, grenade launchers—everything! They obviously intended to blow it away before it got them. For some unknown reason, water buffalo didn't like Americans, and they knew it.

Suddenly, a shrill cry rang out from the direction of the village. Looking in that direction, I saw a frail-looking old woman running in our direction, arms flailing in the air.

"*Kaum*! *Kaum*! (*No*! *No*!)" she screamed. I guess she did not want to lose her buffalo.

"Hold your fire!" I yelled. "Stay away from him!"

She ran into the middle of the platoon, jabbering something unintelligible, grabbed the buffalo's nose ring, jerked its head around and led it back toward the village. The buffalo lowered its head and followed her docilely back to the village. The guys lowered their weapons and looked around at each other sheepishly. That little old lady made them all feel like real he-men. Big, bad Americans!

"Okay, Gormley, get your people together and get going. We're wasting time here."

"Roger."

While I was waiting for the rest of the company to come up, I called Harrold.

"Falcon 6, Bravo 6."

"Falcon 6."

"Bravo 6. We're near the village, about a click out. We should close in about one-zero mikes."

"Roger. Meet me at the perimeter at the head of your unit."

"Roger that."

I saw first platoon coming up and waved them on. Then I and the RTOs moved out to catch the point platoon and to see what battalion wanted us for so badly.

As we closed on the perimeter, I turned to Atkinson. "Tell the platoon leaders to move back to their perimeter positions. I'll fill them in as soon as I can. You guys go on back to the CP."

"Yessir."

I walked over to the Battalion Commander. "Morning, sir. Wish somebody would turn this heat down a bit. What the hell's going on? Somebody having a party and didn't invite us?"

"Morning, Bob. Yeah, and we're invited. Whole bunch of stuff going on. Preliminary reports indicate that the NVA and VC launched a nation-wide offensive against every major population center in South Vietnam. The American Embassy may even have gooks inside right now. That report's still a little sketchy—nobody knows what's going on down there."

"Holy crap! So that's what 3-X-ray meant about those guys finally earning their CIB's. Where do we fit in this mess?"

"Two NVA companies knocked over a district head-quarters and killed the District Chief and his American advisors down south of Cu Chi. Got your map? Okay, here, I'll show you . . . there, about ten clicks south of Cu Chi base camp, below the point where that dirt road meets Highway 1. They're reportedly headed for Cu Chi City. The only thing between them and Cu Chi are a couple of Ruff-Puff platoons, which probably won't slow them down very much. Our mission is to set up a defensive line to defend Cu Chi. We will go in alone and set up from Highway 1, here, through these trees, across the dirt road and around the base camp this way. You'll go in first, followed by Alpha and Charlie. Delta will stay back here and make sure the battalion and company rear personnel and equipment get back to Cu Chi. Your sector is from

Highway 1, here, to the dirt road, where you will tie in with Alpha. Travel light. Take only what you need to fight. Your field first sergeant can work with the S-4 to get your stuff back to Cu Chi. They're sending some trucks out to pick up our stuff. Questions?" ("Ruff-Puff" was a nickname we applied to the Vietnamese Regional Force/Popular Force—RF/PF—Territorial militia units which served mainly to guard District and Provincial Headquarters, although some RF units actually conducted regular combat operations. None of the units was well-trained nor well-equipped, and all were rife with VC infiltrators.)

"No, it's pretty clear."

"How soon can you be ready for pick-up?"

"Ten minutes—we'll be ready in ten minutes."

Harrold looked at me skeptically, but he didn't doubt me. "Okay, that's good. You'll take the command and control ship and C&C your company in. After everyone's on the ground, send it back here for us. You'll have ten ships to work with, plus the C&C. Good luck, Bravo 6-give 'em hell!"

"You got it. See you on the ground."

Back at the company CP, I got things moving. I told Atkinson to get me the platoon leaders ASAP, then I turned to the field first, SFC Johnson, and the artillery FO, Lieutenant Bennett.

"Top, I'm taking the RTOs and the FO team. We're travelling light and quick. We don't have much time. I want you to help the RTOs get their equipment together. We're taking only weapons, webbing, radios, water, flak vest, and a couple of Cs. No packs except for radios. After we leave, you'll pack up everything we leave behind and coordinate with S-4 for transportation to get it back to Cu Chi. They're sending some trucks out to pick it up. You'll have one man per platoon to help ya. We'll link up with you at Cu Chi whenever we get there. Questions? Okay, do it!"

Turning to the platoon leaders, I gave them a one-minute rundown on the situation, what we were going to do, what to take, and how we were going to break down into aircraft loads. They moved out at the trot.

Ten minutes from the time I had left Harrold, Bravo was on the PZ, ready for pick-up. I glanced over at the wood line and saw Harrold and the S-3, Major Davis, standing there watching us. I looked back over my shoulder to the east and spotted a line of dots growing larger and headed our way.

"Okay, first lift, get ready. Here they come!" First and second platoons would go in on the first lift on Highway 1 and move eastward into the woods to a clearing. Third and weapons platoons on the second lift would land on the dirt road, move west into the woods, and link up at the clearing. Third platoon would tie in with Alfa at the dirt road. Weapons platoon had brought its 81-millimeter mortars, which would be set up at the back of the clearing. It was a hot day to be humping the 81s, but we expected a set-piece battle with little or no preparation of positions. The extra firepower would be most helpful, I thought. I was glad my guys would not have to carry them more than a few hundred meters to Cu Chi base camp when this was all over!

The C&C set down ahead of the slicks. As I crawled aboard, the crew chief handed me a headset and pointed to the seat behind the pilot, who was an old Chief Warrant Officer whom I had seen a few times at the Officers Club bar in Dau Tieng. I did not remember his name, but that is not unusual—I always was bad with names, but I never forget a face. My RTOs and FO team settled into the rear seats and we took off just ahead of the first lift.

"Welcome aboard, sir."

"Thanks, Chief. Peaceful TET, huh?"

"Yeah, I wish. Sons of bitches got me out of bed this morning at 0-dark-30. They should have started their little offensive at a reasonable hour, say around noon or something. I could skin 'em."

"Maybe we'll give you a chance to do just that."

"I'm ready. So you're going to save Cu Chi, huh?"

"Yeah, so they tell me. I'd be surprised if they get that far. Some Birddog pilot will probably shoot some Willie-Pete into them and scare 'em away."

"Don't think so. All them Birddogs are down in Saigon protecting all those generals' asses. Won't be no Tac Air up this far today."

"Well, whatever happens, we'll take them on."

"Your about to get your chance. We're about zero-two away from your little spot of Highway 1."

"Okay, let's put this sucker in orbit over that clearing in the middle of the woods there. I can see both LZs from there, and that's the place I want you to put me down when we're finished here."

"Rog, can do easy."

From our orbit, we could see the birds set down along Highway 1 and disgorge the first two platoons. Then they lifted off to return to the PZ for the other two. I watched the troops disappear rapidly into the trees.

I flicked the switch on the headset wire to transmit. "1-6, 2-6, this is Bravo 6. How do you read?"

"Bravo 6, 1-6. Got you five by."

"This is 2-6. Samo-samo."

"Okay, give me an up when you're in position. I'll let you know when 3-6 is on the ground so he and 1-6 can link up."

"1-6 roger."

"2-6 roger."

"Bravo 6 out."

As we waited for the other lift, I looked around toward the villages to the south, trying to see some activity. No luck. I guess it was too far away. As I contemplated taking the C&C down for a look, I saw the second lift approaching with the rest of the company. Of course, if I had tried to take this thing down where they might get shot up, I'd probably piss-off somebody. Just as well the others were coming in. It kept my idle mind occupied.

As the birds lifted away, I flicked the switch again. "1-6, Bravo 6."

"1-6."

"3-6 is on the ground. Are you in position yet?"

"Roger, just got here. I was about to call you."

"Okay, talk to 3-6, guide him in. Let me know when you link up."

"Roger."

We orbited another five minutes, then: "Bravo 6, 1-6. Over."

"Bravo 6."

"1-6. We're tied in at the clearing."

"Roger. Pop smoke. I'm coming down."

"Smoke out."

"Tally-ho goofy grape."

"Roger grape."

The Chief set the C&C down in the clearing. As we cleared the door, I turned and gave him the thumbs-up sign and grinned. He waved back and pulled pitch, taking the chopper up and away.

I turned to Atkinson. "Get 3-6 and 4-6 here as soon as they get their people in."

"Yessir."

I walked over to Lieutenants Sam Monroe (an alias) and Randy Lorne. "Well, I wonder what they'll call this screwed-up mess in the history books. Probably the 'TET Offensive' or some other catchy term. If this is as widespread as it sounds, this is going to be the death knell for the VC and maybe even the NVA. This won't be an offensive, it'll be a funeral. If they're trying to take on the American Army on an open battlefield, they'll their asses kicked. It may take a while, but they'll pay for this stupid mistake."

"I think you're right, Sir," said Monroe, "but we'll have an interesting week." Monroe took First Platoon after Walker died.

"Yeah. Well, down to business. Here come the other two. Okay, gents, here's what we're going to do. Randy,

make sure you cover Highway 1 with a couple of M-60s.
Put a couple of M-79s and LAWs over there, too. There's
no one to tie in with over there. We must protect our own
flank. If you think they're trying to circle around you
there, let me know ASAP. All of you make sure you're
tied in tight with each other. The only reserve you have
is Atkinson, MacKenzie, and me, and a helluva lot of
good we'll do you, unless battalion forms one later. Art,
be sure you cover that dirt road with automatic fire 'til
Alpha closes in. Then make sure you tie in with his right
flank platoon. Jim, I want those mortars laid in to shoot
forward of the treeline. Put your FOs up in trees or somewhere to make sure they can see. If those bastards get this
far, I want as many of them as possible dead before they
get in rifle range. Once they get into the treeline, they'll
be hard to see. Coordinate your fire with Bennett after he
finishes firing in his DEFCONs. Frank, what artillery is
available for us?"

"First of the Fifth is supporting the battalion. At the
moment we have priority of fire. No 155s, just 105s."

"Hell, they'd *better* give us priority—we're protecting
their collective asses! Okay, tell them we want *155s*
pointed this way ASAP. We may need them. Line platoons, listen up. We don't have time to dig in. Get your
people behind some kind of concealment. The trees will
give them some cover, too. Try to clear some fields of
fire while we're waiting. Push out LPs in front of each
platoon. Put them out along the treeline if you can. Helmets and vests stay on, no matter how the hell hot it gets.
Have everyone locked and loaded and fully alert. When
you get your people ready and your crew-serveds in, let
me know. I'll come check you out. Questions? Okay, if I
hear anything about the location of those NVA companies, I'll let you know. Now get moving."

They took off for their platoons. I walked over to a
tree, sat down and leaned against it. We did not set up a
CP. MacKenzie and Atkinson plopped down nearby
where they could hand me the handset easily. Bennett

started calling in his DEFCON coordinates. I took out my map and looked at our defensive area. Not the best place in the world, but we could do it from here. Let them come.

All the platoon leaders called in, and I left to check out their positions. I felt that they were all good lieutenants, although Sam Monroe and Randy Lorne were relatively new. They knew what they had to do. The main things I was concerned with were heavy weapons positions and flank security. After the inspection was finished, I returned to the RTOs' position, just as I heard Alpha Company landing.

"MacKenzie, hand me the phone."

"Here you go, sir."

"Falcon 6, Bravo 6. Over."

"Bravo 6, this is Falcon 6. Over."

"Bravo 6. We're as ready for those bastards as we'll get. What's the latest on their position?"

"Falcon 6. The 3 is trying to get some word on that now. We'll let you know anything we hear. Alpha 6 is now on the ground."

"Rog. My flank platoon has contact with his. The road's covered."

"Okay. Sit tight. I think it'll take awhile for them to reach us. That last contact was at least ten clicks away. Falcon 6 out."

"Hey, Alphagator, it's the Bull. Over."

"Bull, this is Gator. What're you boys doing out here, sleeping? It's mighty quiet over there." Captain Herb Chancey was a good troop. He had taken a burst of .45-calibre from a greasegun on his first tour and came back to command a company. Dumb SOB. Alpha was almost as good as Bravo, although we had had to save their asses a few times. Back on the fifteenth of January, they were ready to try to save ours. Good group!

"Just sitting around, sipping a cool one, waiting for you folks to decide to come out here and join us. Welcome to the war."

"Thanks, Bull. Heard anything lately?"

"Naw. 3's supposed to be trying to get a sitrep. You'll probably hear it when I do. I wonder if Cu Chi is worth saving?"

" 'Course they are. That's where the Bud and Cokes are, instead of this rusty Ballantine and Wink crap they keep sending us."

"Yeah, I guess that does make them worth saving. Well, catch you later."

"Rog. Gator out."

I leaned back against the radios with a handset in each hand. Now the waiting began. I was drenched with sweat from the heat and physical exertion of the last couple of hours. It was time to get a little breather before the enemy attacked. We had been going heavy on the adrenalin since we had left the perimeter. Wearing those flak vests made it much hotter. I was glad we didn't wear them often.

Thirty minutes later, the squawk box blared with Major Davis' lovely sarcastic voice. "Falcon, Falcon, this is Falcon 3. Over."

The company commanders answered in turn.

"Falcon 3. Looks like some ARVNs tied up those two companies at a little place called Ap Cho, about eight clicks south of your position, where the dirt road hits Highway 1. This may not be a reprieve, just a delay. We're not sure what's going on down there, but we'll keep trying to find out. Do you copy? Over"

"Roger, copy." All acknowledged receipt of the transmission and went back to their preparations.

I handed the handsets back to the RTOs and told Atkinson, "Tell the platoons that I want a sitrep every thirty minutes. Let me know ASAP if their LPs spot anything. They can go to fifty percent alert and fifty percent eating. Drink plenty of water. I don't want any heat strokes out here."

"Yessir." He picked up the handset and began relaying my instructions. I broke out my Cs and started eating. I did not know how long it would be before I would have time to eat again. Everyone else did the same.

About an hour later, Major Davis came up on the net. "Falcon, this is Falcon 3. Over."

Company commanders answered in turn.

"Falcon 3. You're not going to believe this, but those Ruff-Puffs really did tie up those two NVA companies in Ap Cho. Their movement toward Cu Chi is temporarily halted."

"Bravo 6. Tell me again where Ap Cho is."

"South of Tan Phu Trung, where that dirt road you're on meets Highway 1. About eight clicks south of your position."

"Great. Ruff-Puffs must be getting tough. That mean we can go home?"

" 'Fraid not, Bravo 6. In fact, our new orders are to go down and help them out."

"You're kidding me. In this heat, with all this gear? Where the hell is Delta company when you need cannon fodder?"

"Yep, we have to do it. Here's the skinny. Battalion (minus) will take the dirt road south to Ap Cho in a movement to contact. Order of march will be Alpha, Bravo, Charlie. Once contact is made, presumably in the village, Alpha will take the right half of the village and Bravo the left. Charlie will stay in reserve. Looking at your picto map, the boundary between the two forward companies will be the center street at coordinates X-ray Tango 3618. If we have to extract from there by air, we'll try to use that dry rice paddy to the east of the village, with Bravo providing security. We'll work that out when we have to. Any questions?"

None.

"Okay. Alpha's LD time is 1330 hours. That's twenty minutes from now. Other companies at five minute intervals. Good luck. 3 out."

Really great, I muttered to myself. We're all going to have heat stroke wearing these damn flak vests.

"Atkinson, get me the platoon leaders up here ASAP."

Five minutes later, four lieutenants were squatting on their steel pots around me.

"Got to make this quick. Arvins have tied up those two NVA companies we're expecting about eight clicks south of here in a village called Ap Cho. Battalion's going to go down and help them. Alpha's leading, we follow, and Charlie follows us. The mission is a movement to contact. If we make contact before we get to Ap Cho, we'll support Alpha. If not, we'll go on line with Alpha at the village and attack on the left. Company boundary is the north-south street at grid 3618, here. Order of march is 3-6, 1-6, 4-6, 2-6. We'll plan to attack the village with 3-6 on the left, 1-6 on the right in contact with Alpha, and 2-6 in reserve. Mortars will be prepared to support the attack. Make sure FOs are with each platoon leader. Coordinate fires with Lieutenant Bennett. I'll frag any changes to this plan when we get to the village. And one other thing—I don't have the foggiest idea where either the NVA or those damn Ruff-Puffs are. When we go into the village, try not to shoot the wrong Vietnamese by mistake. But if they get in the way and it puts our guys in the line of fire, it's too bad for them. We move in five minutes. Make sure your guys drink plenty of water and take along all they can carry. I don't want any heat casualties because of all this gear they're carrying. Questions? Good. Get going."

I took the RTOs and the FO team and walked over to the edge of the dirt road. About ten minutes later, Alpha's lead platoon started moving. When Gator walked by, I waved at him. He lifted his trusty rusty .45 and waved back.

"Why don't you take something along besides that pea shooter?" I yelled at him. I carried my CAR-15 submachine gun and felt more comfortable with it.

"This and all these guys around me are all I need," Gator yelled back.

"Yeah, I've heard that before. See you there. Probably have to save your ass again."

"We'll be waiting for you. Wake us up when you get there."

After Alpha company passed, I gave them a couple hundred meters and then signaled third platoon to move out. As they filed by to follow Alpha down the road, I bantered with some of them as they passed. I also made sure they did not have their vests zipped up—they needed to let the air circulate under them. We fell in behind as the first platoon came up behind us. Across the road, I saw Charlie 6 standing by the road. Gus Fishburne waved us on with that smirk of his. Within five minutes, all Bravo platoons had cleared the LD—the line of departure. The platoon leaders pushed security out to the flanks to discourage any locals from trying to fire on us, and third platoon maintained its distance from Alpha. Everyone was locked and loaded and watching the flanks. We were ready for any ambush attempt.

The move toward Ap Cho proved uneventful, and we had no heat casualties. The men were tough and used to the heat, but they were not used to carrying all that equipment with them.

As we approached Ap Cho, we could see smoke rising from the vicinity of the village. The sound of rifle and automatic weapons fire—with the occasional *crump*! of grenades—was discernable as we closed on the outskirts. Alpha deployed to the right, and we moved up on the left and began our sweep of the village. So far, no one fired at us. As we cleared the first row of houses, we came across some little guys in fatigues moving in the direction from which we were coming. They looked as if they had had enough of this crap. Through some primitive sign language and the few words of Vietnamese which I knew, I found out that they had been a Popular Force platoon but had lost over half of their strength, including their platoon leader. They had seen us coming and were leaving the rest of the fight to us. Considering how bad PF units normally were—and obviously how well these little guys had done—I was content to let them go. They had more than done their job. They also told me that the NVA were likely along the eastern edge of the village and were probably trying to get back into the woods, since it was starting to get dark. They may have felt safer there. And with good reason—I had no intention of following them in there at night. I passed on to the other company commanders what I had learned from the Vietnamese.

Ap Cho was a small, square village with dirt streets running north-south and east-west—about six streets in either direction. The village consisted only of small houses, which we called hooches, and no stores. If the villagers wanted to shop, they could go to Cu Chi or south to Hoc Mon. At that point, there *were* no villagers. They were not fools. It was normal for them to take off with what belongings they could carry at the first sign of converging military units. They could readily tell from experience when they were in a danger zone, and they did not stick around to discuss the weather. The hooches were mostly of cheap, flaky Vietnamese masonry with tin or thatched roofs. A few hooches were completely thatch. The masonry walls gave us—and the enemy—good cover from small arms. In addition, some fairly tall trees in the area gave snipers a good vantage point and a place to hide. This place could get to be hazardous to one's health!

As we cleared the third row of hooches, the earth erupted around us with automatic fire. Everyone dived for cover behind hootch walls and returned fire in the general direction from which they thought the fire had come. It sounded like a fireworks display on the Fourth of July, but nobody was hitting anything because they couldn't see anything.

"Atkinson, tell them to hold their fire unless they have a target. The gooks know we're here now." He did, and the firing on our side died out. We received more sporadic incoming fire—the old familiar *"pop-pop-pop"* of AK-47s. It was difficult to determine exactly where the firers were, but it appeared that there were only a half-dozen or so people shooting at us—maybe one was in a tree. Incoming fire was sporadic and ineffective. It felt more like a rear guard action than a main engagement. We would find out.

I reached for Atkinson's handset. "3-6, move your people out carefully. Use fire and movement between hooches. Let's see what we've got here." Gormley acknowledged. From my position, I could see them move—first one man here, then two there, then another and so on until the whole platoon was across the street and continued to move through the hooches. As they spread out and rushed from hootch to hootch, they received sporadic AK fire, but no one was hit. Either those guys were bad shots, or they were just popping of at movement. I suspected the latter, since it was now almost too dark to see, unless someone was stupid enough to allow himself to be illuminated by the burning debris.

"Bravo 6, 3-6. We've reached the village perimeter berm. Nobody's home. It looks like they made it back to the woods. Even the sniper fire has petered out. Want us to check it out?"

"Negative. It's too dark to go wandering around in the woods. Hold your position. I'll send the 1-6 element up to your flank. Take a position behind the berm in case those jokers start shooting again. Just keep your eyes and ears open. Out. Break-Break. 1-6, did you monitor?"

"1-6. Roger. We're moving now."

"Roger that. Out. Break-Break. 2-6, hold your position and watch our rear and left flank. We don't want any surprises."

"2-6. Roger."

I dropped Atkinson's handset and picked up Mac-Kenzie's.

"Falcon 6, Bravo 6. Over."

"Falcon 6."

"Our section of the village is secure. I've got two elements through the village to the berm. The bad boys have scooted out to the woodline to the east. Since it's black as hell out here, I don't propose we go after them. The

Arvins took off when we got here, but I hold no grudges. They lost half their platoon and their leader.

They greatly surpassed our normally mediocre expectations. And besides, they gave us the opportunity for an afternoon stroll through the countryside. What's our orders, boss?"

"This is Falcon 6 . . ." That guy always was too formal, but I guess that's what West Point does to an otherwise normal person. ". . . Alpha's situation is about the same. I guess we've done all we can there for today, so we'll execute the plan to pick you up and to bring you back here to our location. You secure the PZ and will be the last out. We'll lift out Alpha and Charlie when you tell me you're ready. We have only six birds to work with, so it'll probably take a little longer. Over."

Falcon 6 can wait a minute. I grabbed Atkinson's handset. "2-6, move out to that rice paddy outside the village and secure a PZ big enough for six birds. Designate somebody to use the strobelight at the head of the PZ. When your people get in position, go ahead and assign them to aircraft loads. You folks and I will be on the last lift, in case you haven't figured that out by now. Save me three spaces on the lead slick. 1-6 and 3-6, get ready to move when I give you the word. I want 1-6 prepared to support 2-6, if necessary. When our turn comes—after Alpha and Charlie—we'll go out 4-6, 3-6, 1-6, 2-6 in order. 4-6, the FO team will go with you. Questions? Acknowledge."

All acknowledged, just as I heard Falcon 6 on the other squawk box. "Bravo 6, Falcon 6. Did you receive my last transmission? Over."

"Roger, Falcon 6. We're on the move. I'll coordinate with Alpha and Charlie. Tell the C&C to give me one-five mikes and then bring those babies in. Put him on this push so I can coordinate the lift with him."

"Falcon 6. Roger. He should be up in five mikes. 6 out."

"Charlie 6, Bravo 6. Ready to get the hell out of here?"

"Charlie 6. I don't know. I'm having so much fun here."

"Since you're closest to the PZ, we'll have them pick you up first. Six birds are ETA in one-five mikes. Think you can get you're ass in gear by then?"

"Yeah, I think we can handle that."

"OK, good. You may not be in the hands of God, but you'll be in the hands of Bravo. Rest easy, son. Out! Break-Break. 'Gator, you monitor?"

"Roger that, Bull. We'll extract from here and follow Chargin' Chuck. We'll watch for Charlie's last lift and be ready. I'll give you an 'up' when my last lift goes."

"OK, we'll cover your ass in case someone gets brave and ventures out of the woods. Stay in touch. It's dark out there."

"Rog. By the way, Bull, I know January 15th was tough, but welcome back. You sound like your old self again."

"Thanks, Gator. Now cut out the brown-nosing and get the hell out of here! Bravo out."

While we waited for the aircraft, I made sure that the pick-up zone was as secure as we could make it. There would be no "ring of fire" tonight—only a hasty perimeter. I took a couple of minutes to survey the scene around me. The buildings of the village were visible in the glow of numerous, still-burning fires, and the pallor of smoke and the sulfurous smell of cordite hung heavily over the area. Most of the hooches were still standing except for an area of about four square blocks in the eastern half of the village, where everything standing had been burned down or blown away. This small area was cluttered with piles of debris. The hooches outside the area—and along Highway 1 in the southern part—appeared to be in good shape. It was obvious where most of the fighting had occurred. Had I only known how familiar I would become with that area in the next two weeks, maybe I would have not been so eager to leave it that night.

During the next two hours, I stood at the edge of the

village and watched as the slicks ferried Charlie and Alpha back to Cu Chi base camp.

As the size of the force shrunk, I felt increasingly uneasy, but that was normal when you knew you would be hanging out alone for awhile. Then it was our turn. Fourth and third platoons departed. Then as the first platoon lifted off, I walked over to Lieutenant Lorne.

"OK, we're next. Remember, there's nobody out there covering your ass. Tell your guys to empty a magazine to their front—as soon as the birds touch down—on your signal—and then haul ass to their assigned choppers as fast as they can. Make damn sure no one's left behind. If we get incoming, tell them just to keep moving. As soon as they reach the birds, the door gunners will cover them and do the shooting back. If anybody gets hit, for God's sake, go get him. I don't want *anyone* left. Now, get moving and let's go get a cold beer."

Ten minutes later, I saw the blinking lights of the approaching slicks as they guided in on the flashing strobe. I walked over to the strobe man where the first slick would set down.

"Ready for a cold one, Price?" (Price is an alias.)

"You bet, Captain, 'specially after a hot day like today. I don't much like doing this crap at night. Kind of hard to keep a low profile out here, you know what I mean?"

"Yeah, I know. But, with a little luck, the fun's almost over. Here comes our ride home."

As the slicks touched down, I climbed aboard, followed by my RTOs, as I heard the second platoon fire off their M-16s, M-60s and M-79 grenade launchers. I waited tensely for any sound of return fire but heard none, as I watched the shadowy figures of men running for the choppers. As the last ones dived in, the aircraft lifted off and headed back to Cu Chi.

The trip was uneventful. When we landed, the battalion CO and S-3 were there to greet us.

"Good job, Bob. Tell the men they did well."

"Thanks, sir. I will. Where do we go here?"

Major Davis chimed in, pointing to his base camp map. "Bravo has been allocated four hooches in 5*th* Mech's area. Bobcat is out running around the HoBo Woods and won't be using it for awhile. You, your officers and senior NCO's will be in their BOQ. Your field first sergeant is waiting over there with your jeep, and he has your area ready for you. Your first three platoons are there, and I understand that the beer is cold. We'll have a Command and Staff meeting in one hour. Battalion is located at Brigade Headquarters. Your driver knows where that is. Go get settled in."

"OK, thanks. Catch you later."

Walking over to my jeep, I called Lieutenant Lorne over. "We've been given space in Bobcat's area. Put your guys on those trucks over there. Top will take you to your area. Pass the word to the other platoon leaders that I have to be at battalion in one hour, and I expect that we'll get together at my BOQ room after that to plan tomorrow's operation. I'll let you know when I leave battalion. Make sure they get a cold beer and get their weapons cleaned and get resupplied before they do anything else. Questions? OK, get going. See you later."

I turned to SFC Johnson. "OK, Top, tell me how everything went getting all the company's gear in here."

Johnson scratched his rather large belly and grinned. "Hell, sir, it was a little hairy getting back in. One of the 25*th* S&T trucks took an RPG through the cab, but nobody was hurt seriously. But we got it here. One thing kind of bothers me, though."

"What's that?"

"That damn Bobcat area they gave us. It's right next to an ammo dump. If that thing blows, we all might just fly along with it. Think you can get us moved to another area?"

"I'll check with the S-4. See what he says. I'll let you know when I get back from battalion. Now take Lorne and his guys to their hotel. Tell the platoon sergeants to make sure everybody gets some rest after they get their

gear ready for tomorrow. If this offensive continues, they
might not get much over the next few days. Take the
RTOs with you and get them settled in. If I need them,
I'll call 'em."

"OK, sir. We'll get it done."

"Now, Miller," I told my driver, "take me to the cold
beer." (Miller is an alias.)

"Roger that, Captain. We're on our way."

A few minutes later, I entered the door of the com-
paratively large wooden building known euphemistically
as the Bachelor Officers Quarters, or BOQ. The building
was partitioned with plywood into several small "rooms,"
each of which was barely large enough to hold a few
pieces of Army-issue furniture, specifically a small bed, a
dresser, a small coffee table, and a reasonably
comfortable-looking, partially upholstered chair. Each
room had a small window air conditioner, which practi-
cally filled the window cut into the wooden wall, and
which gave the room a musty smell when it was not running. Oh, well, when compared to my little nylon hammock, that room was a palace! I tossed my rucksack in
the corner, threw my CAR-15 on the bed, plopped down
in the chair, cracked open a can of Bud, and breathed a
deep sigh. This had been one helluva day—I wondered
what was in store for the next day.

CHAPTER SEVEN

TET: WEEK ONE

The TET Offensive, Day Two (February 1st): It really seemed like the first day of the rest of our lives—which we hoped would last out the week. At that point, we were not sure about our futures—either personally or as a fighting force. Our Vietnam experience, to that point involved very little extended, set-piece fighting in the traditional sense, with the exception of an occasional, coordinated fire base defense like we had had at Burt. Most of what we had done to that point had been called such pseudonyms as "Search and Destroy," "Reconnaissance in Force," and other odious, action-specific names for walking around in the jungle a lot, hacking away at Vietnamese bamboo and vegetation, and finding very little sign of an enemy. When we did find them, the action was very intense and short-lived.

On February 1st, we were going into the village of Cu Chi ("Cu Chi City") to see if any bad guys had reached the village after we had left them the previous evening down in Ap Cho. Since the NVA had seemed intent on taking Cu Chi the day before, Brigade thought they may have infiltrated into the village during the night. If they had, then the District headquarters would be their likely target. Alpha and Bravo were designated to check out the area. If we made it through the village without incident, then we had RIF AQs beyond the village. The plan was for Alpha to lead along the road from the base camp until we reached the intersection with Highway 1, then turn north to their AO. Bravo would follow Alpha and turn south toward the village of Tan Phu Trung along Highway 1.

Due to our late hours the night before, we did not get

out the gate until 1000 hours, trailing along down the dirt road about two hundred meters behind Alpha in normal company column. Second platoon led, followed by the CP group, first platoon and fourth platoon, with third platoon bringing up the rear. Because of Alpha's proximity, we had no point out.

On our left, the terrain was open out to about three hundred meters before reaching the woods. We could observe anything occurring there. On our right, for most of the distance to Cu Chi City, was a banana grove. The thickness of the plants caused us some concern. But then, would Conchita Banana really want to hurt us?

As we walked along, we passed, on our left, a line of small shanties containing souvenir stands and other shops designed to bilk the American GI out of his hard-earned money. They stretched from just outside the base camp gate halfway to Cu Chi. Since the troops were either confined to base or out on operations, and because of the waves of enemy attacks, the shops were deserted that day—probably because the owners had joined their local force VC company or battalion to participate in the attacks. We observed these shanties very carefully as we passed them.

Nothing happened until Alpha reached the edge of the village. His point platoon entered the edge of the village, passing the first row of hooches. Suddenly, they started taking fire from their front. Alpha 6 reported that the fire was coming from positions on the ground and from tree snipers. I think they saw us coming . . .

From my position back down the road, I really could not see the action or tell what was going on. We just heard the firing and saw Alpha's column halt ahead of us. I halted my column and had everyone down on one knee along the ditches on each side of the road, facing outward. We would wait there until Alpha took care of its problem—unless, of course, they needed our assistance. We waited . . . waited . . . waited. . . .

Suddenly, the *pop-pop-pop* of AK fire crackled over our heads from the banana trees.

"Hit the ground!" I barked loud enough for the whole column to hear. "If you can find a target, return fire!"

I crouched down in the ditch behind an embankment between my two RTOs, Atkinson and MacKenzie, and surveyed the situation. All the fire seemed to be confined to an area opposite the front of my column, directed primarily against second and first platoons—and the CP Group. The fourth platoon was in a position to assist by providing flanking fire, but they were substantially outside the beaten zone. The third platoon was not really in the fight.

The second, first and fourth platoon leaders were within earshot, but it was hard to hear over the firing. I reached for the company handset and articulated my desires that only those men in the ditch on the right side of the road nearest the banana grove do the shooting, and that the men in the left ditch should *quit shooting up their damn buddies and keep their asses down*! The platoon leaders indicated in return that they fully concurred with my remarks and would do their very best to communicate my concerns and desires to those in their charge.

"I've got to get those AKs turned off," I muttered to myself.

"3-6, Bravo 6."

"3-6."

"Bravo 6. I want you to get ready to execute a flanking maneuver and try to roll up these bad boys. I want you moving in zero-two."

"3-6 roger. I'll let you know when we're ready."

"Roger. 6 out." My thoughts were interrupted by the drone of an approaching helicopter, which I could hear above the clatter of the firing going on around me. I looked up and saw a Huey flying directly at us from the base camp. Abruptly, the squawk box attached to the battalion radio blared.

"Falcon unit on the road, this is Diamondhead 3. Over."

"This is Falcon Bravo 6."

"Diamondhead 3. We're almost over your head right now. We're only a slick, but we have door guns. Could we offer you some assistance?"

"Bravo 6. Roger, wait." I switched handsets. "3-6, Bravo 6. Do not move until I give you the word. I'm going to see if this slick can do us some good before I send you in."

"3-6 standing by."

"6 out." Back to the other mike: "Diamondhead 3, Bravo 6. Do you see anything in the banana grove? It sounds like they're about thirty meters off the road. We've been returning fire, but we're still getting incoming, which means they must be in some kind of hole or something below ground."

"Roger, Bravo 6. We can see a line of men in a trench down there. Want us to give them some door guns?"

"Affirmative, Diamondhead."

"Okay, we're making a pass now."

I watched the chopper turn slightly and start its run along the road just to the north of my column. Suddenly, the ditch in which we were kneeling exploded all around us, throwing dirt and gravel all over us and everything nearby! *The sons of bitches were shooting at us*!

"Diamondhead, cease fire! Cease fire! That's us you're shooting at! Get that damn helicopter out of here, or I'm going to personally shoot your asses out of the sky! Do you roger?"

"Diamondhead 3. Roger. Sorry about that." The bird turned and flew off to the north.

Stupid damn staff officers and their little playtoys, I mumbled to myself. They're more dangerous to us than the VC are!

"Damn, sir, I thought they got you!" shouted Sergeant Reece (an alias) in the opposite ditch.

"Yeah, close but no gravy. I'm beginning to like the VC better all the time."

I looked around to see who was hurt. Miraculously, we had no casualties. Then I glanced around where Mac-Kenzie, Atkinson and I were still kneeling—and I froze momentarily when I realized how close we had come to getting killed by American fire. Since I had been using the radios with MacKenzie on one side and Atkinson on the other, we had been kneeling no more than two feet apart. I could see bullet strikes in the ditch spaced between us—one on MacKenzie's right, one between us, one between me and Atkinson and one on Atkinson's left. We had been exactly in synch with the spacing between the bullets in the burst of fire from the M-60 machine gun—a most unusual phenomenon! I had never seen that happen at any other time—and I hoped I would not see it again!

"3-6, Bravo 6. Move!"

"3-6 roger. Moving now."

The firing from the banana trees had diminished. I thought our return fire had taken some toll on the enemy. Of course, some of them could have bugged out. I looked down the road and watched as the third platoon rose up out of the ditches and rushed into the banana grove. After about thirty seconds, I heard a burst of M-16 and M-60 fire and passed the word down the line to cease fire. As the third platoon's fire increased as they moved through the banana trees, the sound of AKs slowly died out. Then there was silence. Gormley worked his platoon down to the end of the grove at the edge of the village. At my instructions, he then outposted the grove along the whole company column to provide security against any possible return of the VC. I motioned to the RTOs to stay in place. I walked over to the edge of the grove and met Gormley.

"What did you get, Art?"

"Most of them ran when we came in, but we got five of them, all dead. I estimate we saw at least twelve others. Carrying AKs and a couple of RPDs. None of my guys got hit. What do you want me to do with the body count?"

"Bring them out here by the road. We'll notify battalion for disposition."

I walked back over to the road and took the mike from MacKenzie. "Falcon 3, Bravo 6."

"Falcon 3."

"Bravo 6. Since the Gator left us back here with nothing to do, we decided to have a little fun of our own. Estimate seventeen bad boys tried to shoot us up from the banana grove along the road. Results were five body count. The rest decided that discretion was the best part of valor and bugged out when 3-6 came calling. We had no friendly casualties, although we almost bagged a helicopter for dinner, as you probably monitored. Request disposition of these bodies. You want to pick them up or what? Over."

"Roger, Bravo 6. Good copy. Stand by."

"Bravo 6 standing by. Out. Break-Break. Gator, Bull. Over."

"Gator."

"Bull. What are you guys doing up there? You left us back here in this hot sun, while you're up there lounging around in that shady village. Are you going to make it through there today?"

"Sounds like you found something to occupy your time. Five body count, huh? That's more than we got up here. I think we've picked up three so far. We're not getting anything more than an occasional sniper now. We should be through here in another few minutes. We're doing a hooch-to-hooch search now, and my lead element is almost to the Highway 1 intersection. As soon as they get beyond it, they'll turn north, and I'll move the rest of the company up. Then you boys can come on into town."

About thirty minutes later, Alpha made it through the village and we were able to move again. We passed through without further incident and headed for our AO along the road to the south. Our AO started about three clicks south of Cu Chi and encompassed the village of Tan Phu Trung on the west side of Highway 1 and the forest on the east side of the road. We would stay in the trees, until we reached the southern edge of Tan Phu Trung, then cross the road and sweep back through the village in the direction of Cu Chi. We had no idea what to expect there, but those guys who were in this area yesterday were *somewhere*, and that was as good a place as any to start looking.

We found nothing on the east side of the highway. We crossed the highway without incident and started back through the village. About three kilometers long, Tan Phu Trung was bordered on the south and west by a dirt berm, which separated it from the open rice paddies beyond. Two dirt roads, which ran its length and paralleled the highway, divided its narrow three-hundred-meter width roughly into thirds. Several crossroads ran from the berm to Highway 1, generally dividing the village into blocks, each of which contained several small one-room hooches. A number of trees growing throughout the village shaded the villagers from the hot tropical sun. The hooches were similarly constructed out of bricks and thin, flaky concrete, covered by tin or thatched roofs. Although the aroma of Vietnamese fermented fish sauce, or *nuoc mam*, hung faintly in the air, it was obvious that the villagers had left with their belongings when the TET fighting started.

I assigned a platoon to each of the thirds created by the north-south roads, and we started a hooch-to-hooch search for enemy signs. Since the village was empty, we had no occupants to hinder our search.

Shortly after we started the sweep through the village, I heard a rumbling coming up Highway 1 from the south. I sauntered over to the road and saw two M-48 tanks moving north. As the first tank approached, I flagged it down and motioned the tank commander to come down and talk. As he climbed down, I noticed that he wore the four stripes of a staff sergeant.

As he approached, he saluted and said, "Afternoon, sir.

I'm Sergeant Holbrook of the Thirty-fourth Armor." (Holbrook is an alias.)

"Afternoon. I'm Captain Hemphill. What are you doing and where are you going?"

"Back to Cu Chi to rejoin the battalion. We had been detached to Third Brigade at Hoc Mon."

"Well, Sergeant, I want to use you for a couple of hours. We're trying to get through this village by searching the hooches. We could use your tanks for support in case we run into something stronger than we are. Will you do it, or do I have to call Brigade?"

"Sir, we have to get back to the battalion." Sergeant Holbrook nervously shifted his weight and glanced around at the second tank. Obviously, he was not thrilled about the possibility of a fight.

I motioned MacKenzie over and took the battalion push. "Falcon 3, Bravo 6."

"Falcon 3."

"Bravo 6. I've flagged down a couple of tanks from Tropic's armor element. I want to use them to get through this village in case we run into something bigger than we are. Will you clear through your higher?"

"Roger, Bravo 6. Stand by."

A couple of minutes later, the squawk box crackled again. "Bravo 6, Falcon 3."

"Bravo 6."

"Falcon 3. Okay, you can use those two tanks. When you finish with them, send them home. Don't keep them past sixteen hundred hours. They need to close into the base camp before dark."

"Roger, out."

I turned to Sergeant Holbrook. "Well, Sergeant, for the next three hours, you are mine. There are two roads in the village. Put one tank on each road. Stay on line with my platoons, and stay in radio contact with me. Atkinson will give you the freq. I'm particularly concerned about bunkers or gooks in masonry buildings. If we run into anything like that, I want you to fire into the obstacle.

When we get through the village, I'll release you to go to Cu Chi. Any questions?"

"Nossir." He climbed back into the turret. Three minutes later, their engines belched into action amidst a cloud of black smoke, and they rumbled up on line with my platoons. I imagine my guys were rather surprised to look up and see two tanks coming up beside them. Maybe they would save a few lives if we made contact.

The line moved out, my infantry going from hooch to hooch, with the tanks overwatching them as they moved. A few minutes later, I heard the roar of a tank gun up to the left in Gormley's sector.

I grabbed the handset. "3-6, what's going on up there?"

"6, 3-6. That tank just fired a pellet round through a hooch with one of my squads in it."

"Anybody hurt?"

"3-6. Nothing the medics can't handle. A few guys are a little shaken up, though."

"Did you order that fire?"

"3-6 negative. He fired on his own."

"Roger, out." I tossed the handset back to Atkinson, motioned for them to follow me, and set off at a determined pace toward the errant tank. "Tell the tank commander I'm coming."

Approaching the tank, I saw the hatch open and Sergeant Holbrook stick his head out. The expression on his face was one of confusion and meekness.

"Sergeant, why in hell did you fire on that hooch with one of my squads in it? Can't you see anything in that damn thing?"

"Yessir, I can see. I saw movement over there. I didn't know it was your guys."

"Sergeant, it's your damn *job* to know what you're shooting at. You had damn well better *identify* your target before you fire next time, you understand?" He nodded. "Now get back up in that turret and let's get this show back on the road."

"Yessir." He climbed back up and started moving

again. I walked back to a position where I could observe all three platoons working. For the next thirty minutes or so, the platoons moved through the hooches without finding any sign of recent occupancy.

About two-thirds of the way through the village, I suddenly heard the chatter of automatic weapons up ahead in the center of the sector. From my position, I could see the second platoon firing, but I could not see what they were shooting at. As both tanks fired their main guns, I grabbed the handset.

"2-6, Bravo 6. What have you got up there?"

"6, this is 2-6. There's a big building across our path up here. Looks like there are a couple of bunkers at the base of it. We've taken AK and machine gun fire . . . *Look out! DUCK!*" *Boom! Boom!* "Bravo 6, there went two RPGs at the tanks! Looks like they missed. The tanks are shooting back at the base of the house."

I heard about six tank rounds crash somewhere ahead, punctuated by the *Boom! Boom!* of two more RPG rounds.

"2-6, Bravo 6. In relation to the two roads, how big is that building?"

"2-6. It is in the center of the village, stretching across both roads."

"Bravo 6 roger. Are you engaging the bunkers?"

"Roger, Bravo 6. We're throwing everything we've got at them."

"Bravo 6 roger. Stay in place and help the tanks suppress the firing. Try to get a LAW or two inside the openings up there. Out. Break-Break. 1-6, 3-6, this is Bravo 6."

They answered in turn. "Bravo 6. Are you able to engage the bunkers in the base of that building ahead of you?"

"This is 1-6. Negative, but we're trying to move up to a position—where we can. Over."

"Roger, 1-6. Keep me informed. Do *not* move in front of 2-6's engagement. Out. 3-6, what's your situation?"

"3-6. Roger. My left two elements are now engaging the bunkers."

"6 roger. Use your other element to secure the right flank. We don't want any end runs here."

"3-6 roger."

"6 out."

After another exchange of tank and RPG fire, I noticed the tanks were backing back along the roads, obviously disengaging from the fight. I grabbed the handset and called—Sergeant Holbrook.

"This is Bravo 6. Where the hell are you two going? The action is ahead, not back here!"

"It's too dangerous up there, Bravo 6. Too many Romeo Papa Golfs. We gotta save this equipment. We're getting out of here."

"You have the firepower we need to take that place. You're a hell of a lot better protected than my elements are. If you leave before you're released, I'm going to report your departure in the face of the enemy to higher. Over."

"Sorry, Bravo 6. We have to get back to the battalion."

"Bravo 6 out." I tossed the mike back to Atkinson and reached for the other one.

"Falcon 3, Bravo 6."

"Falcon 3."

"Bravo 6. Two things. First, we've got some pretty good contact about two-thirds of the way through the village. Appears to be a couple of bunkers at the base of the south side of a big masonry building. We are engaging with all we have here. We'll see what we can do. Don't believe we can get arty in here from your location—unless you care to hotfoot them down here behind us. Failing that, we'll press on. We're getting AK, Romeo Papa Delta and Romeo Papa Golf fire. Roger so far?"

"3 roger."

"The second thing is that the two tanks I was using bugged out at the first sign of RPG fire. They were *not*—I repeat—*not* released. Those brave tanker boys seemed mighty fidgety and nervous when somebody was throwing something at them which might hurt them a little. They ought to try doing this with these real protective fatigue shirts. Might make them appreciate those hard shells they ride around in. As far as I'm concerned, they are a bunch of damn yellow cowards. You might want to relay that to higher. End of report. Did you roger?"

"Falcon 3. I roger that. I'll also notify higher about the tanks. By the way, keep your eyes open for a supply convoy moving up from your rear heading this way. Should be passing your location before long. Over."

"Bravo 6 roger. Just what we need—a bunch of damn REMFs tromping around in our AO here. Okay, we'll try not to shoot them up. Might spoil the beer supply. They know we're here?"

"Falcon 3. Higher's TOC notified the convoy commander of your approximate location. They may be a bit nervous, though. They're not really used to this combat stuff."

"Roger. Great. Bravo 6 out."

While I had been talking to Falcon 3, I kept an eye on the events to my front, at least as much as I could see. The sound of the firing rose and fell in waves as the enemy fired and my guys returned the fire.

"2-6, Bravo 6. Sitrep."

"This is 2-6. We've moved a little closer, but they have pretty good fields of fire to their front. We just crossed a road about thirty meters in front of the building. I have two elements down in the ditch along the road. I'm not sure we can get much closer. Over."

"Bravo 6. Okay. I want you to lay down a base of fire. I'll see if I can get somebody else up there. Out. Break-Break. 3-6, Bravo 6."

"This is 3-6."

"Bravo 6. What's your view of the right bunker? Can you get somebody to its flank with a granade?"

"3-6. Roger, Bravo 6. I think I can get one of my elements around there if 2-6 can keep their heads down."

"Bravo 6. Okay. 2-6 is laying down a base a fire now. Get 'em going now, but keep your eye on them. Let 2-6 know when to shift fire. Now you keep control, understand? I *do not* want any of our people shooting each other up! Also, notify your right flank guard that a supply convoy is due by any time. Have them make contact with the convoy so they know we're in here. I don't want us dodging their bullets, too. Do you roger?"

"2-6. Roger, Bravo 6. Over."

"6 out. Break-Break. 1-6, Bravo 6."

"This is 1-6. Over."

"Bravo 6. Did you monitor my last with 3-6?"

"Roger, Bravo 6."

"Bravo 6. Okay. Can you get somebody up to the flank of that left bunker with a grenade or two?"

"1-6. Roger, Bravo 6. It seems that 2-6 has their full attention. As long as 2-6 keeps firing, we should be able to approach the bunker."

"Bravo 6. Then get going. Like I told 3-6, I want you to tell 2-6 when to shift or cease firing. You guys *better not* get anybody shot up by our own side. Also, have your left flank element outpost that berm on the left. I don't want any flanking fire from that side. Do you *fully* roger?"

"1-6 roger. Over."

"Bravo 6 out." I handed the mike back to Atkinson and dropped to one knee. When the firing started, my CP group had taken cover in a wide, shallow hole in the ground between two rows of hooches. The hole was about one-and-a-half feet deep, with vertical sides and flat bottom. It was wide enough for all six of us to take cover inside.

As the two flank platoons began moving, out of the corner of my eye I noticed movement to the right. I glanced in that direction and saw, through the hooches and trees, the first vehicles of the supply convoy passing by. Since I presumed that 3-6's element would take care of them, I turned my attention back to the fight up ahead. *Crack—Crack—Crack!* Suddenly, bullets pierced the

air all around us, flying around our heads and kicking up
dust around the hole! Everybody hit the ground in the bottom of the hole. For some reason, I landed on top of Atkinson, on my back with my head up against the side of the
hole. Some of the incoming bullets were stitching a pattern
on the inside of the hole just above my helmet. They were
so close, and I was pushing down on Atkinson so hard already, that I could not move away from them. I had already
determined that they were coming from the convoy.

I reached over for the handset. "3-6, Bravo 6. Get out
there *now* and shut off the firing from those fuckin' supply
clerks! They're shooting up the CP. Tell them to cease
fire ASAP or we'll open up on them. To hell with the
VC—those sons of bitches are rapidly becoming *my* enemy! Now get moving!"

It took about one minute for the firing to cease. I sat
up in the hole, giving Atkinson a chance to get his breath.
"3-6, Bravo 6. Put the convoy commander on the push
now!"

"3-6 roger. He's right over here. Stand by."

"Bravo 6, this is the convoy commander. Over."

"Bravo 6. Were you not advised that we were in this
village?" My voice was deliberate and expressionless.

"Roger, I knew you were in here somewhere, but some
of my guys saw movement and opened fire on their own.
Sorry about that."

My voice now took on a hard, steely tone. "Bravo 6.
Listen, you dumb son of a bitch. They opened up because
you did not exercise control over your own people. Either
you did not brief them properly, or they're a bunch a
untrained Rear Echelon Mother Fuckers* who get scared
and run at their own shadow. Now you listen to me carefully. You get those dumb sons of bitches and your damn
trucks out of here *now*, or *I'm* going to blow you to hell.
Do you understand?"

"Roger, Bravo 6. We're moving now. Over."

---

*These were more popularly known as REMFs.

"Bravo 6 out."

I glanced over at the edge of the hole. There could not have been more than two inches between my helmet and the top of the hole. I counted twelve bullet strikes within that two inches. I slowly shook my head and thought to myself, "This is getting too damn close, and I'm not really sure who the enemy is." That was twice in one day that I—and my people—came very close to getting killed, and in both cases it was from American guns. One more day like today . . .

Just then, I noticed that the firing up ahead had stopped. As I reached for the handset again, I heard two explosions, followed shortly by two more. "1-6, Bravo 6. Sitrep."

"1-6. We just blew the left bunker. I'm on the way up there now. I'll let you know what I find ASAP. Over."

"Bravo 6 roger. Out. Break-Break. 3-6, Bravo 6. Sitrep."

"3-6. We got the right bunker. My element dug out three enemy kilos, two AKs, one RPD, and an RPG-7. We're getting no more incoming. Over."

"Roger. Make sure you have security on the other side of that building and on your right flank. Provide cover for 2-6 to sweep the building. Consolidate the kilos and weapons up near the highway with those from 1-6."

"3-6 roger."

"6 out. Break-Break. 2-6, Bravo 6. I want you to sweep the building to make sure it's empty and we have no surprises waiting for us in there. 1-6 and 3-6 will provide outside security. Check it out thoroughly but as quickly as you can. I don't want to be out here after dark."

"2-6 roger. We'll move in zero-five."

"6 out. Break-Break. 1-6, Bravo 6. Did you monitor my last with 3-6 and 2-6?"

"1-6 roger. I'm sending out security now. We got two Victor Charlie kilos, one AK, one RPD, and one RPG-7 out of the bunker. We're taking them up by the road now."

"Okay, good. 6 out."

I reached for the battalion push. "Falcon 3, Bravo 6."

"Falcon 3."

"Bravo 6. Contact is concluded. No friendly casualties. We've got five enemy KIA, three AKs, two Romeo Papa Deltas and—get this—two Romeo Papa Golf Sevens."

"Falcon 3. RPG-7s, huh? Those are battalion weapons. Wonder who they belong to?"

"Bravo 6. Well, they're waiting right here for you to come get them and ask them. Request disposition instructions. We would like to get back to base camp before it gets dark out here. It's after seventeen hundred hours now, and we have a long walk back."

"Falcon 3. Roger. Stand by."

I switched handsets. "2-6, Bravo 6. Sitrep."

"Bravo 6, 2-6. We've just finished the top floor with negative results. The buildin is clear. We're coming back down now."

"Bravo 6 roger. When you get back down, I'll send you the engineer I have back here. I want him to blow those bunkers. Give him security. When he has set the charges and is ready, give me the word."

"2-6 roger."

"6 out."

The other radio crackled. "Bravo 6, Falcon 3."

"Bravo 6."

"Falcon 3. You'll have a slick inbound in three-zero mikes to pick up your cargo. Once that is done, give me an 'up.' Since it's getting late and you have a pretty long walk back, I've laid on a lift for you. After the slick departs, you will need to secure a Papa Zulu and conduct an extraction. You'll have ten birds to work with."

"Bravo 6. Roger. Thanks for the lift. With ten birds, we'll make it out in two trips. We'll be ready. We'll bring them in on the highway. Because of the trees along the road, they'll have to land in trail."

For the next one-and-a-half hours, we blew the bunkers, finished sweeping the village, sent out the enemy bodies and weapons, and extracted the company without further incident. As the last chopper lifted off Highway 1, I looked out at the last vestiges of daylight and thought about how peaceful it was. It was hard to believe at that moment that we were right in the middle of the biggest enemy offensive of the war. I was sure that the next day would bring us back to reality.

At 0700 hours on February 2nd, I was sitting in my jeep at the 1st Brigade helicopter pad, awaiting an observation bird to conduct an aerial recon of that day's operations area. The company would be saddled up and ready to move by the time I returned. We were assigned to conduct a RIF to the south of Cu Chi City, back toward Ap Cho hamlet, as part of the security operations to protect the capital of Cu Chi District—and, of course, the District Chief and District Advisor.

As I waited for the chopper, I took the time to study the area on my tactical map. Suddenly, I heard the telltale *whoosh! whoosh! whoosh!* of incoming rocket fire, punctuated by three explosions not far away. Noticing that we were sitting out in the open, I decided it was time to do something about it.

"Get the hell out of here! There. Over behind those buildings!" I pointed to the nearest cover as Miller started the engine, slammed the gears into first and popped the clutch, all in one motion. In ten seconds, we screeched to a stop behind the first building, jumped out of the jeep and took cover.

We waited about five minutes and decided nothing else was coming in. As the rockets landed, I heard a large explosion and a lot of smaller ones nearby. As we got back into the jeep and drove around the building to return to the helipad, I saw a column of black smoke over toward Bobcat's area where the company was billeted.

"Looks like one of those rockets hit something over near us."

"Sure does, Captain."

I looked at my watch. 0725 and no chopper. I reached for the radio handset.

"Falcon 3, Bravo 6."

"Falcon 3. Glad you called. The chopper is cancelled for now. You had better get back to your company area ASAP. One of those rockets hit the ammo dump next door to your company's billets. Over."

"Bravo 6. Roger, on the way. I'll get back to you later. Out."

I hung up the mike and told Miller to get us back to the company area ASAP.

As we approached the company area, I saw all the men standing out in the street adjacent to Bobcat's area. As Miller stopped the jeep, Gormley walked up.

"What happened, Art?"

"One of those rockets hit the ammo dump. The explosion threw dud four-deuce, eighty-one, and artillery rounds into the company area. It also set off other ammo, which popped more duds over the fence into our area. We all ran like hell out of there, carrying only what we were wearing at the time. EOD won't let us back in until they clear the duds out."

"Anybody hurt?"

"Negative."

"Get the other platoon leaders up here."

"Roger, sir." Off he went to round up the other lieutenants.

While I waited, I looked over the company area from where I stood. The black smoke continued to billow from the ammo dump. I could see at least two hooches which had been blown down, their roofs caved in down to the level of the sandbag walls which protected the lower half of the hooch. None of the hooches were burning.

I turned around to face the four lieutenants standing there. "Give me your status. First Platoon?"

Lieutenant Monroe looked a mite perturbed. "All my men got out when things started blowing, but only six brought their weapons, and none have their webbing."

"Second Platoon?"

"All personnel out and okay, ten weapons and no webbing."

"Third Platoon?"

Gormley shifted nervously from foot to foot. "All personnel accounted for, and everyone has their webbing. We had just saddled up when the ammo dump went up. But I have only half with weapons."

"Fourth Platoon"

"All out, but we have no webbing or weapons. Everybody just took off as those unexploded shells came raining in. We lost two hooches, though."

"Okay. Sounds like we have about one platoon's worth of weapons and equipment. Go back and reorganize your units. I'll get back to you."

As they walked away, I called over the two RTOs and the field first sergeant. I noticed that both radios had been rescued.

"I'm glad to see you guys saved those radios. We would be lost without them. Top, did all our CP people make it out okay?"

"Yes, Captain. We're all here. Except what you see, all our stuff is back in there, though. I talked to the EOD sergeant, and he told me it may be three or four days before they clear out all that crap in there. He says we can't go back in 'til then."

"Okay, Top. Get the CP people together and hang loose here until I get back. I'm going over to battalion to see what's going on."

"Okay, Captain."

Five minutes later, Miller screeched to a halt in front of our make-shift battalion headquarters. Falcon had taken over one of the Wolfhounds' buildings and established a CP there.

I walked up to Davis, who was perusing a large area map taped to the wall.

"Morning, Bravo 6. I see Murphy's Law is still in effect."

"Roger that. Why did that rocket have to land next to my people? Why couldn't it have done something useful, like land on Brigade headquarters or something."

"What's your situation?" Typical—when a staff officer has nothing important to say, he can always ask for your situation.

"All my people got out unscathed. My problem is that I have only enough weapons and webbing for one platoon, if we pool everything together. My field first tells me EOD won't let us back in at all until they clear all those duds out of there."

"That's right, they won't. They don't want anyone getting hurt."

"Hell, sir, this isn't a training exercise!" I had had enough of this pussy crap. "We're in the middle of the biggest enemy offensive of the war, and they're afraid somebody might get hurt? That's really stupid! Just have them clear us some paths back to the hooches so we can get our weapons and webbing, and they can have the joint! We can't do our job without them."

"They won't do that. They're afraid of a cook-off as somebody walks past, or of somebody setting one off *inside* a hooch when he picks up his rifle or something, not knowing there's a dud under it. Nobody knows what's inside those hooches."

"Nothing we can do to speed this up?"

"Not now anyway. We'll keep you informed about their progress."

"Will somebody lend us some gear until we can get to ours?"

"Negative. All other infantry units are out in the boonies and nobody else wants to take a chance on losing accountability."

"That's a bunch of crap! If we lose something, they can combat-loss it. I guarantee we'll give them enough combat to get it through! We'll probably have to do some of that for stuff in those two hooches that were blown down. Hell, all we're asking for are some M-16s, M-60s,

M-79s, and a little TA-50. Anybody could lend us that."

"Sorry, Bravo 6. I know how you feel, but Brigade told us to take care of our own problems."

"Yeah, that sounds like that damn screwed-up Brigade. Okay, I hear you. This has got to be the most screwed-up situation I've ever been in. That means I have one combat-effective platoon. Until we can get in to recover our gear, give us a platoon mission. I'll rotate platoons and equipment to spread out the wealth. EOD says it will take three or four days."

"Yeah, I've already discussed this with Falcon 6. That's what we plan to do." He turned to the wall map. "We want to send your platoon on a sweep through these woods south of Cu Chi where you did your helicopter insertion on the first day of the offensive. The extent of their sweep is here." He pointed out a small road on the map. "That's about three clicks out from Cu Chi. This is more of a security mission. We don't think anything is in there, but we want to make sure. As you know, it's pretty thick in there. How soon can your platoon be ready to depart?"

"We can have them out in one hour. Meanwhile, I'll have my field first get with the sergeant major on new billets. I need to get the rest of the company off the street. We also need a re-issue of C-rations for today."

"Okay, sounds good to me. Look, I know you're frustrated and pissed off about this situation and being left out of the action, but right now, there's nothing else we can do about it. You know Bravo is our best company, and we would certainly use you if we could. But in this brigade, we're bastard step-children. Nobody's going to give us a damn thing. The fact that we're here to help protect their asses doesn't mean a thing to them. So just consider this a standdown. Anything else?"

"Not that I can think of." I marked the AO on my map and left the CP.

Back at the company area, I sent the field first to see

the sergeant major and S-4 about billeting and rations. Then I turned to the platoon leaders.

"Okay, listen up. EOD won't let us back in to get the rest of our weapons and equipment until they clear the area. They say it will take three or four days. In the meantime, we have to work with what we've got. Since we have only one platoon's worth of weapons and web gear, I'm going to send you out one platoon at a time. You'll swap off equipment between platoons, but I want you to make sure you account for every piece so everybody gets his own stuff back. I've sent top over to get us other billets and re draw Cs for today. Now for the platoon rotations. Third platoon will go out today, First gets the next mission, and Second the next one. Missions may be day or night. Unless I tell you differently, you're off if you are not out or getting ready to go out. Should give the guys a little break, but I don't want anybody getting out of control. Understand? If this country-wide offensive continues, it may be a long time before they get another break. So, Art, you're first. The only equipment needed for this mission is basic webbing, weapon, and radio. I want you to give the other platoon leaders a list of what you need now. I want a list kept of all serial numbered items, who they belong to, and who will be using them. Update this list every time it changes. You must be on the move in one hour. So I want you other guys to get him what he needs ASAP. Art, I'll go over your mission after the others leave. Any questions? Okay, go."

Gormley passed out his list and the others left. I briefed him on his mission and sent him on his way.

For the next three days, Bravo company killed time. We were tasked each day to send platoons on such missions as road security, area sweeps and night security ambushes. We rotated a platoon package of weapons and equipment for each mission.

During that period, Captain Herb Chancey's Alpha company was detached for a couple of days to the 25th Infantry Division's cavalry squadron, the 3rd Squadron,

4*th* Armored Cavalry, which we called the "3/4 Horse," to keep Highway 1 open from Tay Ninh, north of Cu Chi, to Saigon. The VC continuously built roadblocks in several key places along the road. The Division's intent was to keep the road open for supply convoys and other mission-essential vehicular traffic. However, no convoys were venturing out of base camps and moving on that road. Therefore, the 3/4 Horse was knocking down roadblocks because they were there and to deny success to the VC. Had to keep 'em busy.

Charlie company, with First Lieutenant Charlie Boyle now in command, was running company sweeps beyond Cu Chi City, helping to screen the area around the District headquarters and the Division base camp. Delta company, under Captain Bill Montague (an alias), drew the duty of guarding the Phu Cuong bridge from VC/NVA sappers.

On the night of February 4th, Delta company, which had returned to the base camp, was the reaction company. At about 2200 hours, Falcon was notified that the Cu Chi District compound was under attack. They initially received heavy fire from several 82mm mortars, followed by automatic weapons fire from the rooftops of buildings which surrounded the compound. One of the mortar rounds had started a fire in the living quarters of the MACV advisors. As the situation unfolded, several VC entered the compound through a back gate opened by a Popular Forces soldier. Delta 6 found out about how the gate had been opened. As far as could be determined, the PFs manning the bunkers in the compound perimeter wall had fired very little, if at all, at the attacking enemy. I am not sure exactly what they had done, but fighting to protect the District Chief and his headquarters—their mission—was certainly not it. The VC, however, were blocked from reaching the District Command Bunker—containing the District Chief and his American advisory team from MACV—by the fire in the living quarters.

Once the District headquarters came under fire, the senior advisor requested assistance from the Division, which

was about one click away. Delta company and the Recon
Platoon from 1st Battalion/5th Mech—Bobcat Romeo—
responded with most of Delta's men riding on Romeo's
tracks. To discourage ambush en route, Romeo's track
commanders reconned with their 50s as they moved down
the road from the back gate of the base camp to the village.

When the VC in the District compound heard the 50s
firing and getting closer, they gave up on trying to get
through or around the fire and withdrew from the compound. By the time the reaction force had reached the
compound, the only VC they found were a few snipers
shooting at them from the brick schoolhouse behind the
compound. A few bursts of 50 caliber fire through the
brick silenced most of that.

Delta and Bobcat Romeo secured the compound,
helped extinguish the fire and conducted a security sweep
around the immediate area. After they were satisfied that
the VC had left the village, they returned to the base
camp.

On February 5th, Alpha was released and returned to
Falcon. For the day's operation, they were assigned an
AO beyond Cu Chi City to the south of Charlie's. That
was an area called "The Pineapple" because of the numerous pineapple fields in the area. It was also near the
Division's boundary with the 25th ARVN Division, then
known among the US military as the World's Worst Division, a dubious title earned by its almost complete lack
of success in most tactical operations. It seemed that,
every time they went out, they were either shot up or
found nothing. It sounded to me like they had a VC in-
filtrator in some key position in their organization. In any
case, we were extremely reluctant to work with or near
them.

On February 6th, Lieutenant Colonel Harrold was
scheduled to depart to rotate back to the States. The good
part was that he was taking his asshole of a sergeant major
with him. He was being replaced by some general's horse-

holder from Headquarters, US Army, Vietnam (USARV). Great! Just what we needed right in the middle of a major enemy offensive—a rear-area type coming out to get his command time and his ticket punched so he could get promoted. At least Harrold had come from the Division G-4 shop, which was a lot closer to the fighting than USARV. In any case, Falcon 6 was scheduled to depart that afternoon for Camp Alpha to outprocess, and the new Falcon 6 was due in that evening sometime.

That day's operational missions for Alpha, Charlie and Delta remained unchanged. After Alpha, Charlie, and my third platoon left the base camp, I had Miller drive me over to Bobcat's area to check on EOD's progress.

As I stepped out of the jeep, the EOD sergeant came up to me.

"Good morning, Sergeant James," I said, glancing at his name tag. (James ia an alias.) "I just wanted to find out how much longer before we can get our equipment out of here and get back on the road."

"Well, sir, I think by noon today, you can get most of your stuff out. We're still not completely through here, so I want to avoid having everyone rushing in here at once. Also, we haven't finished with the two hooches which were destroyed."

"I'm particularly interested right now in getting those weapons and web gear out of there. We can get the other stuff later."

"Okay, Captain, that you can do. It would be better if only a couple of people went into each hootch and brought out everyone's stuff. I'll send one of our guys in with them. When do you want to go in?"

"It's 0900 now. How about 1200? The only problem is that the third platoon is out on a sweep. They have most of their webbing and a few of their weapons already. I'll have platoon reps here at noon. I'll send the third platoon over as soon as they get back in. I'll have the platoon sergeant find you then."

"Okay, sir, sounds good to me. We'll be waiting."

We drove back to the Wolfhound area where we were then billeted. As we drove up, I motioned to the two RTOs. "Atkinson, get me the platoon leaders and field first. Also, tell 3-6 to get back here by 1400."

After everyone arrived, I explained what each man was to do, including meeting 3-6 to get back their equipment. They were to let me know when all platoon members had their webbing, weapons and radios. They needed to get with the first sergeant to draw ammunition and rations. I expected all to be equipped not later than 1500 and supplies drawn by 1600. Top was also responsible for insuring CP personnel recovered their equipment and were supplied. They roger'd and left.

I climbed back into the jeep. "To battalion."

When I walked into the S-3 shop, I found Major Davis studying the wall map (I guess he spent most of his time studying the map).

"Morning, Bravo 6."

"Morning, sir. Thought you might like to know that Bravo should be mission-capable by 1600 hours today. We should have at least our weapons, webbing, radios, bullets, and chow by then. That's all we need to function."

"That's good. In fact, I just happen to have a little something for you to do. Come over here to the map." He pointed to the area east of Cu Chi City. "This is Charlie's AO and Alpha's AO, here. Today's mission is expected to take them to at least 2100 to complete, which will be after dark. They are expected to link up and move back here. Moving at night probably means they won't close base camp before 2230 or 2300. Considering what happened down at the District compound night before last, they could run into trouble in Cu Chi City as they pass back through. They will also be pretty tired that late at night. What we want you to do is to take some trucks down to Cu Chi City, secure the highway intersection outside the front gate of the District headquarters to make their passage easier, and to haul them back here. You'll have enough trucks for all three companies. I'll coordinate your move and link-up with Alpha and Charlie. Comments? Questions?"

"No questions. I'll move out around 2000, which should be just before dark. Where do I pick up the trucks?"

"25th S&T Battalion will provide you with twelve trucks. They'll be positioned at the front gate at 1900 hours."

"Okay. Tell them we'll be there around 1930. Anything else?"

"No. Let me know when you're ready to depart the camp."

"Okay. Any more word on when the new Falcon 6 arrives?"

"Not really. All we know is that he is due in sometime around 1800 or so."

"Not much help. Guess we won't see much of him tonight. When will we meet him?"

"We'll have a command and staff meeting first thing in the morning before you go out. We'll do introductions then."

"When will we git our missions for tomorrow?"

"I'll have them written for all of you by the time you all close back in here from Cu Chi."

"Okay. Where's Colonel Harrold?"

"He's over in the BOQ packing. The S-4 had all his stuff shipped up here from Dau Tieng. He'll be leaving the battalion around noon."

"Guess I'll drop in and tell him good-bye. See you later."

"Okay." He turned back his map board.

When I walked into the colonel's BOQ room, he was just locking up a footlocker. An almost full suitcase lay open on the bed, and a freshly-starched khaki uniform was hanging in the open closet.

"Well, sir, looks like you're almost ready to un-ass the AO."

"Yeah, Bob, I think it's time to get back to the world.

This is a good battalion, and it's time to get back to the world. This is a good battalion, and it's been a good year, but I want to move on."

"Where are you going?"

"They're sending me to the War College, so I'll kill a little time at Carlisle until the class starts in the summer."

"Pennsylvania in the springtime. Sure beats this dry and dusty season here. Anyway, I wanted to drop by and say good-bye before we got tied up again. Hope you have a good trip home. Those bastards are all over Saigon. Don't let them get you before you can get out of here. Keep your head down over at Camp Alpha. I hear Ton Son Nhut is being rocketed regularly. It would be a shame getting blown away on the day you're going home."

"Don't I know it!"

"Do you know anything about your replacement?"

"Only that his name is Roy Fulton, and he is coming from USARV. I think he worked for the Chief of Staff, General Tabor, up there. I don't know anything about him." (Ray Fulton is an alias).

"Will you see him?"

"I don't think so. He's not expected until this evening sometime. He's flying down in General Palmer's personal helicopter. I'll be through at Division and watching the movie at Camp Alpha by then."

"Well, I'll let you know how he turns out if I see you again. Got to go now. We're getting our stuff out of Bobcat's area. It looks like we're going out tonight and act like a company again."

"Okay, take it easy, Bob, and thanks for all you have done with Bravo. Watch out for Coloniel Dunn. He can be a real asshole."

"I will, Take it easy, sir."

"The rest of the afternoon went as planned. By 1600, Bravo was sufficiently supplied and equipped for that night's mission, which, admittedly, was not very demand-

ing—help get the other two companies back to base camp
a little earlier—but it was something for us to do. On the
next day, we would be back in full mission rotation.

By 1930 hours and gathering darkness, we had loaded
on the trucks and were on our way out the front gate. The
District Senior Advisor, Major McWhorter (an alias), was
advised that we were on our way. We wanted to make
sure that we did not get shot up by the Ruff-Puffs. We
drove down the main road to the village and District compound without incident. The trucks were parked in single
file along the side of the road next to the southern compound wall. The fourth platoon secured the intersection
near the front compound gate, and the other three platoons
were sent to outpost the roads out to 100 meters to the
north, south, and east. Once all were in position, we settled in to await word that Alpha and Charlie were coming
in.

I walked into the compound and up to the door of the
MACV TOC (Tactical Operations Center) where an
American major stood watching and puffing on a pipe. As
his eyes crinkled through the blue smoke reflecting the
light from the doorway, he smiled and held out his hand.

"Mac McWhorter. Glad you guys stopped by for a
visit. We could have used you for a little while a couple
of night ago."

"Evening, Major. Bob Hemphill. Thought I'd touch
base with you to let you know what I am doing out there."

"Good. The District Chief and I were wondering about
that when we were alerted that you were coming."

"Well, sir, we are here to secure this intersection and
pick up two of our companies who are operating out to
the west in 'the Pineapple.' Let's see—it's 2030 now. I
expect them around 2200. So we'll hang around for another hour or two. Then we'll load them up in the trucks
and be off."

"Okay, we can breathe a little easier for the next couple
hours anyway."

"I heard what happened the other night." I looked over

the compound in the weak illumination from a few ill-placed perimeter lights, and I could see the dark hulk of the remains of the MACV living quarters. "I hear you are pretty lucky your living area caught fire. Has the Chief found out who opened the gate?"

"Yeah, he got two of them. They're now on a quick one-way trip to Phu Quoc Island. They will not likely have a very pleasant life there."

"What is Phu Quoc Island?"

"A Vietnamese maximum security POW compound, run by Vietnamese MPs. Those fellows are tough! They keep some of them in underground tiger cages and the like. Phu Quoc is an island in the Gulf of Thailand off the west coast of the Mekong Delta."

"Good riddance. Anything on the VC who hit this place?"

"Since we had no bodies lying around, we have not identified the unit, either VC or NVA. They were obviously trying to knock over another District compound."

"And kill the American advisors. I heard they've gotten quite a few of them since this mess started."

"They've overrun three in this province so far, not counting the ones they have taken in the rest of the country. They missed us the first time, but we think they'll be back again sometime to try to get at us again. That's why we are happy to see you—for however long you may stay."

"Don't forget we're not far away. Obviously, you need to call sooner next time."

"Yeah, we thought we had some degree of protection, but that proved to be an erroneous presumption. Next time, I'll call as soon as anything happens."

"That would be smart. Well, let me go back out to see how we're doing. I'll check back in later."

"Okay, Bob. See you later."

I motioned to the RTOs and turned toward the gate. Suddenly I froze, listening. I heard a very faint "poop-poop-poop" in the distance back toward the base camp.

Mortars! Ours or theirs? *What are they doing? Mortaring the Division base camp?* With all that firepower, that's pretty damn stupid! Then I had another, more sinister thought: maybe they're not aiming at the base camp.

Crash! Crash! Crash! The rounds started landing around and inside *that* compound!

I crouched and ran to the gate, yelling at Constantino: "Jim, get all your people inside here *now*! Spread them out in the wall bunkers!" They jumped up and started sprinting for the gate through the pounding mortar barrage, most of which was falling beyond the intersection and along the back edge of the compound.

I ran back to the TOC door, where the RTOs had taken cover, and grabbed the company push.

"Falcon Bravo, Falcon Bravo, Bravo 6. Get your elements back into this compound ASAP! Bring 'em in the front gate and spread them out in the wall bunkers. I'll show you where your sectors are when you arrive. *Haul ass now!*"

All platoons roger'd.

Checking the impact area of the exploding mortars, I motioned the RTOs to stay put and, keeping low, I sprinted to the gate. This could be a mortar preparation for a ground attack. If this was them coming back to finish the job, they would probably come with more force to make sure the job gets done this time.

"Jim!" I called 4-6. He ran over at a crouch. "I'm putting a rifle platoon on each side of thy gate. I want you to slide around to those bunkers over there." I pointed out his limits. "Move your people now."

"What about the Ruff-Puffs in the bunkers?"

"Live with them. Share the bunkers with them. Take over the bunkers. Do whatever you have to, but watch your back. I don't want any of my people getting shot from *inside* the bunker. If they give you trouble, shoot first and ask questions later. Understand?"

"Yessir." Off he went, just as the first squad from first platoon arrived, followed closely by the rest of the platoon. I put them in the bunkers starting from the right of the gate back to 4-6's first bunker. As second platoon arrived, I sent them left of the gate, and third platoon filled the bunkers between second and fourth platoons. As I pointed out their sectors, I told the platoon leaders to make sure they had all their people. I also gave them the same instructions about the Ruff-Puffs that I had given 4-6. I also told 1-6 to lock the front gate as soon as everybody was inside.

Within ten minutes from the time the first mortar round fell, all of Bravo company had closed into the compound, had completely occupied the compound perimeter and were ready for whatever might come. This was accomplished without a single serious casualty, in spite of their dash through the mortars falling around the intersection outside and around the compound.

As I ran at a crouch toward the TOC entrance, the mortars started hitting the center part of the compound and bursts of AK fire streaked over my head. One mortar landed in the MACV living area to my right, but I made it to the entrance unscathed. I stood just inside the sandbag-protected entrance, caught my breath and listened for a moment. Our biggest problem seemed to be the mortars falling into the compound. The increasingly intense automatic fire from machine guns and AKs was being fired from the rooftops of buildings across the roads to the south and west of the compound, and 4-6 was getting some fire from the top floor of the two-story school building to the rear. Diagonally across the intersection from the front gate was the local headquarters of the National Police Field Force (NPFF), which had a protective bunker by its front door. From his position by the gate, 1-6 saw no one in the bunker, neither NPFF guards nor VC, but that could change. As I listened, I heard an occasional loud *Crump!* from an RPG hitting the wall. The crescendo of firing began to build up as my people returned fire. I noted that I heard only M-16s, M-60s, and M-79 grenades. I heard *no* outgoing .30 caliber fire—the

Ruff-Puffs were mostly armed with older caliber weapons, which were big and heavy in comparison to our weapons, which could be part of the reason for their unwillingness to fight.

I motioned the RTOs over and took the company push. "Falcon Bravo, Bravo 6."

They all answered in turn.

"Bravo 6. Okay, I want you all to control your fire. Ammo is *not* unlimited. Return fire at observed targets or at sources of incoming fire. Conserve ammo as best you can in case they rush us. Try to knock out as many of those RPGs as you can. I'm going to try to get those mortars turned off. Until I do, I want everyone to stay inside those bunkers. Do you roger?"

All roger'd in turn.

I tossed the handset back to Atkinson and took the battalion push. "Falcon 3, Bravo 6."

"Falcon 3."

"Bravo 6. We are under attack in the District compound. I'll get back to you with more detail in a few minutes. Meanwhile, I need gunships up here ASAP."

"Falcon 3. Roger. I'll get back to you soonest. Out."

"Alpha 6, Charlie 6, this is Bravo 6."

"This is the Gator. Go."

"Charlie 6."

"Bull here. We've got a little activity going on here in town which just might delay your return a bit. You need to lie low out there for awhile until we take care of it. Do not approach the intersection or village until I give you the word. Stay at least one click out. I don't know what we've got here yet. Over."

"Gator. Roger, we'll wait. If you need help, let us know."

"Roger, Gator. I'll let you know if I need you. Charlie 6, you roger?"

"Charlie 6 roger. We'll be standing by."

"Bravo 6 out. Break. Falcon 3, Bravo 6."

"Falcon 3. Be advised Little Bear is on the way and

should be over you in zero-five. I am trying to get another light fire team up, too."

"Roger, sounds good. Okay, here's what we have so far. We have eighty-deuces coming into the compound. It sounds like at least three tubes firing. We also have AK and machine gun fire being directed down into the compound from rooftops to the south and west and from the school building to the north. We're getting RPG fire against the eastern wall from the vicinity of the NPFF building. I have the perimeter wall completely manned with Bravo personnel. We are returning fire. If this keeps up much longer, we will need an ammo resupply. I'll find out what they have here, but since they mostly use thirty caliber, I don't expect much. Will keep you advised. Over."

"Roger, Bravo 6. What seems to be the enemy's purpose?"

"First, I don't think they knew we were here, since we came in when it was almost dark and with no lights. I think they are coming back to finish what they started the other night."

"Okay, that's our guess, too. Let me know what happens. Out."

I turned to see Major McWhorter walking to the entrance. He was wearing his helmet and flak vest—and his trusty rusty .45 pistol. He looked real combat ready— except that he was still smoking that pipe. Just as he reached the spot where I was standing, the whole TOC suddenly shook with a deafening *Ka-Boom*! Everybody hit the floor. We had taken a direct hit on the TOC by an 82mm mortar round. We lay there a minute or so, then started getting up slowly. We dusted ourselves off and returned to our duty stations.

As McWhorter dragged himself upright, I noticed that his pipe had gone out. He dusted himself off. "Boy, that was a close one! Bob, I wanted to say that I'm certainly glad you and your men are on our perimeter right now. I wouldn't want to go through again what we went through the other night."

"Well, unfortunately, Major, as long as you rely on these Ruff-Puffs, that possibility will continue to exist. They don't give you any kind of a personal bodyguard?"

"No. I don't think they have anyone they trust enough to do that."

"By the way, have you got any 5.56 or 7.62 ammo? Or M-79 rounds?"

"Sure do. We stock for contingencies in case something strange and wonderful happens—like we get modern weapons or something."

"Okay, I'll need access to that ammo if this keeps up. Please arrange it."

"Can do. Just let me know when you want it."

Just then the battalion radio crackled, "Falcon Bravo 6, this is Little Bear."

"Little Bear, Bravo 6. Great to hear you. What have you got on board?"

"We are a light fire team, and we have rockets and miniguns. Wowee! From up here, it looks like the Fourth of July down there!"

"Yeah, welcome to the celebration. Okay, here's what I need. We are taking mortars here. Can you locate the tubes from there?"

"Roger, Bravo 6. We see three tubes working. Funny thing is, they're in a clearing that is only about three hundred meters from the front gate of Cu Chi base camp."

"Okay, first thing, close them down and get those mortars off us."

"Roger. Rolling out now."

"Bravo 6 out."

I looked through the smokey pall and made out the faintly blinking running lights of the two passing helicopters. As they passed overhead, they assumed their angle of attack and unleashed their rockets. They made three rocket passes and two minigun passes. There were no more incoming mortar rounds.

"Bravo 6, Little Bear. Think we took those boys out. Only flashes we see down there now are exploding ammo. We've fully expended, so we're going back to re-arm. Then we'll be back to help you."

"Roger, Little Bear. We're not getting any more mortars now. Looks like you did a good job. We're still getting a lot of automatic fire and RPGs. Look forward to your return."

"Roger. Thanks. We'll be back."

"Bravo 6 out."

Just as I was handing the mike back to MacKenzie, it squawked again. "Falcon Bravo 6, this is Black Widow."

"Black Widow, Bravo 6."

"We're a light fire team up here to give you a hand."

"Roger, Black Widow. Can you make out the compound?"

"It's pretty smokey down there."

"Okay, it's on the northwest corner of the intersection of Highway 1 and the road to the front gate of the base camp. There are a few dim lights around the perimeter and a flagpole in the center with an RVN flag on it."

"Okay, Bravo 6. I can faintly make out the perimeter wall, but I do see the flagpole and the intersection."

"Roger. Tell me what activity you see outside the compound."

"I see massive weapons flashes from the buildings across the street from the compound on the south and east. I see other flashes to the northwest coming from some large building."

"Yeah, that's the school. I want you to engage the targets in the buildings to the south of the compound."

"Roger. Do we have clearance to fire in the village?"

"Stand by."

I turned to McWhorter across the room. "Major, do we have clearance to use gunship fire in Cu Chi City?"

He glanced toward the District Chief, who nodded. "Roger, the village is yours."

"Roger, Black Widow. We have clearance for the whole village. Go get 'em!"

"Roger. We'll be coming in west to east. Stand by."

"Roger. Standing by. Out."

"Bravo 6, 1-6."

"6. Go."

"1-6. An RPG from across the street just blew open the front gate. Also be advised that dinks are inside the NPFF bunker. They can shoot directly into the compound from there."

"Roger. I want you to reinforce the bunker next to the gate and make sure nobody gets through it. Are there any LAWs in those bunkers?"

"Negative."

"Okay, try to drop some M-79 rounds in the apertures of that bunker. Try to pin them down in there. Put an M-60 on it, too."

"1-6 roger."

"Bravo 6 out. Break. 2-6, 6."

"2-6."

"Reinforce that bunker next to the front gate which is now standing open. I don't want anybody coming in there."

"2-6 roger."

"6 out."

I turned to McWhorter. "Major, do you have any LAWs?"

"Affirmative. We have a few."

"I need them."

"We'll get them up here."

Back to the radio: "1-6, 2-6, Bravo 6. Send a runner to the TOC for LAW's. 1-6, use a couple of them against that NPFF bunker and let me know what happens."

"1-6 roger."

2-6 roger."

A few minutes later, one of McWhorter's sergeants brought about a dozen LAWs to the front of the TOC, just as the runners arrived. I gave them each six.

I leaned against the TOC door, listening to the bursts of fire going back and forth across the streets. I listened to the bullets rattling around inside the compound. I listened to the numerous explosions caused by Black Widow's rockets. Those two birds were really hosing down those small buildings over there. Most were on fire, and there was a noticeable reduction in incoming fire from that side of the street. That had been the origin of most of the fire coming inside the compound, because those buildings—housing mostly small shops and stores—were closer and taller than the ones on the east. (As a passing thought, I wondered how the trucks outside the wall were holding up to all that fire. The drivers were inside the compound with us.) The incoming fire from the school building in the rear was less intense because the building was considerably farther away.

—or so I had thought.

I looked up as Lieutenant Constantino stumbled into the TOC. "Jim, what the hell are you doing here? I told everybody to stay in the bunkers."

"Yessir, but we need ammo. Also, I wanted to tell you that I have two wounded. Not very serious, but I set up an aid station with my medic in my rightmost bunker."

"How the hell did they get shot?"

"I was redistributing my men between bunkers, and a couple strayed a little too far from the protection of the wall. They were shot from the school."

"That's real great. I kind of hoped that people would do what I told them to do so nobody would get hurt. Guess I must have been dreaming. Okay, the ammo is over there. Get what you need and get back in that bunker."

"I can drop some off to the other platoon on my way back."

"What's the matter with you? You have a death wish or something? Okay, do that. I guess it's better getting you killed than three others. But don't expose yourself any more than you have to. And next time, delegate this little chore to someone else. My platoon leaders are not runners or ammo bearers. Understand?"

"Yessir." He grabbed several ammo cans and took off.

I glanced over at McWhorter, who had observed all this with a bemused look on his face. I took a long swig from my canteen and said, "You know, that guy is two left feet and four thumbs at any normal time, but get in a fire fight, and I can't keep the son of a bitch down. He runs around everywhere, moving men, distributing supplies, pulling out wounded, and so on. I don't know whether he's trying to prove something or not, but he'll be mighty lucky to make it out of here without getting his ass blown off."

Suddenly, I heard a big *Ka-Boom*! and saw a large fireball shoot up from beyond the burning row of stores.

"What the hell was that?" I asked McWhorter.

"The VC or the rockets or somebody just blew up the Esso station." That was the only gas station in the Cu Chi vicinity. I could see the flicker and glow of a major fire raging in that direction. The breeze was carrying the fire from the burning stores back in that direction as well.

"Falcon Bravo 6, Black Widow."

"Bravo 6."

"We've expended on the area to your south. Don't see very many flashes coming from that area now, but there sure is a lot of smoke."

"Yeah, looks like we're burning out Cu Chi South. Thanks for your help. Will you be able to return?"

"Roger, as soon as we get some more gas and bullets. We'll be around as long as you need us."

"Okay, we'll leave the light on for you."

"Falcon Bravo 6, Little Bear. We're back."

"Roger, Little Bear. Glad to see you back. The main fire against us now is from the area east of us, to the east of Highway 1. I am particularly interested in that big building on the corner. That's NPFF Headquarters with a bunker right across the intersection from our gate. You have your bearings?"

"Roger, we can see enough to tell where the building is. Can't see any bunker, though."

"I didn't think you could. Just aim a few at the corner of the building nearest the intersection. The whole area east of Highway 1 is yours. I'd certainly appreciate it if you would turn off those weapons flashes."

"Roger, we'll see what we can do. We'll be coming in north to south. Little Bear out."

I listened to the choppers roll in on their first pass. *Whoosh! Whoosh! Whoosh!* Three rocket salvos plowed in the row of stores to the east. The bird turned as the second one rolled into attack angle. *Whoosh! Whoosh! Whoosh!* The northwest corner of the NPFF building disintegrated into one big cloud of dust and debris, propelling pieces of masonry across the road toward the open gate.

"Bravo 6, 1-6."

"Bravo 6."

"1-6. Believe it or not, two of those rockets just took out the bunker. Blew the top right off. We'll keep an eye on it for movement, but I don't think we'll see much else there."

"Bravo 6, roger."

Flames now lit up the sky to the east of the compound. Since most of Cu Chi City was to our east and south, it appeared to me that most of the village was on fire. A few minutes later, Little Bear came up on the radio: "Bravo 6, Little Bear. We've expended in that area. How's the fire situation? We don't see many flashes anymore, but it's hard to see through the smoke."

"Bravo 6. Except for a few snipers in those trees behind those stores, most of the firing has died down. Our remaining problem is the school building in the rear. You guys did a good job. Coming back for more?"

"Roger, thanks. We'll be back shortly. Out."

"Falcon Bravo 6, Black Widow. We've replenished and have returned. What's next?"

"Looks like the village to our south and east is pretty

well cleaned out, but we still have some in the school building to the rear. How about trying to level that damn place?"

"Roger. We'll see what we can do."

Over the next twenty minutes, Black Widow methodically reduced the school building to a burning hulk of ghostly masonry walls, roofless—and empty. No more fire from there!

"Bravo 6, Black Widow. We've expended our rocket load, but we still have miniguns. Any use for those?"

"Affirmative. We're still getting some sniper fire from the treeline to the east, just behind the burning buildings. How about hosing them down for us? Be advised that Falcon Alpha and Charlie are out in that direction somewhere, but they're not very close. So approach from the north or south and stay in the treeline."

"Black Widow roger."

Black Widow made two minigun passes, saturating the treeline with a shower of bullets as thick as an afternoon monsoon rain. That should have taken care of the last vestiges of the VC attack.

"Black Widow, Bravo 6. I think that takes pretty good care of most of our problems. I appreciate your help. If we need you to come back tonight, we'll notify you through Falcon 3. Over."

"Roger, Bravo 6. Glad to oblige. Call anytime. Black Widow out."

"Falcon 3, Bravo 6."

"Falcon 3."

"Bravo 6. The firing seems to have stopped. I think they have decided that discretion is the better part of valor and un-assed the AO. Request you notify Little Bear that we won't need him to return at this time."

"Falcon 3. Roger. Be advised that Falcon 6 is present and has monitored your action."

"Bravo 6. Roger. We're going to wait a bit before calling in Alpha and Charlie to make sure this is over and to

see if the trucks still work. Will advise when we're ready
for them."

"Falcon 3. Roger. Anything else?"

"Bravo 6. Negative at this time. Out."

I turned to McWhorter. "Major, as soon as I'm sure
they have left the area, I'll call in the other two companies
and get back to base camp. I'll leave the security sweep
to your people. I'd sure appreciate knowing a body count
if you find anything out there. Judging by the volume of
incoming fire, I would say you had at least one company
and maybe more coming after you. Between the fire and
them taking their dead with them, I doubt you'll find anything, but let our TOC know if you do."

"Wilco. We'll go out at first light. One of my people
will go with them to keep 'em honest."

"Good." I turned to Atkinson. "Tell 1-6 to come to my
location."

A couple minutes later, Lieutenant Monroe walked up
to the TOC entrance. "Sam, take a couple of guys for
security and check out the trucks. Take the drivers with
you. Find out how badly damaged they are. Make sure
there are no satchel charges or other booby traps under or
around them. Make it quick and let me know what you
find."

He nodded and off he went.

I picked up the Battalion push. "Alpha 6, Charlie 6,
this is Bravo 6. Did you monitor my last with 3?"

"Alphagator roger."

"Charlie roger."

"Okay, I'll call you when we're ready to meet you.
Out."

Fifteen minutes later, Monroe returned. "Sir, you won't
believe it, but the only damage to the trucks is two flat
tires, and both of those are on rear duals. That means they
can all move out as they are. We didn't find any explo-
sives, either. It doesn't look like anybody crossed the road
at all."

"Okay, thanks, Sam. When you go back up there, tell the

drivers to turn them around while we are waiting for the other companies. Tell them to be careful. I don't want them hitting any duds. When the troops load up, I want to head out quickly. After they turn the trucks around, have them line up again next to the compound." I turned to Atkinson: "Get the other platoon leaders up here."

My orders to the platoon leaders were to move back to their security positions near the road junction, making sure they were careful not to set off any duds or booby traps that may have been left out there. Once the other two companies passed through, they were to follow them back.

As they left the TOC, I glanced at my watch. 0135. This was really going to be a long day and a short night.

I picked up the battalion mike. "Alpha 6, Charlie 6, Bravo 6. Come on in. Be advised that, as you approach the village, you should run into my elements, so don't shoot 'em up."

"This is the Gator. We're on our way."

"Charlie 6. Roger."

"Bravo 6 out."

By 0230, all companies had closed, been loaded on the trucks and were passing through the front gate of the base camp. The ride back had been a little hairy, since we expected the enemy to try to ambush us going back, but nothing materialized. Maybe they had had enough for one night. I know I had. We breathed a collective sigh of relief as we rumbled back to the Wolfhound area. As the troops unloaded and headed for the hooches, Chancey, Boyle, and I headed to the TOC for the next day's mission orders, and I had to make a final report of our little live fire defensive exercise.

As we ambled into the TOC, we immediately noticed a frazzled-looking stranger sitting with Major Davis at the table next to the bank of radios. As he realized who we were, he leaned over and said something to Davis that we couldn't hear.

Davis motioned us over. "Come on over, guys, and meet Falcon 6."

We approached the table. "Colonel Fulton, here are three of your line company commanders, Captain Chancey, Captain Hemphill, and Lieutenant Boyle." We all shook hands with him. I looked at him closely. He was slender like Harrold, but he had a more tanned complexion with a receding hairline and a somewhat slouched posture. Harrold had a very white complexion with freckles, a thick crew-cut, and stood ramrod straight. Besides appearance, I wondered how else they differed. I guessed that we would find out very soon.

"Glad to meet all of you. I know we are all going to fit together very well, and I look forward to working with each one of you. Captain Hemphill, I have spent the last five hours listening to your action in Cu Chi. That was the damnedest thing I ever heard. That was a hell of a fine operation!"

"Thanks, sir, but I know either of these guys could have done the same thing. The important thing is that we stopped the enemy from doing something he badly wanted to, and we didn't get anybody killed or seriously wounded doing it."

"That's fine, Captain. How many of them did you get?"

"I don't know, Colonel. We didn't take the time to look around. We couldn't get to much of the area anyway 'til the fire dies down. The District Advisor, Major Mc-Whorter, will send out a patrol at first light to see what is out there. I doubt they'll find much, though, given the intensity of the fire and the fact that the VC like to take their dead home with them. Probably so they can screw up our body count."

"Who made that decision?" Fulton frowned. Oh, hell, I thought, I hope we don't have another rabid body counter on our hands.

I looked him right in the eye. "I did. I'm not about to run my people around that mess in the dark. Also, I fig-

ured you wanted your three companies back in here sometime before tomorrow morning."

He glanced at the other commanders. Chancey looked
at him and offered: "Yessir, I would have done the same
thing."

"Okay. Well, it's good to meet you guys. I think Major
Davis has your orders for tomorrow." He checked his
watch. "It's 0300. Tomorrow will come early. I think I'll
hit the sack. See you tomorrow."

He waved to his driver and left the TOC. We walked
over to Davis, went over his map and our missions, and
headed to the BOQ to get a little rest.

We did not know it at the time, but Chancey and I had
just established the basis of our relationship with Lieutenant Colonel Fulton. He proved to be a battalion commander who over-controlled and micro-managed his other
company commanders, many of whom would be first lieutenants, but Herb and I were generally left alone to command our companies as we saw fit. I think we developed
a mutual respect for each other on that basis.

Later, as I lay on the bunk, thinking back over the
day's activities, I had mixed emotions. We had gone from
being unprepared to full combat in one day. We had gone
out on a baby-sitting mission and ended up being the main
attraction. Bravo company had once again proved its met-
tle after having had to sit out much of the first week of
the TET offensive. But most of all, that night will be long
remembered as the night we burned Cu Chi City.

CHAPTER EIGHT

TET: WEEK TWO

The second week of the TET offensive started out with a bang—or lots of bangs—mostly left over from the *first* week of TET. At the beginning of the week, we thought all was going just fine for us and our side. We had met the enemy several times, but I don't believe he was very appreciative of our hospitality. We were able to serve him some pretty hot stuff, but he didn't much like the tang. By the end of the week, we had discovered Ap Cho.

On the 7th of February, we received the mission to sweep the village of Tan Phu Trung, where we had run into the VC in the bunkered basement of the large building six days before. This time we would do it without messing with cowardly tankers from the Land of Oz. We were to start in the north and sweep to the southern edge of the village.

From our previous operation, we recalled that Tan Phu Trung was a long, narrow village bordering the west side of Highway 1 south of Cù Chi City. The village was only about three hundred meters wide and stretched three clicks along the road. The hooches were interspersed with quite a few trees, and, across the road, the southern portion of the wooded area stretched down from Cu Chi City. The village had a berm around its perimeter which stood about three feet high on the inside, with the outside wall sloping at least fifteen feet. About four hundred meters south of the village boundary was the village of Ap Cho, where we had been tied up reacting to the ARVNs on the first day of Tet. Ap Cho straddled Highway 1, with most of the village east of the road, and measured about one click square.

On the previous day, the Falcon battalion had moved the line companies and a jump CP (primarily a TOC) out of Cu Chi base camp and into a perimeter position about one-and-a-half clicks west of Tan Phu Trung in the middle of an extensive, dry rice paddy area. The nearest vegetation or terrain feature in sight of the perimeter was the village itself. We could see anybody or anything approaching us at several clicks' distance in all directions. Our new location allowed us to work the two villages without having to travel an hour or two back and forth to the base camp. That was important, because the biggest threats to Cu Chi District at that moment were the VC/NVA unit or units in those two villages. Presumably because of the chaotic situation country-wide, we had no intelligence whatsoever concerning the estimated size of this force, but they were, obviously, the ones who had tried twice to take the District Compound, including the night when we were there. We were also in a position to respond to other areas should we be required to do so.

At 0800 hours, we lined up in our movement formation inside the perimeter and were just about ready to move, when Lieutenant Gormley hurried up to me.

"What is it, Art?"

"Sergeant McCracken is a little nervous in the service today. He is refusing to go out and wants the day off. Says he has a bad feeling about today." (McCracken is an alias.)

"Send him to me. Keep this quiet. I don't want this idea to spread."

"Yessir." He hurried off.

I turned to Atkinson. "Tell 1-6 on point to start moving. Then tell 2-6 to give 1-6 three hundred meters and then he can move out."

I glanced over toward third platoon and saw Sergeant McCracken walking toward me with a dark expression on his face. I could see that he was worried and scared.

"Sergeant McCracken reporting as ordered, sir." He saluted smartly. I returned it.

"What's the matter, Sergeant?"

"I am not going out today, sir. No way I'm going out there!"

"Here, walk with me a minute or so, Sergeant Mc-Cracken, and tell me what your problem is." I started walking slowly in the direction the company had begun to move. Everyone is afraid at times—if he has any sense at all—and sometimes one lets his fear get the best of him. Given an opportunity to confront that fear, they normally regain control of themselves. If they let that fear get out of hand, and they refuse an order to move out, the result is a General Court-Martial. And I really hate General Courts!

McCracken fell into step beside me, a deeply worried look knotting his brow. I could feel the fear emanating from him. When he spoke, his voice was earnest and measured, and his eyes bore a hole into the ground, although he probably saw nothing. "You know, sir, I had a nightmare last night and woke up sweating bad. Sir, I don't want to refuse to fight. I have been fighting this whole week and ever since I got here, it seems. I did well, too, and made sergeant. But, sir, I know if I go out there today, I won't come back. I'm going to die out there. I don't want to do that."

McCracken did not notice that the company was now moving out through the perimeter toward the village as he talked.

"Believe me, Sergeant, I know exactly how you feel. It's unnatural to walk out there and make ourselves a target. We all are sometimes afraid and have nightmares and premonitions about dying. Most of the time, they don't mean anything. In the end, nothing happens to most of us. We're all afraid. If somebody says they aren't afraid, they're either numb or stupid. Either case, I don't want them around me. They're walking dead men. The way we usually come through this is, we buck up and get control of ourselves. We get control of our fear. We can't let it rule us. We must rule it. Do you understand what I'm trying to tell you?"

"Yessir, but I can't shake this feeling I have. Sir, can't I be given some sort of detail in the perimeter today until I can get over it? I'm sure I'll be alright by tonight. This isn't like me. Can I stay back today, sir?"

"You know that if I make this a matter of record, and you won't go, they'll court-martial you?"

"Yessir, but I don't want that. I'll go before that happens. But I'm really scared today, sir."

"What about your men? You're a squad leader, right?"

"Yessir, but Maddox can handle them for a few hours. He's good with them. Not as good as I am, but he's pretty good." (Maddox is an alias.)

As we walked and talked, the company continued to move. McCracken was not aware of where we were. The point platoon had reached the village. The end of the column was about one click away from the perimeter across the open paddy.

"Okay, Sergeant McCracken, just this one time, I'll let you stay back. But you're going out tomorrow with your men, or I'm going to relieve you and send you back for a court-martial, do you understand?" He nodded. "Report to the battalion S-3 for duty while we're out."

"Yessir! Thank you, sir!" He stopped, saluted and turned to go back. Only then did he notice the great expanse of open area between the company and the perimeter—open area which could be covered by a sniper or gunner from the village. No one in his right mind would go wandering out there alone. His predicament began to dawn on him. He stopped and turned back to where I was still standing.

"But, sir, we're pretty far from the perimeter. Who can I take back with me for security?"

"I'm sorry, Sergeant, but we have a mission to do. I can't spare any one to take you back. You'll just have to go back on your own."

"Damn, sir, I can't do that! That's too far to go by

myself. I'd never make it! What will I do?"

"If you don't want to take a chance of getting shot trying to get back to the perimeter, your only other choice is to rejoin your platoon and stay with the company. We're about to get busy here. What's it going to be?"

He cocked his head and looked at me a moment, then looked back at the perimeter in the distance, then back at me. After a long minute, he sighed, squared his shoulders, looked me straight in the eye, and croaked: "Sir, I'll rejoin my squad, if it's all right with you."

"Very good, Sergeant. I knew you would do your duty. Keep your chin up, son. You'll be all right." I hoped . . .

"Thank you, sir." He turned and walked away in the direction of third platoon.

As we moved into the northern end of the village, the platoons spread out in their search sectors, stretching from Highway One on the left to the perimeter berm on the right, and we started moving through on line. Other than the one large building previously mentioned, the remainder of the village consisted of small one-or two-room hooches with masonry walls and tin or thatched roofs.

One thing about operating in Vietnamese villages: there were no inhabitants around. Any time the military approached a village, the people would hit the roads and vacate the area. I do not know where they went, but they were never there. When we would conduct a cordon-and-search of a village, that is why we had to move quietly and completely surround the village before daylight. We wanted the villagers to find the cordon in place when they awoke—and by the end of the standing government curfew.

For the next three hours, we searched the village, moving from hooch to hooch, checking under fireplaces, bedding, furniture, and any other place we could think of, looking for tunnels and hiding places. Generally, all we found were a bunch of deserted hooches.

At around 1100 hours, a supply convoy from Cu Chi passed through, heading for Saigon or Long Binh to pick up supplies for the base camp. I guess they had to keep up the REMFs' supply of Budweiser and Cokes. One of these days, we field grunts will see some of that stuff, instead of the rusty crap that we usually get, I thought to myself. Because of our previous experience with supply convoys around there, we were sure to take good cover as they passed. I also had 1-6, on the left, send a couple of troops out to let them know we were Americans in here. They managed to pass without further incident.

We approached the southern edge of the village without having found anything of tactical importance: a few extra bags of rice, a couple of empty hiding places, etc., but no tunnels, underground bunkers, or VC.

Suddenly, all hell broke loose!

Sniper rounds ricocheted all around us and echoed throughout the company area.

"Take cover!" I bellowed, diving into a hooch, followed closely by my RTOs. As I poked my head around the masonry wall, I noticed that everyone had been way ahead of me in taking cover. As I tried to assess the situation, I determined that we were receiving sniper fire from about four different locations. There were at least two firing from the trees across the road, one from directly to the east across from us and one from a position to the north. There appeared to be two different snipers firing from the trees behind us, near the road. They must have slipped across the road after we passed. I was pretty certain all were up in trees.

I grabbed the company push. "Falcon Bravo, Falcon Bravo, this is Bravo 6. Make sure everyone is behind cover. Return fire only if you can determine where the fire is coming from or if you have a definite target. I don't want people wasting ammo just spraying the trees. Roger in turn."

All platoon leaders roger'd. I heard a few bursts of fire, but, generally, there was little return fire, although the snipers continued to fire at targets throughout the company. There is a reason for that. All that stuff you see in

Hollywood movies about blasting snipers out of trees is not likely to happen in real combat. You can determine the general direction from which a sniper is shooting, but it is extremely difficult to pinpoint his position, unless, of course, you are standing directly under him. The best tactic in a case like that was to get out of the snipers' target area.

With that in mind, I looked around our location to see whether or not there was a reasonable way out. The company was spread out all across the southern end of the village. Except for the side along the highway, the rest of this portion of the village was surrounded by the berm. I studied the southwest corner of the berm. I was located in the next-to-the-last hooch from that corner, which would have to be our way out. It would be about a fifteen-meter dash from the last hooch to the berm. I hoped they were good at speed diving.

I picked up the battalion handset. "Falcon 3, Bravo 6. Sitrep. Over."

"Falcon 3. Go ahead."

"Bravo 6. We've reached the southern end of the village and are now receiving sniper fire from at least four sniper positions. Because of their locations, we've got no real targets for return fire or for indirect fire support. However, since I have no Foxtrot Oscar out here, request you have your Foxtrot Sierra Charlie plot some arty fire on the other side of the highway. As far as I know, there is no village over there except Ap Cho to the south. The fire should be plotted from across from the southern end of this village to five hundred meters north of that line, along the highway. Let's see if we can knock a couple of them out of their tree. Meanwhile, I'm going to try to get us out of here. I'll get back to you if I need any help. Over."

"Falcon 3. Roger copy. We'll be standing by. We'll plot the fire mission ASAP. Anything else?"

"Negative. Bravo 6 out."

I turned to the two RTOs. "I want us in that hooch over there, now!" I pointed to the one nearest the corner.

"I'll go first, then you follow one at a time, ten seconds apart." I stood up and stuck my head out. Nothing was coming in from that direction at the moment. I crouched and ran for the left side of the hooch, getting around the corner just as two AK rounds smashed into the masonry. That wasn't even close; they missed by a good six inches, I breathed with a sigh of relief. I scooted around and into the hooch just as Atkinson came tumbling in, followed by the *pop-pop-pop* of AK fire flying over the hooch. He looked up at me and grinned. I gave him the thumbs-up. "Fun, ain't it?" He nodded. Then MacKenzie slid in, punctuated by the AKs.

Across the highway, I could hear the artillery begin to arrive, crashing in among the trees. That should disturb their sight picture a bit.

"Okay, fellows, we're staying here for awhile. Make yourselves at home. Give me the company push."

Atkinson passed it over. "Falcon Bravo, Falcon Bravo. Respond in turn with your initials." I was always mindful of security.

They all logged in properly.

"Bravo 6. Okay, this is the plan. The only thing to do with this many snipers is un-ass the AO. So here's how we're going to do it. I'm located in the hooch nearest the southwest corner of the berm. We're going over it, and we're going to do it one or two at a time, at my command only. We'll launch from the hooch I'm in and the one five meters to the right of it, where I can see it. We'll start with 3-6 since he's closest, then 2-6, 4-6 and 1-6 last. As the element in front of you vacates a hooch, I want you to move up and occupy it, until you reach the two here that I'm controlling. Do you roger so far?"

All roger'd.

"As your element approaches this location, I want you personally in the hooch directly behind this one to control movement into these last two hooches. At no time will you move more than two men at a time within your element, and alternate them side to side. I can take up to five at a time in each hooch. When they reach these hooches, I'll tell them what to do then. Just get them here without getting shot! But keep 'em coming. I don't want this to take all day. Those bad boys might catch on after awhile. Do you roger the concept?"

All roger'd in turn. I could imagine what they were thinking about then.

"Okay, we start now. 3-6, move in behind me now, and start moving people into these hooches. Out."

Besides me and my RTOs, there two other men in the hooch where I was and three in the next hooch.

"Okay, guys," I addressed both hooches. "Here's what I want you to do. Get on the left and right of this hooch, and on the left of that hooch over there, where you can see me. When I point at you, I want you to get up and run like hell to that berm over there and *dive* over it, and I mean *dive!* Don't worry about the other side. It slopes about fifteen feet down. Hit it and roll down to the bottom. It's a helluva lot better getting skinned up a little rolling down a hill than getting a bullet up your ass! Do you understand?"

They all nodded. "When you get to the bottom of the berm, make sure you have all your gear, and then move quickly out of the way, because other guys will be coming right after you. Move down to the right, but make sure you hug the berm for cover. Make sure the others come join you when they come over. Okay? Now when I point at you, run like hell and don't hesitate at the berm. And don't look back! Okay, now, get ready."

I pointed to the guy in the other hooch on the right. "Go!" He took off and dove over the berm, leaving a staccato of AK rounds kicking up dust along the top of the berm.

I pointed to the left. "Go!" He also made it over before the bullets came flying over the berm.

I pointed to the middle and the right at the same time. "Go!" Both made it over. The AK was a bit late, meaning that I probably confused him by sending two targets at the same time.

It took about forty-five minutes to get the whole company over the berm. In spite of the artillery, we continued to get sniper fire, but I noticed a lessened volume of fire which seemed to come mostly from our side of the road. I alternated the men as best I could, pointing right, then left, then right and center together, then left, then all three together, and so on. As each platoon leader came into the hooch, I gave directions concerning where to assemble the platoons on the other side of the berm and where to set up security. As the exercise proceeded, I had that dreaded feeling that those snipers would get smart, eventually, and start sighting directly on the berm, but I guess they never did. Maybe I fooled them just enough by alternating the guys. Whatever the reason, not one of my men was hit going over the berm.

Then it was our turn. Only I and my RTOs were left. "Okay, guys, be swift, but don't break the radios. Go!" They made it over.

"Last chance, you dumb son of a bitch," I breathed. Then it was up, run as fast as I could, over, rolling, rolling, rolling . . . *Pop-pop-pop*! *Pop-pop-pop*! I thought I would never stop rolling, but, finally, I hit the paddy with a thud. I stood up, checking for bullet holes and finding none. "That was interesting," I muttered to no one in particular. I walked over to the RTOs and checked the radios, which were okay.

"Atkinson, go tell the platoon leaders to come over here." I picked up the battalion push.

"Falcon 3, Bravo 6. Sitrep."

"Falcon 3."

"Bravo 6. We're now located outside the berm. You won't believe how we did it, but we did, and without anybody getting hit. Judging by the volume of sniper fire as we evacuated the village, I think the Redlegs were effective across the road. Most of the fire at the end sounded like it came from this side of the road. We had completed our sweep when the sniper fire started. There is nothing significant in this village. I'm sure the snipers will slip away just as they slipped in."

"Okay, Bravo 6. Come on home. We'll check out those woods another day."

"Roger. Out."

I turned around to face the platoon leaders. "Everybody okay?" They nodded. "Where's 2-6?" I looked over toward second platoon. I saw Lieutenant Lorne sitting on the side of the berm without his helmet.

"Wait here."

I walked over to where Lorne sat. As I walked up, I saw that he was flushed and shaking, and seemed to be in a daze.

"What's the matter, Lieutenant?"

"I . . . I l-lost my glasses," he stammered without looking up. I looked closely at him. Here was a guy who was scared to death. He was mighty pale, his skin was clammy, and he was shaking with fear. Although he was new in country—he had replaced Lieutenant Wilder after the January 15th fight when Wilder had gone to battalion—and had just gone through a pretty harrowing experience, there was no excuse for a troop leader to show such fear and to lose control of himself like this in front of the men. I suspected that he had either thrown away his glasses or ground them into the dirt somewhere on the side of the berm, which, if true, was an act of cowardice.

"Where did you lose them? Have you looked for them?" If I could prove that he threw them away, I would court-martial his young ass.

"I . . . I think I lost them when I came over the berm," he mumbled.

"You think? Don't you know when you first noticed you couldn't see? Come on, Lieutenant, act like an officer! Your men are watching you." My voice had turned cold and steely. This man was totally useless. I had to get him out of there.

I turned to the platoon sergeant. "Sergeant Hughes, I

want you to take command of this platoon for now. Send a squad back over there where we came over the berm and see if they can find the lieutenant's glasses. You've got ten minutes. Let me know what you find. Questions?"

"Nossir. On the way." He turned, grabbed the nearest squad leader, gave him rapid instructions and sent him and his squad on the way.

I motioned to the lieutenant and the platoon sergeant. "Come with me." I turned and walked back to where the other platoon leaders stood.

"Lieutenant, go sit over there on that berm 'til we're ready to move out. You'll stay with the company CP 'til we get back to the perimeter. Sergeant Hughes, join the meeting."

I faced the platoon leaders. "Okay, let's go home. Order of march is as you stand. 3-6, take point, followed by 2-6, 4-6 and 1-6. 1-6, I'm particularly interested in you making sure that none of those bad boys follow us or take shots at us as we move out across the paddy in the open. Mount a rear guard. We move out in fifteen minutes. Questions? Okay, get 'em ready."

As I suspected, the squad found no glasses. We moved back to the perimeter without further incident. I motioned for Lieutenant Lorne to follow me, and I walked over to the TOC.

"Well, that was an attention-getter," I drawled as I entered the TOC. I left Lorne cooling his heels outside.

Major Davis looked up, a grin playing along the corners of his mouth. "I'd like to hear how you pulled that one off—especially without getting anyone hurt."

Lieutenant Colonel Fulton, coming out from behind a curtain which separated his field desk from the rest of the TOC, spoke up: "Yeah, so would I." Then he noticed the frown on my face, which did not fit in with their lighter mood.

I began slowly. "Nobody hurt by bullets, but I have a lieutenant outside I want sent back to the rear by earliest available means. He needs to replace his glasses. I don't want him back, and I don't want to see him in the area when we get back there. He froze up on me in front of his platoon. I suspect he threw his glasses away, but I can't prove it. If I could, I'd draw up charges. I don't want him getting a CIB, either. He's no infantryman, combat or otherwise."

Davis frowned. "Okay, we'll get him out tonight. I'll pass your comments back to Falcon 1. He should be able to reassign him out of the battalion right away. Now get on with the story!"

"Okay, keep your shirt on. As far as the village is concerned, it's been deserted ever since we started operating there. We swept the whole damn thing and found nothing significant. But as we got to the southern end of it, at least four or five snipers opened up on us from the trees behind us and from across the highway. They must have slipped in behind us after we swept the area. We found no tunnels or any kind of hiding places. I think they came out of the trees on the other side, maybe from that unit we ran into last week down at Ap Cho. And maybe the same one we drove out of Cu Chi City. Which I think is the same unit. Maybe they're now dug-in in Ap Cho and operating out of there. It's something to think about. Whatever happened, they were popping AK rounds around us like the Fourth of July! After the arty started, the firing from across the road slowly died out. Now here's what we did. . . . " For the next twenty minutes, I described in detail our exit from Tan Phu Trung.

Fulton leaned back and shook his head. "Good job, Bob. No wonder Lorne froze up. That probably scared the hell out of most of them."

"Scared them, yes, but it didn't stop them. The bottom line is, they did what I told them and it worked. They did fine. Lorne couldn't take it and he flipped out. I hope we don't have to do that again anytime soon!"

Davis stood up. "So do I. By the way, your comments about Ap Cho are interesting. Somebody else agrees with you, it seems. Tomorrow, we start operating against the hamlet. There's been too much going on in this area, and that seems to be the logical starting point, since that is where we found the most resistance. It could be a good base for operating against Cu Chi. The only problem is, we don't know what might be in there. So tomorrow, we're sending Alpha and Charlie in there to check it out. I want you to go back and check out that wooded area across the road from Tan Phu Trung where the snipers were. A small paddy area separates the northern end of Ap Cho from the woods. Start there and move north, guiding on the highway. If your theory is correct and you find something in there, you may end up cutting them off from their base at Ap Cho. The northern limit of your advance is across from the northern end of Tan Phu Trung. Your only available support is artillery. All the gunships are dedicated to Cu Chi base camp defense, whatever that means. We might be able to get something up if you have major contact. As for Tac air, we would play hell trying to get some of that. Seems all the air is committed to protecting all the Saigon warriors, especially all those other Air Force weenies at Ton Son Nhut. Our request for an air strike in Ap Cho tomorrow was denied. They said if we had contact, we could try again. So be sure to take your FO with you. We will have priority of fire from Killer tomorrow, just in case our suspicions are correct. We'll have a supply bird in later today. They'll be bringing what your field first called in this morning. Your LD time is 0800 hours. Any questions?"

I shook my head. "No questions. One thing: when you talk to Falcon 1, tell him I need another lieutenant as soon as he can scare one up."

"Okay, but considering what's going on, they may be in short supply."

"Understand." I turned and walked out of the TOC.

I walked over to where Lorne was still standing. "They'll get you back to the rear as soon as they can. Go back to the company area and get your gear and report back here. When you get to the rear, report to the S-1 for

further instructions. Clear? Then get going." He trotted
off toward the second platoon's area. I watched him for
few moments and then turned away, shaking my head,
mumbling to myself: "Poor, dumb bastard. He shouldn't
even be here. Doesn't have th' stuff for an infantryman.
Maybe they'll make him an AG officer or something for
the rest of his time in the Army. Just don't send him back
to the field again. He'll either get somebody killed or get
himself killed. Helluva thing . . ."

The next day, we swept the woods almost all the way
up to Cu Chi City but found nothing of interest except a
lot of trees. There were no signs of caches, bunkers, or
other indications of a base camp of any type. That meant
that our visitors the day before came from elsewhere. This
fact, coupled with the stiff contact that Alpha and Charlie
had in Ap Cho the same day, reinforced the theory that
whoever was dug-in in Ap Cho was conducting the various actions in that area.

The following day, we drew the Ap Cho mission, along
with Dufus Delta. Referring to my map, I noticed that Ap
Cho was a square-shaped hamlet of hooches with criss-
crossing streets, set astride Highway 1 with most of the
parallel streets—about twelve—lying east of the highway,
and two streets on the western side. From the night TET
started, I remembered that Ap Cho was virtually treeless,
except for a stand of trees to the east just outside the
village berm. Judging by Alpha and Charlie Companies'
action the previous day, the VC appeared to have dug in
near the eastern boundary in the section of the hamlet east
of the highway. They had seen nothing nor met any resistance until they had crossed the highway and at least
two side streets. Then they had emerged into an open area,
about seventy-five meters wide, where hooches had been
cleared out. Once they had stepped out into that open area,
they had received substantial small arms fire from their
front. It was apparent that the VC were firing from a bunker complex and were using the cleared area as a "no-
man's land" killing zone. How effective that killing zone

had been could be attested to by the battered hulk of a
burned-out M-113 armored personnel carrier that rose out
of the middle of the clearing—presumably left there by
fleeing ARVNs, since, as far as I knew, no other American units had been through there since this offensive
started.

The basic plan was for us to follow Delta around the
western edge of the hamlet, turn east along the southern
boundary, cross Highway 1, split up and approach it from
different directions. Delta was to proceed eastward, enter
from the east, and attack in one sector toward the northwest. We were to enter right at Highway 1 and attack
toward the northeast. Using such a pincer movement by
attacking from two directions would allow us to turn the
flanks of the bunker complex one way or the other and
take it out from behind. It sounded good to us anyway.
Falcon 3 had requested air strikes on the village but had
been told that they were only available in case of actual
contact—no matter what we *thought* we knew was in
there. All aircraft were being used to protect Saigon and
other *higher* headquarters. The troops on the ground
would have to get along without them unless significant
contact was certain. *Support the troops!* However, we
were not totally alone out there—if we were lucky, we
might get some artillery support if we *really* needed it!

So, at 0800 hours, we crossed the LD—that is, we left
the perimeter—and, following Delta, walked the click-
and-a-half to Ap Cho. I had first platoon on point. Near
the southwest corner of the village, we held up a few
minutes while Delta executed a secured crossing of the
highway. Once they were across, we moved up so that
my point platoon reached the edge of the highway. Just
as we were about to send out security to begin the
crossing, the battalion radio suddenly blared.

"Falcon Bravo, Falcon Delta, this is Falcon 3."

"Falcon Bravo."

"Falcon Delta."

"Falcon 3. Believe it or not, we have an airstrike com-

ing in. You need to pull back across Highway I and take
cover. FAC should be up in zero-five."

"Bravo 6 roger. We haven't started crossing yet. We'll
give Delta some room."

"Delta 6. Roger. We're turning around now. Over."

"Falcon 3. Okay. I'll have FAC talk directly to Delta
6 to make sure you're out of the target area. Out."

We moved back around the corner of the village and
put out security. Delta moved back across the highway
and took up positions there. For the next forty-five
minutes, we watched as the FAC marked the target with
white phosphorous rockets fired from his Birddog and two
F-4 Phantoms began making repeated passes over the target, releasing their load of five-hundred and two-hundred-
fifty-pound bombs, then spraying the target with twenty
millimeter machine guns. Those silver birds were a plea-
sure to watch, circling overhead and then swooping down
toward the target in a steep dive, pulling up at the last
minute as they released their ordnance a virtual aerial bal-
let, of sorts.

As the aircraft finished the strike, I mused that there
couldn't be much left of the center of beautiful downtown
Ap Cho! Hopefully, there wasn't much left of the bad
boys dug in there.

Monitoring the battalion push, MacKenzie suddenly
turned and handed me the handset. "Captain, you ought
to hear this. It's the FAC talking to the 3." I put the
handset to my ear and heard part of the conversation:

". . . you should know that I saw several people scur-
rying from the village to the trees to the east. Looks like
they were vacating the village as I fired my markers, an-
ticipating the strike. They might try to get back in when
they are sure the fighters are gone."

"Falcon 3. Roger. Do you have a BDA for us?" That
would do us a lot of good, I thought. A Battle Damage
Assessment is merely the FAC's best guess of the damage
his aircraft caused—assuming he could see the ground
through the smoke.

"Roger, Falcon. Looks like we hit the right spots in the middle of that cleared area, but all I see is smoke and dust. Sorry I can't be more specific." At least, he was honest about his limitations.

"Roger, FAC. Thanks for your help. If you have any more birds available, we would welcome a return appearance any time."

"Roger. I'll keep you in mind. FAC out."

"Falcon Bravo, Falcon Delta, this is Falcon 3. Did you monitor FAC?"

"Bravo 6 affirmative. We probably missed them all when they scooted out of the village. Maybe we scared 'em to death."

"Delta 6. Affirmative."

"Falcon 3. Okay, now you need to move on to accomplish your assigned mission. Maybe it will be a little easier now."

We both acknowledged, and Delta re-crossed the road.

As my point platoon leader reached the highway, he suddenly held up his hand and stopped, his men taking a knee facing alternating directions. I thought he was about to send security across, which we did not need to do since Delta had just crossed. I started to move up to jump his ass when I froze in my tracks. To my surprise, an M-113 APC rattled out of the village and turned right and stopped, taking a security position—right beside 1-6! A few seconds later, a second M-113 passed the first one, moved about fifty meters down the highway and took a position facing left. A third took a position beyond these two. As I grabbed my battalion handset, an M-48 tank came rumbling out of the village and proceeded down the road.

"Falcon 3, Bravo 6. What the hell is happening out here?! I have an armored convoy that just came out of the village right in front of me!"

"Bravo 6, Falcon 3. Wait. Out."

As I waited for a return call from the 3, I watched a second tank pass through, followed by a mixture of ar-

mored vehicles and trucks, including gas tankers. I could
not believe this was happening, right in the middle of an
operation.

"Bravo 6, Falcon 3. What we have is a supply convoy
from Cu Chi en route to Saigon for resupply. They are
being escorted by Alpha troop. You may not believe this,
but we've been ordered to secure their passage through
Ap Cho. You need to outpost the village on both sides of
the highway to make sure nobody shoots 'em up or fires
an RPG at them. Do you roger?"

"Bravo 6. Yeah, I roger. Well, there goes the effect of
the airstrike, whatever there might have been. We're moving shortly. Any more good news?"

"Negative. 3 out."

I sent 1-6 across the road with instructions to outpost
the west side of the highway along the second street back,
which should be enough space to keep out the RPGs. 3-
6 was dispatched on the east side one street back.

With the cav's leap-frogging overwatch movements
and the slow-moving trucks and gas tankers, it took one
hour for the convoy to pass through. As the last rear-guard
APC pulled away, I called first and third platoons back to
my location.

"Falcon 3, Bravo 6. Any chance for another airstrike
or some artillery on call?"

"Falcon 3. Negative on the strike. You can try the arty
through your Foxtrot Oscar."

"Roger. What's Delta's situation?"

"Delta is waiting in its attack position until you're
ready to proceed."

"I'm ready." I motioned to 1-6. "We're starting our
crossing now. We should be in attack position in one-zero.
Delta can push off then."

"Roger. I'll pass it on. Out. Break. Delta 6 . . ."

I handed the mike back to MacKenzie and, noticing
that first platoon was already across, motioned the others
to move. 1-6 moved about seventy-five meters beyond the
highway and took up security positions until the company

closed on him. Then we spread out with three platoons on line and the fourth platoon in reserve and started our sweep through the village. As we began moving, I heard pretty intense firing coming from Delta's area. We encountered absolutely nothing until we reached the cleared "no-man's land" area near the middle of the village. It was patently obvious that the VC were not interested in leaving their bunkers and coming out to meet us. They resisted the temptation to try to pick off some of the sofa-sided vehicles in the supply convoy, and they did not try to engage us in the open. That was a definite sign of an experienced and disciplined unit, whatever size the unit was in there.

As we approached the edge of the remaining hooches, we started receiving a few rounds of sixty millimeter mortar fire! It seemed to be coming from within the village! That was a cute trick—considering how small the village was. We moved through the mortar fire unscathed, but as we reached the cleared area, we were greeted with the *pop-pop-pop* of AKs and RPD machine guns. The men on the assault line hit the ground or took cover behind hooch walls and began returning fire. The sound of M-16s and M-60s, punctuated by the *crump! crump*! of M-79 grenades, joined the chorus of lethality. The good thing about the airstrike was that the bombs had created several craters and piles of dirt in the cleared area. I decided to try to employ a little fire-and-maneuver to see how close to the bunkers we could get. I was not about to try a frontal assault and rush the position. Meat-grinders were not my cup of tea.

"Falcon 3, Bravo 6. We have contact. Any chance for another airstrike?"

"Falcon 3. Negative. When Delta made contact, we requested one, but it was denied."

"Bravo 6. What's Delta's status?"

"Delta made no headway against the bunkers. They broke contact and backed out of the no-man's land. They are still nearby in case you need help."

"We'll call if we need them. I'm not sure what they can do. What we really need is armor, but I guess that's not available like everything else."

"Negative."

"Okay. I've got a war to fight. Bravo 6 out."

While second and third platoons concentrated their fire on what appeared to be the bunkers from which the firing was coming, I signaled first platoon to try to work its way closer. As 2-6 and 3-6 poured fire into the objective (whatever it was—I was not really sure what kind of bunker configuration we had there, but it had to be extensive), 1-6 began moving his people forward in short rushes. They made it about one-third of the way across the cleared area when they were pinned down from the bunkers. They then established a base of fire as I moved 3-6 forward. They made it a little farther than 1-6 had, but not by much. I then had 1-6 and 3-6 fire as I moved 2-6, with me along with them. We rushed from mound to crater, from crater to mound, hugging the ground in between as best we could, diving behind the next mound, helmet bouncing off and rolling around, grabbing it and slamming it back on tighter, peeking over the mound, finding the next cover, doing it all over again. Being the platoon in the middle had its definite disadvantages. The fire became fiercer, it became increasingly harder to spot that next cover, and it became difficult to peek out without being perforated by a stream of bullets. Our advance bogged down at about the same point as that of the other two platoons.

I rapidly contemplated our situation. Fourth platoon would do us no good here. We had run out of mounds and craters. There was no way to go farther without unnecessary losses. I knew we already had had several casualties. With us this close and Delta's whereabouts unknown, there was no question of trying to get any kind of fire support. I decided it was time to get the hell out of there!

Over the next thirty minutes, we withdrew slowly back

to the nearest hooches, moving in the reverse order in which we had advanced. As we disappeared out of sight of the bunker complex into the village streets, the firing died out. They made no attempt to mortar us on the way out. I guess that was just their way of greeting us. All casualties were brought out, five all together. The good thing was that no one was killed, in spite of the intensity of the incoming fire.

I reached for the battalion push. "Falcon 3, Bravo 6."

"Falcon 3."

"Bravo 6. We tried to crack this nut, but the shell is too tough at this time. We got almost halfway across the no-man's land, but all elements were pinned down at that point and couldn't get any further without getting shot up. I won't do the Light Brigade trick. We've pulled back to the hooches. Everything's quieted down now. I have five whiskies, two serious. Request Dustoff. I'll set up at the southwest corner of the village and wait for him. If Delta's still waiting, you can tell him to go home. Recommend he return by the northern route. We'll be a little busy blocking the southern edge of the village for the medevac. When we get that done, we'll be ready to return home, too. Over."

"Roger, Bravo 6. Okay, we'll get the Dustoff request in right away. Let me know when you're ready for him. If he gets here early, we'll have him orbit. Then you're clear to return to the perimeter."

"Roger. We should be ready in one-zero to one-five. Out."

I signaled for first platoon to take the point and move out. We re-crossed the highway and halted at the southwest corner of the village. I left third platoon on the east side of the highway as security in the village and along that side of the highway. I did not want those guys in those bunkers to suddenly get reckless and to come out to try to interrupt our medevac. I sent first platoon to screen to portion of the village west of the highway, and second and fourth platoons formed a defensive perimeter.

Just as we finished these preparations, the radio crackled. "Falcon Bravo 6, Dustoff 23."

"Bravo 6. What's your location?"

"We're about three minutes from your location. You can go ahead and pop smoke."

"Roger." I took a smoke from MacKenzie's rucksack, pulled the pin and tossed it into the middle of the perimeter. "Smoke out."

After a few seconds: "Roger. I tally-ho lovely lemon."

"Affirmative yellow. Come on in. Your best approach and departure is from southwest to northeast across the paddy."

"Roger, coming in now."

The helo rolled in and landed. My guys moved the casualties up and loaded them as quickly as they could. I waved and gave the pilot a "thumbs up" salute, and he pulled pitch and skimmed the rice paddy on his way back out. The whole evacuation took less than five minutes. Those Dustoff guys were good!

We left the village at that point and snaked out across the dry paddy, heading directly for the perimeter, which we could see in the distance. As we closed the perimeter, I sent the company back to our sector and then walked into the TOC. I wanted some answers.

"That was the stupidest damn screw-up I've ever seen," I growled to no one in particular as I walked across the tent. I approached Major Davis, who was eyeing me warily, not really sure what I was going to do. "Where in almighty hell did that convoy come from?"

Davis responded. "It was a Cu Chi Base Camp resupply convoy. It was the first time they had attempted to get to Saigon since TET started. The first time they went out last week, they only went to the bridge to the south to get some things from the Third Brigade CP set up down there. It was on the way back from there that they tried to shoot you up, which I'm sure you remember."

"Yeah, I remember. I still owe them one for that. Why the hell didn't we know they were coming so we wouldn't waste an air strike? Doesn't anybody ever talk to anybody in this damn Division?"

"I know how you feel. I didn't know they were coming either. I've already raised hell with Brigade for not letting us know. They said they would let us know next time, but I'm not sure how much time we'll get. I guess anything is better than nothing."

"Well, if they pull this again, I just might shoot up those dumb sons of bitches! It would serve them right for getting my people hurt." I turned and trudged out of the tent. As I left, I heard Davis say to Fulton, "That guy's really pissed off!"

"Don't blame him," Fulton responded.

For the next two days, this same scenario replayed twice. Each day, we would start out with no air support. Each day, we would make contact with the enemy at the same place as the day before. Each day, we would get air strikes after physically making contact. And each day the supply convoy would show up, unannounced, at just the appropriate time to prevent us from taking advantage of the strikes. We continually bitched to First Brigade about the convoys, but it did no good. Either those idiots were totally incompetent to run a battlefield operation, or they were being overruled higher up the line. It seemed that the higher up you went, the less they knew about what went on in the field.

The bottom line was that, by the time we actually made our attack each day, we ran into a brick wall of fire. Because of the delay between the strike and the attack, the enemy had recovered from any ill effects caused by the strike, and was ready for us. We made little progress against those bunkers, but we did manage to get some of our people shot each day. In fact, by the end of the week, Falcon 6 had attached the Battalion Recon Platoon to Bravo Company so we would look

like a company again. Although Bravo lost none killed
during those days, my wounded casualties amounted to
almost half the company, although not all were evacuated. I considered it to have been a waste of valuable
manpower to keep butting our heads against this thing
without effective fire support. I wished that someone
would listen to us about that.

Falcon 6 had listened. Daily, he had gone to the new
First Brigade Commander—who had taken command
the week before TET started—and requested additional
resources. Daily, he was refused. The Brigade Commander's priorities were elsewhere. Wherever they were,
they certainly were not with a combat battalion in contact. After a week of that, however, it became obvious,
even to him, that one shirt-armored, foot-mobile battalion was not likely to make it through that well-prepared
position.

During the afternoon of 11 February, as we returned
to the perimeter, Falcon 3 called the company commanders to the TOC before I went back to our sector of the
perimeter. As we lumbered in and plopped down on the
folding chairs which had been set up, Davis straightened
his notes.

"Okay, I just wanted to let you know that Brigade finally relented and gave us some more resources to help
us crack this nut. We expect to be joined today by Alpha
Troop of the Three-Quarter Horse with their five tanks,
two mech companies from 4th of the 23rd Tomahawks,
two M-113 flamethrowers and one eight-inch howitzer.
We'll have a briefing at 1900 hours with you and the
commanders of the other units. Until then, we will be
trying to figure out how we will use them. That's all I
have."

I wondered briefly how the hell we were going to get
all that stuff inside Ap Cho. When it rains, it pours, but
those droughts are hell. I dismissed the thought. That was
Falcon 3's problem. I returned to the company area.

At 1900 hours, the company commanders and separate

platoon leaders gathered in the TOC for the briefing. We introduced ourselves to the mech company and cavalry troop commanders and took our seats on the folding chairs which had been set up in front of the map.

Major Davis and Colonel Fulton hustled in. Davis stopped by the map board. Fulton approached the podium and introduced himself, Davis, and his commanders. He welcomed the newly-attached commanders and briefly outlined what Davis was going to tell us in detail. When he finished glad-handing the newcomers, Davis took over and outlined the next day's operation. The basic plan was for a three-company attack from northeast to southwest roughly parallel to Highway 1, with a mech company on the left, Falcon Bravo in the center, and Alpha Troop on the right. Bravo would be squeezed out by the armored units about half-way through the enemy position. One flame-thrower track ("Zippo") would be attached to the mech company and one to the cav troop. Two of Alpha's tanks were attached to the mech, and I got one. The other two remained with the cav. The other mech company would form a blocking position to the northeast of the village to prevent the enemy troops from escaping to the woods as they had done when the air strikes had been delivered. Falcon Alpha would form a blocking position to the southeast to prevent escape in that direction. Falcon Charlie would protect the rear of the attack by screening the woods east of Highway 1 and by providing security for the howitzer. Falcon Delta drew the perimeter security mission. The 8-inch howitzer would be used at a minimum range of 750 meters to fire directly into the mouths of bunkers as directed by the FOs of the attacking companies.

I observed Davis with a humorous glint in my eye as he finished his briefing. He must have taken a long time coming up with this plan. It was obvious to me that he had to deal with more units than he really needed, but, after bitching to Brigade for a week for more help, he was not about to turn anything down. It was also obvious he was going to let the armored units bear the brunt of the action—except for us stuck between them. That seemed fair to me. Rolled aluminum armor was somewhat more protective than rip-stop nylon. I wondered how many of them would still be around the next day.

I returned to my sector and briefed my platoon leaders. As they heard the details, they looked around nervously at each other.

"I know you are uneasy about all these RPG magnets around. Just don't get too close to them so you won't get it when they blow up. Get plenty of sleep, gents. Tomorrow's going to be interesting."

At 0700 the next morning, Bravo departed the perimeter en route to Ap Cho. Strung out across the dry, flat, and open rice paddy, we took the most direct route to the northern edge of the village, guiding on the stand of trees near the village's east side, which we could see in the distance. When we arrived, both armored units were in place. The two blocking companies had sneaked into position before daylight. Of course, I was not really sure how a mech company could "sneak" anywhere . . . I radioed to Falcon 3 that we were in position.

Two minutes later, I winced and involuntarily ducked as an 8-inch round came shrieking low overhead and crashed into the middle of the bunker complex ahead.

"Who called that in?" I shouted over the explosion to Bennett.

"The mech," he shouted back.

For the next ten minutes, we watched as 8-inch rounds were walked slowly back and forth across the enemy position. "That should give them a hangover," I muttered to no one in particular.

Then the word came from the S-3: "GO!" That was unusually succinct for Davis, I thought.

The mech and the cav moved out with fifty-cals blazing, pouring fire into the few bunker mouths which we could see from that angle. We were somewhat quieter, firing a few LAWs and M-79s at the bunkers, but I ordered my guys to hold fire with the rifles and M-60s until they had a target or started getting fire and could identify the source. I wanted to conserve ammunition until we needed it—and there was no doubt that we would need it! That had become particularly evident over the previous week or so as we busted our heads daily against this wall—a level of combat experience obviously not enjoyed by the mech and cav units. Of course, maybe that was their only way to ward off the RPGs.

As we emerged from the rubble of hooches and started across the no-man's land, a veritable deluge of automatic and RPG fire poured out of the bunkers toward us. My infantry hit the ground as I felt a sudden surge of heat from my left. Glancing in that direction, I saw two tracks disintegrate into balls of flame, as a broad finger of fiery death spewed forth from the Zippo, flicking back and forth between two bunkers.

I glanced to my right and saw one of Alpha troop's tanks stopped, one of its tracks blown off. It was still firing its ninety millimeter main gun and coaxial machine guns. Suddenly, with a *whoosh!*, an RPG found its mark, hitting the stalled tank just at the base of the turret. As the ammunition inside exploded wildly, the turret was blown off and flew up into the air. It landed twenty meters away, barely missing one of the command tracks. Poor bastards . . .

But I did not have time to think about them right then. My platoons were receiving direct automatic fire and were conducting fire and maneuver, trying to get close to the bunkers. The tank which we had was moving with the second platoon on the left, which allowed it to coordinate its fire and movement not only with the platoon, but also with the tanks with the mech on the left. The infantry moved with the tank, using it as a shield between them and the bunker, but not getting very close to it. RPGs flew around the tank, several glancing off the turret, but none scored a damaging hit.

They moved on, my men firing as they slowly advanced into the hail of bullets.

Due to the intense heavy-caliber fire from the mech and cav across the front, my infantry platoons were getting ever closer to the bunkers. Three more tracks on the left went up, along with one tank. On the right, two of Alpha's ACAV tracks joined the wreckage.

My first platoon came to within twenty meters of the first bunker before being pinned down by fire from within that bunker. Third platoon on its left shifted fire to the bunker to first platoon's front, throwing grenades and firing two LAWs into the mouth of the bunker. The firing from the bunker faltered momentarily, then picked up momentum again, still not allowing first platoon to advance. My tank was about forty meters from the bunker, almost at its flank. I directed his main gun fire against the bunker. As he was firing on that bunker, an RPG from another bunker directly to his front suddenly whizzed by, just barely missing the top of the turret. The tanker quickly rotated his turret, firing his coax into the bunker mouth, moved forward the short distance to the bunker, stuck his main gun almost into the opening, and fired point-blank. As he was doing that, I radioed Lieutenant Constantino, whose fourth platoon was in reserve but very close to the tank's position, to send three men down to clear that bunker. He roger'd.

From my vantage point, I could look directly down on the bunker to my front. I saw three men rushing up to the bunker just as the tanker fired a second round into the opening. The tanker then backed off as he saw the infantrymen arriving. As I watched the three men squat down by the side of the bunker, using it for cover, I suddenly realized that one of them was Lieutenant Constantino himself!

"What the hell is that guy doing there?" I yelled in the general direction of my RTOs. "I didn't mean for the damn platoon leader to go blow that bunker *himself!*" All they could do is shrug and look deeply concerned. "Tell his RTO that I want him here just as soon as this dies down." They nodded.

As I watched the action at the bunker, I saw the first two men stick their M-16s inside the aperture and empty a magazine into the inside of the bunker. Then Constantino pulled the pin on a grenade, swung around to the front of the bunker and reached for the opening with his right hand. Just as he released the grenade, I saw his body suddenly jerk and fall back on the ground, just lying there. It was obvious that he had been shot from the same bunker into which he had just thrown the grenade. The other two men grabbed him and dragged him back past the tank and through the no-man's land to the cover of the rubbled hooches.

I reached for the radio. "4-6, Bravo 6."

"This is 4-6 X-ray. Over."

"Bravo 6. Put 4–5 on the horn."

"Roger, Bravo 6. Here he is."

"Bravo 6, this is 4-5. Over."

"Okay, 4-5. I saw what happened to 4-6. You are now 4-6. I want a status on 4-6's condition as soon as your doc has one. In the future, I don't want platoon leaders running off to do squads' work. Understand?"

"This is 4-5-er, 4-6. I roger that, Bravo 6. Over."

"Bravo 6 out."

I contemplated for a moment what I had seen. A man had been gut-shot from a bunker which had just received at least two ninety-millimeter, high-explosive tank rounds, whole belts of 7.62 millimeter machine gun rounds, and two magazines of 5.56 millimeter M-16 rounds fired inside the bunker! *What the hell do they have down there?*

I was shaken from my thoughts by a sudden, ear-shattering explosion from my left. I quickly turned in that direction and observed a sight unlike any other. The Zippo had evidently taken an RPG and was burning furiously, an orange-red column of flame shooting at least two hundred feet up into the cloudless sky. Anything or anyone inside that track could only have been a cinder by now. What a helluva way to die, I thought, as I turned back to what my units were doing.

In spite of the tank fire, first platoon was still mostly pinned down. Third platoon was still moving toward the bunkers, but by inches. They had some low ground which gave them some protection from the bunkers, but such cover was minimal. Second platoon had spread out around the tank and had taken cover when it started engaging the bunkers. They were starting to move again.

I looked to my left and noticed that the mech company had ground to a halt. Some of its tracks were slowly backing away while continuing to lay down a curtain of fifty-cal fire. It looked like they were calling it quits for the day. I glanced at my watch. 1400. The attack had been going on for over four hours! Time flies when you're having fun. Four hours with all these assets, and we still had not penetrated that position!

On the right, I observed that Alpha Troop had also ground to a halt, but there was no sign of them beginning to pull back. They were just sitting there, pouring out machine gun and tank fire, still dodging numerous RPGs. They were a well-experienced unit, having fought continuously since TET had begun, mostly in the area around Ton Son Nhut airport. I wondered if they had also had had enough for the day.

I turned to MacKenzie on the battalion radio. "What have you heard from our flanks?"

"Well, sir, the mech said they're pulling back. Falcon 3 told them to stay put for the moment 'til he could decide what to do about the attack. I've heard nothing from the cav."

"Okay." I reached for his handset.

"Falcon 3, Bravo 6. What's going on my flanks? Looks like my left flank element's bugging out. On my right, everything's stopped. We're still trying to push forward. Over."

"Roger, Bravo 6. Stand by for orders."

After five minutes, the radio squawked again. "Falcon, Falcon, this is Falcon 3. Terminate operation at this time and return to this location. Roger in turn."

All companies roger'd.

I swapped handsets. "Falcon Bravo, this is Bravo 6. Break contact *now* and pull back to the hooch line. I want you moving back just as carefully as you moved up. Do fire and maneuver in reverse until you get out of the open. 2-6, don't forget to bring that tank back with you. Roger in turn. Over."

All platoons roger'd.

"*Move now*! Bravo 6 out."

For the next thirty minutes, all platoons slowly disengaged from the bunkers, hugging the ground or crouching behind the tank as they moved. Finally, we reached the relative cover of the rubbled hooches. I gave the troops a much-deserved rest break, with a security element to the front to watch the bunkers, and I released the tank to return to Alpha troop. At least this guy did not run at the first sign of enemy fire like the last ones did. Such action could restore my faith in armor if I wasn't careful. Maybe there *is* a difference between cav and armor units.

I took a sitrep. We had lost eight—two believed dead and six wounded seriously enough to evacuate, including one platoon leader. Lieutenant Constantino was in pretty serious condition, but doc said he was stable and would most likely recover, provided we could get him out of there.

I reached for MacKenzie's battalion radio. "Falcon 3, Bravo 6. Request Dustoff, same location and approach pattern as last time. Pick-up is for five whiskies and two kilos. Need it ASAP. A couple of these guys are serious. By the way, one is Bravo 4-6. Will need replacement ASAP. That makes two LTs you owe me. Over."

"This is Falcon 3. Roger copy. Stand by."

For the next five minutes, I observed the men. It had

been a hell of a day for them, and fatigue showed in most of their grimy faces. The fire had been real intense up there. They had seen tanks and APCs blown away right next to them, and they had heard the screams of the vehicles' crews as they were roasted alive. They had ducked repeatedly as the 8-inch shells screamed over at minimum range—and they had seen all that heavy equipment fail to take the objective. *How the hell had they expected us to take it alone?* I sure hoped that someone would pay hell for that screw-up!

"Bravo 6, Falcon 3. Dustoff inbound in zero-five. Roger two LTs. Sorry about 4-6. Request you report to th' TOC when you get back. I contacted Falcon 4. A cold one will be waiting for all you guys. Over."

"Bravo 6 roger. Out." Sometimes Davis was not such a bad guy!

After the medevac was complete, we moved back to the perimeter. I called the platoon leaders together as we entered the perimeter. As they gathered around, I slipped off my helmet, wiped my brow, took out my canteen, and drew a long swig of tepid water. Replacing the canteen, I looked them square in their faces.

"Get the men back to the perimeter and let them get some rest. I want 30% alert—that's one on alert and two resting. Tell them they did a helluva job today and I'm proud of them. Tell them that we may have to do it again tomorrow. I suspect somebody's going to do this every day until we get through that God-forsaken place. TOC says they should have some cold ones back there. Check it out. If it isn't there, send a runner back here and let me know. Questions? Okay, get going—all except 4-6."

They meandered off. Sergeant First Class Mitchell (an alias) looked at me with nervous expectation.

"Sergeant Mitchell, I regret what happened to your lieutenant today. I hope he'll eventually be okay. I also hope you men learned a lesson today. It isn't a platoon leader's job to go blow bunkers unless he's the only one

available to do the job. I don't want to lose anybody, but
it hurts the company a lot more to lose a lieutenant or
senior NCO than a private or a corporal. I know much of
the problem lies with his personality. When the firing
starts, I can't seem to keep the son of a bitch down.
Maybe he'll learn a lesson from this, and it just might
save his life next time. You need to do whatever reorgan-
izing you want to do in your platoon this afternoon just
in case we go out again tomorrow. It's your platoon 'til
you get a new lieutenant. The way TET's going, that may
be awhile. So good luck, Sergeant. I know you'll do a
good job."

"Thank you, sir. I'll do my best, sir."

"I know you will. You know I'm counting on you.
Now go take care of your men."

He walked quickly away as I ambled into the TOC.
Davis and Fulton were in deep conversation in the corner
of the tent. They looked up as I entered.

Davis smiled. "Come on in, Bravo 6. Pull up a chair.
You're getting kind of rough on lieutenants, aren't you?"

"Yeah. But you know, they're a dime a dozen."

Fulton shook his head. "That was a helluva fight out
there today."

"Yessir. Didn't do us a lot of good, did it? Got kind
of hot out there around all those burning vehicles."

Davis shifted the papers he was holding. "Well, we
have to do the same thing tomorrow, but with fewer
forces. One of the mech companies has departed. It was
the one in today's attack."

"Sounds like they couldn't take the heat. Guess they
must have figured they had lost enough tracks for one
battle. How many did they lose?"

"Six."

"What was the damage today? Looked like a lot of
RPGs were hitting what they were aimed at."

"Yeah. The mech company lost six tracks, plus the
zippo. The cav lost two tanks and three ACAVs. I don't

have the final personnel casualty figures yet. You know what yours were."

"What's up for tomorrow?"

"We'll have a briefing for all the commanders later, but, basically, we'll go in there again like we did today. We were on the verge of getting through there when the mech backed off. The cav was willing to keep going, but without the mech on their flank, we felt they were over-exposed."

"We were there."

"Yeah, but those fifties were more comforting to them. Besides, tracks crush bunkers better than combat boots."

"Yeah, I reckon."

Fulton cleared his throat. "Tell me what happened to your lieutenant."

"You won't believe this." I recited the whole story to him.

When I finished, he leaned back in his chair and shook his head. "Damnedest thing I ever heard. You think they have tunnels down there between the bunkers?"

"That would be my guess. I don't believe they could have survived in a simple bunker with all that ordnance coming inside there." I turned to Davis. "What's my job tomorrow?"

"You get to be reserve tomorrow. We're using the other mech company with the remaining zippo, along with the cav. I'm sending Charlie in between them. Bravo will be in a reserve position to the rear, available to be committed if we need you. Alpha and Delta will be in blocking positions. If we get through there, I have a graves registration team and some bulldozers on call. I'll need you to escort the graves people through the area and provide security to the engineers while we level what remains of the village and dig up those bunkers and tunnels. That's going to be the reserve's job whenever we finish this task."

"Okay. After today's little jaunt, I won't argue about taking a little break and give someone else a chance for a little fun. By the way, tell me how the hell some dufus idiot thought we could get through that place without any support? That had to be the most screwed-up planning I have ever heard of—or lack of planning."

"That was a Second Brigade call. I guess the new Brigade Commander got some questionable advice while he was trying to get the hang of his new job."

"Well, as far as I'm concerned, he flunked his first test. He's Armor, right?"

"Yeah, he's Armor."

"That's the damn problem. Tankers have got no business leading infantry. Except for Gus Fishburne, none of them understand infantrymen or infantry tactics. They think you can all go into battle at two thousand meters and at sixty miles an hour. They forget that jungle fatigues don't stop bullets like tanks do. Damn incompetent idiots!"

"Well, maybe he learned something out of this," Fulton ventured.

"I would be happier if Mearns would relieve his ass and send him to USARV or somewhere where he can't get anybody else hurt. Got anything else for me?"

"No, that's all. We just wanted to hear what happened out there."

"See you later."

The next day, we watched the other companies leave the perimeter for the day's operation, then we moved into a position to the rear of Charlie, not far away from the 8-inch howitzer's position. Falcon 6 was taking a gamble by sending out all the companies, leaving only the Recon Platoon to secure the perimeter. I guess he felt that most of the enemy in the immediate area was underground in Ap Cho. I hoped he was right. Of course, Recon could probably hold off almost anything until we could get back there.

It took about half the day, but the task force managed to get through Ap Cho that day. Everybody breathed a great sigh of relief that this thing was finally over. The vehicle losses were much lighter than those of the previous day, with both units together losing only four tracks, with one tank was damaged.

It was about 1300 hours when the battalion radio crackled. "Bravo 6, Falcon 3."

"Bravo 6."

"Falcon 3. The GR team and the engineers are here. You need to send back some security for them and get them into the village as we discussed. Over."

"Roger. I'll send one of my elements now. Out."

I waved Gormley over, briefed him and sent his third platoon back to the perimeter to escort the "visitors" to the village. I then moved the company up and deployed the other three platoons in defensive positions around Ap Cho. As we entered the village, I noticed that the other companies had passed on through the hooches and rubble and were conducting medevacs to get their casualties out. We had the village—what was left of it—to ourselves.

For the next four hours, the bulldozers worked at digging up and filling in the bunker complex from which a determined enemy had taken its toll on our battalion and the other units that had finally come to our support. As they dug them up, we piled all the enemy weapons together for transport back to Cu Chi. Among the weapons found were 61-millimeter and 82-millimeter mortars, 57-millimeter recoilless rifles and numerous machine guns. From the looks of those, we had been up against a battalion. So the illustrious Second Brigade had pitted our shirt-armored, foot-mobile leg battalion against a dug-in enemy battalion. Real smart!

As the dozers worked, I noticed that the bunker from which Lieutenant Constantino had been shot had been opened. I wandered over to get a better look and received a bit of a surprise. This "bunker" was nothing more than a foxhole with overhead cover. Not only were there no connecting tunnels, but also there were no side holes in which one might escape the incoming fire. Those guys had absorbed all that ordnance which we had poured into that hole and were still able to shoot my lieutenant. Amazing!

I then turned my attention to the graves registration team, who were trying to recover remains from the burned-out vehicles and from the battlefield around them. If I had felt elation at finally taking Ap Cho, the sight of those bodies and the condition they were in put a decided damper on that feeling. I saw the body of one soldier just sitting up against a rock, still wearing his helmet and flak vest. Other than some blackened skin, he looked like he was merely taking a nap. I walked on. Near the wreckage of a track, I stared at a piece of charred meat that had been a living, breathing soldier the day before. It was just a hunk of meat—there were no arms, no legs, no head—nothing but the torso. The smell of burned meat was everywhere, worsened by two days in the hot sun. That was a smell that I will never forget as long as I live. In a burned-out tank, the only remains identifiable as human were some blackened pelvic bones which were very carefully removed. In the blown-away zippo, the heat had been so intense that there were no recoverable or identifiable remains at all. Those guys had just simply disintegrated and ceased to exist in any form. The heat had melted much of the cast aluminum armor on the sides and top of the vehicle.

I had been a company commander for almost five months and had been in numerous fights, had seen many casualties in various conditions, had smelled long-decomposing bodies for weeks around Fire Base Burt—and those sights had never affected me physically. But, as I wandered among the wreckage and saw what was left of fine soldiers and smelled that terrible smell of charred flesh, I came very close to being physically ill. Nothing had ever affected me that way before. As I felt the bile rising, I fought back the urge to puke, gritted my teeth, turned on my heel and went out to check the units on the perimeter.

It was nearly sundown when we returned to the perimeter, having completed the leveling of Ap Cho and the evacuation of the graves team and the recovered remains. I was glad that chore was over and we could get on with our normal business.

CHAPTER NINE

BYE, BRAVO

If the TET Offensive had started like a lion, it certainly went out like a lamb. The third and final week of TET in our area was downright boring, which was a welcome change after the first two weeks. And with my R&R coming up, what could be better? To the rest of the world, R&R variously means "Rest and Recuperation," "Rest and Relaxation," and "Rest and Recreation," but we had a somewhat different name for it in Vietnam: "Rape and Run." The intent of this term was not violent in nature, but, rather, it reflected the intent of most soldiers to spend that journey to Fantasyland in bed with someone— whether through an arranged meeting with their spouses or by finding someone else.

After taking Ap Cho, the TET Offensive was pretty much over for us. Although we continued to read about the Marines fighting up north in Hue, most major resistance in our part of Vietnam petered out. For the following week, we continued to conduct company-sized patrols around the Cu Chi area and to run operations against suspected mortar and rocket sites, but there was little further contact. Apparently, what was left of the VC and NVA had gone back into Cambodia to lick its wounds.

We had a little wound-licking of our own to do. We had to replace our personnel and equipment losses and resupply ammunition, clothing and other items which we had foregone while various modes of transportation were being restored. We had a number of our earlier wounded returned to us, and we were glad to see them again.

Lieutenant Colonel Fulton and I had agreed that I would turn over Bravo Company to Lieutenant Prairie on February 18th and return to Dau Tieng to wrap up my paperwork, move my stuff to Battalion Headquarters, go on R&R and return as the Battalion S-2. I did not like the S-2 idea, since Lieutenant Colonel Harrold had promised me the S-3 job. However, I was only a Captain, and we had a couple of inexperienced Majors who felt they needed a little S-3 time. By being the S-2 with very little intelligence work to do, I would be like an assistant S-3 and, perhaps, could keep the Majors from doing something stupid. Little did I know how much help those guys really would need! Not *one* of them could be compared to George Davis. In retrospect, I came to realize, during the following months, that I thought much more of Harrold and Davis than I had admitted during the time I had served with them. They certainly were good for the Battalion and made major contributions to the Battalion's very successful record.

February 18th dawned bright and clear—as did every day during the dry season—except that in Saigon, it dawned bright and smoggy. As the 18th approached, my anticipation at turning over the company and getting rid of that physical and psychological burden grew like kudzu. That seemed more important to me than my imminent R&R.

The physical burden of commanding a line infantry company in the field was obvious, especially in light of what we had gone through during the previous three weeks. Even though I was a bit tired following the demands of the month or so before, I was not particularly concerned with lifting the physical burden. A restful R&R would likely take care of that.

The psychological burden was not so obvious. The responsibility for making decisions and giving orders which directly affected the lives, health, and futures of one-hundred-and-sixty other people was mentally awesome. The emotional impact of having your men killed or wounded would eventually drain the most stalwart of men, but it was part of the job and something with which the commander had to come to terms. The inbred necessity to think through your actions and orders to ensure that there were no hidden faults in your reasoning was mentally taxing, but the degree of one's ability to do that determines his success or failure as a commander. When all these psychological factors are combined together and are experienced daily over a four- or five-month period, the burden becomes more understandable. In any case, I viewed the upcoming command change with elation. (However, within a month thereafter, I regretted giving up command of Bravo Company, even though I had lasted longer than most company commanders in the battalion during that period. I missed the members of the company, the action in the field, and—to be truthful—the sense of responsibility. The R&R break may have been sufficient to clear my mind and recharge my psychological batteries. However, they say you can never go back . . .)

That morning, my thoughts were not so analytical or philosophical. Bravo Company drew perimeter security that day, to permit us to change commanders. As I finished packing my gear, the battalion radio crackled.

"Bravo 6, Falcon 3."

I reached over and grabbed the handset. "Bravo 6."

"Falcon 3. The new Bravo 6 is en route to this location from Delta Tango. Echo Tango Alpha is two-zero mikes. You will have to take the same bird back, so make your exchange brief. The pilot won't shut down. Over."

"Bravo 6 roger."

"3 out."

Well, I thought, this change of command will be longer than when I took over. At least we will both be here at the same time, however briefly. At least I am not being medevac'd out of here like my predecessor was.

Since my stuff was packed up and ready to go, I made a quick round of the company perimeter to say good-bye to the troops and to encourage them to work for Lieutenant Prairie as well as they had for me. I did not take a lot of time doing that, since I promised I would see them

again, either in base camp or out there in the field as a
Battalion Staff officer.

By the time I returned to the CP, the chopper was
landing. I hurriedly shook hands with my CP folks,
grabbed my ruck, weapon, and helmet, and set off at a
fast pace toward the LZ. About half-way there, I met Prairie.

"Welcome, Bravo 6." I stuck out my hand. "I can't
think of anyone I'd rather turn over the company to than
you. You better take good care of them or I'll have your
ass," I grinned at him. He grinned back and shook my
hand. "Since this bird isn't supposed to wait long, I told
Top to brief you on what is going on in the company. I'm
sure Falcon 3 will let you know what they want you to
do next. Good luck, Dick. You're getting a helluva good
bunch of guys. Take care of them, and they will take care
of you. See you later."

With that, I took off for the helicopter. As we lifted
off, I got my last real look at Bravo Company on the
ground. Even though I knew I would see them again—or
at least some of them—at that moment I knew it would
never be the same. For the first time that day, I choked
up a little thinking about that. As I said before, you can
never go back.

For the next two days, I worked in the company area,
getting all the paperwork completed to officially relin-
quish command. This included remaining correspondence,
company punishment documents, officer efficiency
reports, property inventories and anything else that the
Battalion Adjutant could think of. Being a combat commander still had its peacetime ration of bureaucratic crap.
Or, as a guy once said as he came out of the latrine, "The
work isn't over 'til the paperwork's done."

On the second day of the paperwork drill, Victor Charlie
sent me his greetings one more time—or maybe he was just
saying good-bye. It was late morning, and I was sitting in
my office in the corner of the company headquarters closest
to the commo shop next door. My communications team

shop was located inside a fully-sandbagged CONEX container about twenty feet from the headquarters. I was scanning through some document I had just written when . . . *Crash!* A mortar round landed just outside my wall! *Crash! Crash! Crash!* Several more followed rapidly. Yelling *"Incoming!"*, I ducked down behind my desk. After a slight hesitation—probably the result of a short period of disbelief that *anyone* would dare attack a headquarters building in so safe a rear area—I heard the other guys in the building scooting out the front door. It was instantly clear that this tin-roofed, screen-and-plywood hooch was not a whole lot of protection from eighty-two millimeter rounds! As the rounds continued to fall, it seemed that all of them were concentrated around this corner of the building and the commo shop. That meant that *I was smack dab in the middle of the beaten zone!* I took a deep breath and bolted out of the office door and to the back door. Dropping to one knee just inside the entrance, I listened a moment, trying to discern exactly where they were falling. Deciding that this was a futile exercise, I took a running start and dove, head-first, into the protection of the entrance to the commo shop.

As the commo sergeant, Sergeant Brandt (an alias), stuck his head around the corner to see what the hell was going on, I slowly picked myself up, brushed off my shirt, and grinned at him. "Mind if I visit for awhile, Sergeant Brandt? Those rounds were just a little too close for comfort."

He grinned back. "Not at all, Sir. Come on in."

The rounds fell for another five minutes or so and then tapered off. As things quieted down, I walked back outside. The headquarters building had some shrapnel splatters in the wooden walls but, otherwise, had suffered no damage. As I walked back toward the rear door, I stumbled on something buried in the round. Stopping, I bent over and saw that it was an eighty-deuce tail fin, partially imbedded in the dirt. I picked it up, found it to be pretty much in its original shape, and kept it for a souvenir. As I turned back toward the door, I noticed that it had been laying no more than five feet from where I had been sitting. I tossed it in the air and caught it, grinning. "Nice try, Charlie, but no cigar!"

The next day, I left for R&R in Hawaii. Dick Prairie's Assumption of Command order had been published, and I left Bravo Company forever—except in my heart—or so I thought. I have thought about those guys many times over the years—remembering some names, remembering many faces, and remembering all the actions and events. I had no doubt that Bravo was the best company in the Army—because the men were the best, the officers and NCOs as a group were the best, and we were given room to do our job. Those were the ingredients for the perfect recipe for a very successful command. I salute them all!

EPILOGUE

One of the highlights of my military career was serving as Bravo 6. During my almost five months in command, Bravo Company progressed from being the epitome of low morale to becoming what many consider the best company in the Battalion. This was accomplished not because of my specific talents or contributions—whatever they may have been—but more directly because I tried to create an atmosphere which allowed the junior officers and non-commissioned officers to develop and practice *their* leadership talents. Because they were permitted to *act* like officers and NCOs, they assumed the real leadership function on a day-to-day basis in the company. A combat unit without such effective grassroots leadership would eventually prove to be ineffective. Bravo Company was very effective.

In addition to good junior leaders, a successful combat unit must have good soldiers. No unit will be successful with soldiers who lack self-respect or a sense of responsibility for their actions. Soldier must have respect for, and be responsive to, military discipline. Soldiers must contribute consciously to the unit's cohesion and teamwork. Bravo Company had mighty fine soldiers. As a commander, I could not ask for better soldiers than I had in Bravo. Although all units have occasional misfits—that is inherent in any army—I will always love and respect those guys, as a group, for their superb performance of duty in what proved to be a very unpopular undertaking.

Since Vietnam, the men who were in Bravo Company during my tenure have pursued many careers. A few remained in the military, eventually to retire, as Sergeant Hughes (2nd Platoon) and I did. Others became successful in businesses and professions, such as finance and architecture, as John Otte (Company Headquarters), Art Gormley (3rd Platoon), and Larry Robinson (1st Platoon) did. One of our men—Specialist 4 Oliver Stone (2nd Platoon)—became a famous playwright and movie director. In fact, Oliver's movie, *Platoon* was his dramatic representation of his Vietnam experiences and has earned him critical acclaim, including two Oscars. Even though many veterans take exception to some events in the movie, it is certainly a monumental achievement. On the other hand, several of our compatriots have experienced problems in readjusting to civilian life after Vietnam. Regardless of their reaction to their Vietnam service, I believe Bravo Company soldiers share a bond created in the crucible of their experiences in that place, far from home, where they had to depend on each other for their very survival.

The 3/22 Infantry was the last 25th Division battalion to depart Vietnam in 1971. Since that time, numerous former members of Bravo Company tried by various means to maintain contact with their old buddies. Since 1994, my former RTO, John Otte, has developed a society of former Bravo Company members, called *Bravo Regulars*. This society has reestablished direct contact among hundreds of old comrades and has organized and conducted several reunions across the country. *Bravo Regulars* is rapidly facilitating Bravo's reemergence as a cohesive unit.

At the end of the previous chapter, I wrote that I had left Bravo Company forever—*not on your life*!

VIETNAM GLOSSARY

AK or AK-47: Soviet or Chinese-made assault rifle; fires automatic or semi-automatic.

Area of Operation (AO): The maneuver area assigned to a unit, sometimes called a "box."

Arclight: Code name for a B-52 heavy bomber attack, usually consisting of three aircraft.

Armored Personnel Carrier (APC) or "Track": Armored vehicle assigned to mechanized infantry units, equipped with machine guns and designed to carry one infantry squad. Variations are used by armored cavalry squadrons and armor battalions, and as mobile command posts and as field ambulances.

Army of the Republic of Vietnam (ARVN): The standing army of the Vietnamese Republic, consisting of the regular field army and the militia-like units of the Territorial Army.

Article 15: Refers to the sections of the Uniform Code of Military Justice and the Manual for Courts-Martial which prescribe the limits for Company and Battalion Commanders' punishment, designated as company and field-grade punishment.

Beehive: Anti-personnel artillery round filled with flechettes, or small metal darts.

Buzzsaw: Slang expression for a situation where a unit suffers a high number of casualties.

CAR-15: Short carbine version of the M-16 rifle with a telescoping stock.

Claymore Mines: Above-ground, unidirectional anti-personnel mine designed to explode and throw small, round pellets in a designated direction.

Click: Slang expression for a kilometer.

Combat Infantryman Badge (CIB): Permanently awarded badge designating that an Infantryman has been in direct combat at battalion level or below.

Command Post (CP): Designated location of the commander or leader in a military field position.

Cordon-and-Search: Military tactic in which a unit surrounds a village to prevent escape and then conducts a house-to-house search of the village.

Crew-Served: Weapons which require more than one person to fire and to service. For example, a machine gun may require a gunner and an ammunition bearer.

C-Rations: Combat food rations in which the components are packed in cans and may be eaten cold or hot.

C-4 Highly effective plastic explosive which requires a blasting cap to explode. When lit, C-4 burns white-hot.

Defensive Concentration (DEFCON): Artillery fire concentration planned as part of the final protective fires before a defensive field position.

Field First Sergeant: Non-commissioned officer (NCO) designated to function as the company first sergeant in the field, who may or may not be the actual first sergeant.

Final Protective Fires (FPF): Planned final line of fire for all unit weapons in a defensive position. Lines of fire must interlock with similar lines of fire (e.g., machine gun to machine gun), and, when fired, must be fired continuously until the "Cease Fire" order is given.

Fire Support Coordinator (FSCOORD): Direct Support Artillery officer (usually a Captain) who is responsible for coordinating all supporting fires for a combat arms battalion.

(Artillery) Forward Observer (FO): Direct Support Artillery officer (usually a Lieutenant) attached to a combat arms company and responsible for coordinating and calling for all supporting fires for the company.

Grunt: Slang expression for an infantryman or other ground combat soldier.

Gunship: An aircraft configured with weapons for direct combat. Weapons may be a mixture of 2.75" rocket launchers, machine guns, 40 millimeter rocket launchers, rapid-firing mini-guns, and other available weapons.

Heavy Fire Team (HFT): A combat aviation team consisting of three gunships.

Helipad: Specific area designated for the landing of one or more helicopters.

Huey: The UH-1 Iroquois helicopter, used extensively in Vietnam, nicknamed the "Huey" from its UH-1 designation.

Killed in Action (KIA) or "Kilo": Soldier killed as a direct result of combat action.

Laager: Night defensive position (NDP).

Landing Zone (LZ): Specific area designated for unloading troops from helicopters to participate in a combat operation. This may be done under enemy fire (**Hot LZ**) or not (**Cold LZ**).

Light Antitank Weapon (LAW): Small shoulder-fired, pre-loaded, recoilless, free-flight antitank rocket launcher, designed to be fired once and discarded. They were frequently fired against enemy bunkers in Vietnam.

Light Fire Team (LFT): A combat aviation team consisting of two gunships.

Listening Post (LP): One- or two-man position established forward of a platoon defensive position to provide early warning of enemy presence.

Mad Minute: Planned firing of all company weapons to the front of the position for a specified period of time, designed to discourage the presence of enemy personnel.

Mechanized Infantry: Infantry units organized, equipped, and trained to ride into combat aboard APCs. In combat, they may fight while mounted or dismounted.

M-16 Rifle: Standard individual semi-automatic weapon for most personnel in Vietnam; fires 5.56 mm bullets in magazines, but may be equipped with a selector switch to permit automatic firing.

M-60 Machine Gun: Standard platoon automatic assault weapon; fires 7.62 mm bullets in 100-round disintegrating belts, and may be fired from bipod or tripod mounts.

M-79 Grenade Launcher: Shoulder-fired launcher for 40 mm grenade rounds, assigned to the infantry squad and similar units.

Napalm or "Nape": Jet fighter-delivered canisters of incendiary mixture which break and ignite upon ground impact, burning whatever it touches and using available oxygen as it ignites.

North Vietnamese Army (NVA): National combat forces of the People's Republic of (North) Vietnam, normally dressed in standard NVA uniforms.

Officer Candidate School (OCS): Program for training Army enlisted personnel and commissioning them as officers with the rank of Second Lieutenant.

Phonetic Alphabet: Word alphabet for use in radio communications, developed to eliminate pronunciation errors caused by similar sounds of letters of the alphabet. The military alphabet used in Vietnam follows:

Alpha	Hotel	Oscar	Victor
Bravo	India	Papa	Whiskey
Charlie	Juliette	Quebec	X-ray
Delta	Kilo	Romeo	Yankee
Echo	Lima	Sierra	Zulu
Foxtrot	Mike	Tango	
Golf	November	Uniform	

Pick-up-Zone (PZ): Specific area designated from which troops are to be picked up by helicopter following, or a part of, a combat operation for transport to another location. This may be done under enemy fire **(Hot PZ)** or not **(Cold PZ)**.

Push: Slang expression for radio frequency.

Radio-Telephone Operator (RTO): A soldier designated to carry and operate a tactical radio for a commander or other leader.

Reaction Force: Term for a commander's tactical reserve force within a defensive perimeter.

Reconnaissance-in-Force: As used in Vietnam, the employment of a sufficiently strong tactical unit, normally a company, to search for an enemy force or facility and to either destroy what they find or call for additional combat power as required to complete the mission. (See **Search-and-Destroy**.)

Regional Forces/Popular Forces (RF/PF): Territorial militia units of the Army of the Republic of Vietnam (ARVN). These units, poorly equipped and trained, were used mostly to guard Vietnamese government facilities, such as District and Provincial Headquarters. Although frequently considered rife with enemy infiltrators, a small number of these units were very successful in combat operations against the Viet Cong. Americans referred to them as **Ruff-Puffs**.

Rocket-Propelled Grenade (RPG): Soviet or Chinese-made, shoulder-fired, reloadable, free-flight anti-tank rocket launcher, frequently used against personnel. The enemy in Vietnam had the light RPG-2 and the heavier RPG-7 launchers.

RPD: Soviet or Chinese-made light machine gun, firing 7 mm rounds from canister magazines.

Search-and-Destroy: Employment of a sufficiently strong force, normally a company, to search for and destroy an enemy force or facility. This term was replaced by **Reconnaissance-in-Force** in late 1967 and was no longer authorized.

Situation Report (Sitrep): Verbal report by radio of a unit's current tactical situation, covering significant friendly and enemy status.

Slick: A utility helicopter, such as a Huey, configured for the transport of troops and supplies. A slick is not armed for combat.

Squawk Box: Slang expression for a speaker box attached to a tactical radio.

Squelch: Rushing sound emitted from a tactical radio when not transmitting or receiving.

S-1 Officer: Primary battalion/brigade staff officer responsible for personnel and administration.

S-2 Officer: Primary battalion/brigade staff officer responsible for intelligence and field maps.

S-3 Officer: Primary battalion/brigade staff officer responsible for operations, plans and training.

S-4 Officer: Primary battalion/brigade staff officer responsible for supply and logistics.

S-5 Officer: Primary battalion/brigade staff officer responsible for civil-military operations.

Tactical Air Support (TACAIR): Close air support and ground attack provided to ground forces by Air Force or Navy fighter aircraft.

Tactical Operations Center (TOC): Battalion or higher command post occupied by the commander and his primary staff, particularly elements of the intelligence and operations staff sections.

"Top": Slang term for the Company First Sergeant, sometimes extended to the Battalion Sergeant Major. This Term was derived from an earlier reference to the senior enlisted man of a unit as the "Top Soldier."

Viet Cong (VC), "Victor Charlie" or "Charlie": Indigenous South Vietnamese Communist insurgents, organized into guerilla "Local Force" units and more conventional "Main Force" formations.

Wounded in Action (WIA) or "Whiskey": Soldier wounded as a direct result of combat action.

It was a war within a war—and it took no prisoners...

COVERT OPS
The CIA's Secret War in Laos

James E. Parker, Jr.

For the first time, veteran James Parker, codename "Mule," reveals the story of the covert war in Laos—a bloody battle that raged behind the face of the Vietnam War. As Parker takes you inside the hell and devastation of war, he provides a first-person account of the people who courageously fought until the bitter end.

(Previously published in hardcover as *Codename Mule*)

AVAILABLE WHEREVER BOOKS ARE SOLD
FROM ST. MARTIN'S PRESS